Willie K. Vanderbilt II

Willie K. Vanderbilt II

A Biography

STEVEN H. GITTELMAN

McFarland & Company, Inc., Publishers

Jefferson, North Carolina, and London

Frontispiece: William K. Vanderbilt II, aged 47, as painted by Gari Melchers in 1925 (courtesy Suffolk County Vanderbilt Museum).

Library of Congress Cataloguing-in-Publication Data

Gittelman, Steven H., 1949–
    Willie K. Vanderbilt II : a biography / Steven H. Gittelman.
      p.   cm.
    Includes bibliographical references and index.

    ISBN 978-0-7864-4777-0
    softcover : 50# alkaline paper ∞

    1. Vanderbilt, William K. (William Kissam), 1878–1944.
2. Millionaires— United States— Biography.   3. Wealth —
Psychological aspects.   I. Title.
CT275.V238G47   2010
973.9092 — dc22 [B]   2010016061

British Library cataloguing data are available

Front cover: Portrait of Willie with a moustache (courtesy Suffolk
County Vanderbilt Museum); background ©2010 Shutterstock

Manufactured in the United States of America

McFarland & Company, Inc., Publishers
  Box 611, Jefferson, North Carolina 28640
  www.mcfarlandpub.com

To my children,
Michael, Sara and Emily.
The best things in life to leave
behind are art and children.

Acknowledgments

My interest in the Vanderbilts is a product of my twenty years as trustee and later president of the Suffolk County Vanderbilt Museum. The trust that William K. Vanderbilt II bestowed on the people of Suffolk County has provided unending education and joy to the many thousands who have visited his home, Eagle's Nest, the institution which, shortly after Willie K.'s death, became the County of Suffolk's first park.

Perhaps the greatest beneficiaries of Willie's largess have been my own family. While Dad lovingly toiled through fifteen years as museum president, he also played at his role as "John the Gardener," a fictitious character who, in the company of either Margaret, the sea plane pilot's daughter (my own daughter Emily), or Rosemarie (daughters Emily and Sara), Mrs. Vanderbilt's daughter, enjoyed life in the nineteen thirties as a member of the living history cast of characters. All of us tried to stick to the approved script, but "John" wandered shamelessly with each newly discovered story.

The museum grew in those years, and the archives slowly revealed a treasure trove of Mr. Vanderbilt's rich records. I found it impossible to resist the opportunity to settle into the stacks and pass the hours pawing through Mr. V's many albums.

There were three directors who brought renewed professional life to the institution, but the most recent, Carol Ghiorsi Hart, is by far its most passionate champion. We have reveled in exchanging stories, discerning together whether they are "museum folklore" or the latest discovery. Carol read this manuscript and passed on a rich combination of wisdom and enthusiasm that I will always cherish.

Stephanie Gress, natural history curator, provided me with much assistance researching photographs and sharing a day where we "dream walked" through the habitat together. The epilogue is based on that shared experience.

Michael Dooling and Carole Lindsay provided incredibly invaluable research assistance. Trustees Gretchen Oldrin Monas and Carol Ghiorsi Hart were early readers. Elizabeth Peters provided some editorial assistance. My daughter, Sara, authored the brief section on Elsie Janis.

My wife, Jennifer, was endlessly generous in allowing me all of these eccentricities.

People at my place of employment, Mktg. Inc., tolerated my incessant search for material and assisted beyond the call, particularly Danielle Leacock, who was always there to aid in everything from scanning to photocopying. Howard Gershowitz, my business partner, allowed me more time than I deserved for such pursuits, and Elaine Trimarchi, another business partner, has been a willing reader and suffered the telling and retelling of many stories to which she provided a caring and interested ear.

The folks at Galapagos Connection — Greg Estes and Thalia Grant — were quite kind and patient in my search for Willie and Rose's graffiti. I am greatly indebted to the owners and crew of the *Heritage*, a Galapagos tour boat, who kindly went out of their way to assist me in locating the marks of Vanderbilt's travels there. That in itself was quite an adventure.

Heartfelt thanks to Emily Gittelman and Jon Zurn who worked with me as editors.

Lastly, this volume would never have come to pass if the trustees at the Suffolk County Vanderbilt Museum had not encouraged me to pursue it. Indeed, this project began as a special pamphlet to orient visitors. Who would have thought it would take five years? The museum is a great treasure, and it has been my joy to be part of it for these decades. Most of the photos are from the rich collection of the museum. Certainly, all of the inspiration has been found there.

Table of Contents

Preface

Willie K. Vanderbilt II was born in 1878, a member of, in their day, one of the richest families in the world. Stories of the moneyed Vanderbilts still ring of the lavish extravagances of that bygone "Gilded Age." Their mansions still dot the eastern seaboard, historic monuments to a fleeting prominence. Yet Willie's home, Eagle's Nest, just a few miles east of Long Island's "old money" Gold Coast, pales in comparison. Why? Because as a fourth-generation Vanderbilt, Willie was born far from the inherent drive and vigor of its founder, the Commodore, Cornelius Vanderbilt. This scion to a dynasty was an inheritor, not a builder, and somewhere in that space, Willie found himself alone in a world he did not understand. At age twenty-nine, the bank failures of 1907 nearly broke his financial back. The progressive era, begun under one Roosevelt and finished by another, drove Willie from the comforts of his storied past. And the upheaval of the First World War stripped him of his rightful place as head of one of America's most powerful industrial empires. When the music stopped, William Kissam Vanderbilt II was left holding the bag.

Dreams that Willie had for himself, and expectations that the world anticipated of a Vanderbilt, towered over his realities. As history shifted beneath his feet, Willie grasped at his future, seeking countless routes to discover his purpose and his destiny. But at nearly every turn, Vanderbilt found himself instead either too early or too late.

At age twenty-nine, I finished my doctorate in ecology, never to practice my chosen profession. No tenured professorship awaited me. I floated sadly without direction for years, much like Willie, seeking something to call my own. Unable to find employment in the sciences, I grasped at a nearby straw: I volunteered at various science museums to fill the void.

Years later, as a trustee to the museum that now fills Willie's summer home, I came to wonder about the man who filled whole buildings with bottles of preserved fishes and invertebrates. The lexicon was less of a museum and much more of this moneyed individual, a man who left a legacy of ambitious intellectual pursuits, yet most of them unfinished. The house in final form seemed so grand. After all, it was built by the fortune left to him by his father.

1

Steven H. Gittelman at Tower Island, Galapagos, where he retraced Mr. Vanderbilt's romantic 1926 voyage. The wording reads "ARA 1928." The lovers, Willie and Rose, returned after the 1926 voyage, two years later, to update their mark.

Willie never had the dignity of earning his own money. I wondered about a man who practiced an earlier version of my career and had his own wealth to do it. Did he find fulfillment in this chosen pathway? I wondered, too, would I find myself through Willie?

In 1994, I was elected to my first term as president of the board of trustees of the Suffolk County Vanderbilt Museum. It was this leadership role that drew me into Willie's life: no one seemed to know much about this wanderer. Though something of a celebrity in his day, he left little about himself and was not the subject of anyone else's writings.

We began a program of "living history" at the estate. I became a fictional character: "John the Gardener." It allowed me a stage for personal expression. Soon my daughters, Sara and Emily, joined me, each playing her own character. It was great fun to share endless moments as a cantankerous gardener, never short of a story to tell. The joy was in the sharing, especially with my daughters and, of course, with the public.

Emily provided a challenge to me. She has always exhibited a thirst for knowledge. We built living history scripts together and for over a decade spent Sundays acting out our latest discoveries. It has been a father's delight.

In 2008 the world seemed to come apart. Bank failures have been followed by a depression/grade recession; a condition we continue to suffer in a more advanced form in 2009. Remarkably, one hundred years before, Willie had suffered a similar fate when the bank failure of 1907 nearly wrecked him.

Overextended and inattentive, Willie lost a collection of visionary efforts: a vacuum cleaner business, the Day and Night Bank, and a precursor to the toll road, the Vanderbilt Motor Parkway. All this while he still licked his wounds over a land purchase debacle at nearby Lake Success, where he was tripped by his own hubris as he clung to the birthright of his name — to "Vanderbuild" in a scale beyond mere mortals.

Approaching thirty years of age, he was a financial disaster. To make matters worse, his wife, Virginia Fair, was an heiress with plenty of money of her own. To bail himself out, Willie surreptitiously sought to sell her real estate in San Francisco, and worse, her jewelry, to financial real estate mogul and incessant gossip Hetty Green. It was just another in a string of disasters. Within a year he was caught philandering with a French actress and his marriage turned to separation. And so, Willie wandered far out on the north shore of Long Island, building Eagle's Nest to avoid the scrutiny of society and keep precious his access to one of the few happy places in his life: the sea.

Willie struggled with the ghosts of his relative failure but eventually found himself in a mixture of delusion, love and a sizable inheritance. Eagle's Nest became his modest home and, in a way, ours as well. He left behind an incredible collection of scrapbooks, logs, and journals of his own travels. Precious little was of a personal bent, but there was an archive to be proud of, and the materials flowed with signs and clues to this mysterious man.

Through Willie, I have filled some gaps for myself. I have learned to pursue my passions and draw comfort from my own dreams. But I have yet to distance myself from my fear of failures past and those that may still await. After all, it was Willie, always restless, who pondered after he captained his yacht around the world for the first time, "What next?"

When I think about it, this book is about two men and their search for fulfillment: one a Vanderbilt and the other his biographer.

CHAPTER 1

Accidental Heir

Inevitably, death bodes change for those who remain. The demise of Cornelius Vanderbilt II in the autumn of 1899 promised consequences both exceptional and profound. For in his passing, a vast railroad legacy and colossal riches—to either realize or squander—lay behind. Now, solitary and neatly bound, that empire rested on an ornate desk in the old man's stark oceanside mansion, the Breakers: his last will and testament. For those gathered in the gray light of an October afternoon, the air lay thick with simmering passions, long-held resentments, and perhaps most palpable of all, desperation.

Only fourteen years before, William Henry Vanderbilt I, then the wealthiest man in the world, bequeathed to his eldest son, Cornelius II, and his second son, William Kissam, an estate worth one hundred twenty million dollars. At its core was the great railroad network stretching from Long Island to Chicago. Founded by William Henry's father, the ruthless and bold Cornelius Vanderbilt, the railroad spread quickly across the industrial and agricultural heartland. This was the dawn of the locomotive age, and the Vanderbilt lines where the essential arteries to a nation just realizing its inevitable, and seemingly God-given, might. The elder Cornelius, the Commodore, was hailed a self-made genius of his generation. William Henry, in his turn, doubled the family empire. In an era heralded America's "Gilded Age," the Vanderbilt name reigned among titans.

With William Henry's passing, one giant was succeeded by two. Cornelius and William Kissam, working together to harness an estate divided virtually by half, a move considered risky by some and brilliant by others, did not disappoint in their legacy. They made the New York Central Railroad and its myriad constituent lines even stronger and controlled a stranglehold on the world's busiest and most profitable port, New York Harbor. Where the ships arrived, the Vanderbilt trains awaited.

Yet astride the Vanderbilt's immense success came a current of discord of nearly equal proportion.

With Cornelius's death, he left behind the considerable fortune of one hundred million dollars, one of the largest of its time. Cornelius, like his father before him, had a large family with six children: four sons and two daughters. His first-born son, William Henry, a winsome young lad adored by his parents,[1] had died from typhoid at the cusp of manhood. Next in succession by the laws of primogeniture came Cornelius III, known affectionately as Neily, a studious youth, who, though suffering from rheumatism, worked at the family's Grand Central railroad office with diligence, eager to take on increasing responsibilities as the heir apparent.

Neily displayed the same promise as his lost sibling, William Henry, and exhibited many of his elder's talents and pursuits. Ironically, the two also shared one particularly fateful interest: they both loved the same woman, Grace Wilson, a stunning beauty of considerable social ambition. When William Henry passed on, Grace moved on to Neily with remarkable ease. Both Cornelius and his wife, Alice, disapproved of the bewitching young woman, rightly considering her a social climber, and were shocked by her willingness to so quickly consort with yet another Vanderbilt scion. Nonetheless, Neily's obsession for the young woman, three years his senior, did not abate, and despite his parent's obvious discomfort, Neily stubbornly persisted in the courtship.

Yet the rheumatism he had battled in his childhood resurfaced, and Neily was forced home from Yale to recuperate. Sequestered in his family's mansion on Fifth Avenue, Neily grew irritable and frustrated as tension between father and son intensified with each passing day. The elder Cornelius seized this opportune moment to convince his son to forget Grace and move on. But the more he and Alice pled, the more staunchly Neily refused to give in — even despite his father's threats to completely cut him off from his inheritance. Cornelius retaliated by demanding that his son leave Manhattan, where Grace also resided, and instead convalesce at the Breakers, their Newport retreat, miles away from heady distractions.

One hot summer afternoon, a heated exchange of words abruptly erupted into blows. Neily, rebelling violently, struck his father[2] hard, then rushed from the house.

Whether a result of the blow or not, Cornelius suffered a debilitating stroke soon after that left his entire right side paralyzed. It rendered him a pale shadow of his former self, nearly unable to speak. The family turned its outrage on Neily, and in an instant, his future turned to stark uncertainty.

Yet, while the elder Cornelius retreated behind the Breaker's austere walls, his son continued his clandestine courtship. Only a few months later, Neily shocked his family beyond reprieve: Grace Wilson was now his wife.

For father and mother this was too much. Neily had crossed a Rubicon of his own making. Inheritance was out of the question. Though time passed and Neily fathered a son, he and his father would not speak again.

Such are the knotted threads of Fate.

Only in the few years prior to Cornelius's stroke had William Kissam actively engaged in expanding the Vanderbilt roads. Cornelius was far more the

Left: William Kissam Vanderbilt I (1849 to 1920), fourth child of William Henry Vanderbilt I, grandson of the Commodore — railroad man, investment banker, father of
Willie K. Vanderbilt, Jr. Educated on the Continent, he sought refuge from the public eye. He would shock the world in 1902 by announcing that money never made him
happy. He retreated to a life of raising horses and living with his loving second wife,
Anne Harriman Sands Rutherford. *Right:* Alva Erskine Smith (1849–1933), first wife
of William Kissam Vanderbilt I, gave birth to three children: Consuelo (1877–1964),
Harold Sterling (1884–1970) and William Kissam, Jr. (1878–1944). She divorced William Kissam I in 1895, married Oliver Hazard Perry (O.H.P) Belmont in 1896, and
forced a marriage of daughter Consuelo to the Duke of Marlborough and, although
she was active in women's suffrage, was never forgiven by the movement for her earlier activities (courtesy Suffolk County Vanderbilt Museum).

daily manager, diligent and detailed. William Kissam, on the other hand, preferred the long-range view of an investment banker, and balancing work with
pleasure, trusting his brother to execute details. But recently, Kissam had taken
a keen interest in the business, particularly, and somewhat inexplicably, in
acquisition.

He pursued first the extensive Big Four Railroad, a major artery that controlled much of Ohio and extended west to Chicago and St. Louis. His skillful
maneuvering continued when he succeeded in acquiring the Boston and Albany
Railroad on a ninety-nine-year lease. His coup effectively sealed a Vanderbilt web
across the eastern seaboard, locking up all the major ports throughout New
England, eliminating competition, and raising dividends for stockholders.[3] Hot
on the heels of the Boston and Albany merger, Kissam ambitiously planned and

executed a collusive compact between the New York Central and the Pennsylvania lines, one of the largest combinations in railroading. It effectively linked the two largest properties of the northeast into one, non-competing system — a coup even his father and grandfather had never been able to achieve.[4] This extraordinary union further solidified Vanderbilt interests from Baltimore to Pittsburgh and parts southwest, devouring competition by crushing, then acquiring, smaller railroads across his path and, most importantly, paving the way for an "enormous increase in earnings."[5]

It appeared that despite his grandfather's fear that William Kissam and his brother would be "spoilt,"[6] the brothers had in fact exercised sound judgment and pushed forward their own plans for expansion with forcefulness akin to that of the fiery Commodore. Yet William Kissam's style was markedly distinct from that of his family members. He was quiet and unassuming, preferring to work behind the scenes and often in secret. Unlike Cornelius, who had spent time getting to know the clerks at the railroad offices, William Kissam had kept to himself. He possessed a certain "intuitive genius"[7] and knew when to act. His hand, invisible most of the time, was growing more apparent — and impressive — as he had emerged from his brother's shadow. Cornelius's rapid decline suddenly opened another of fortune's doors for Kissam, now to take the helm of the Vanderbilt Empire.

William Kissam left much of the management to the family counsel and longtime railroad man, Chauncey Depew. Instead, he went about his grander designs, quietly but decisively extending the reach of the Vanderbilt dominion from the northeast to the western horizon, swallowing up rival after rival until Kissam had, as some speculated, "welded together a chain of railroads from the Atlantic to the Pacific."[8]

His governance was astute, but always from afar. William Kissam never engaged fully in Vanderbilt finances. Perhaps being keenly aware of his brother Cornelius's steadfast approach to the drudgery of daily work, Kissam often commented, with well-noted irony, on money as a handicap to happiness.[9] His European education was readily apparent in his demeanor and his patronage of the arts. A connoisseur of fine art and a collector of classic books, William Kissam occupied a chalet in France with his second wife, Anne, and spent a great deal of his free time aboard his luxurious yacht, the *Valiant*. Yet, at the dawn of the new century, a shift was underway.

What, then, would happen to Cornelius's fortune? The elder Vanderbilt's two other sons, Alfred Gwynne (a mere twenty-two years of age) and eighteen-year-old Reginald Claypoole, were known more for their social indiscretions than any interest in railroad finances. Two years prior, Alfred had shared quarters at Yale with his older brother, Neily, who had kept him at his books. While Neily diligently prepared for his future in the world of Vanderbilt finance, Alfred concentrated on pursuing women. The young Vanderbilt was handsome, athletic, and cut a dapper figure on campus. Once his older brother graduated, however, Alfred was free to do as he pleased. With more social aptitude than intellectual prowess, he promptly shirked academics, instead gaining a reputation for his nightly escapades and earning the moniker "Social Light" of his class. Nevertheless, Alfred was next in line to the throne.

On October 16, 1899, Cornelius's wife and children gathered in the Breakers' main library, Neily included, though clearly apart from the rest. Across the room, fifty-year-old William Kissam Vanderbilt I stood surveying the morose scene. Two weeks had passed since Cornelius was pronounced dead from a cerebral hemorrhage,[10] followed by a funeral befitting a king.[11] But the will's contents remained sealed until Alfred could return from another of his frequent travels abroad. William Kissam had sent urgent telegrams to every destination trying to locate him. Finally, in China,[12] halfway around the world, he made contact. Alfred rushed home by steamboat, train, and tugboat, but still the wait back in New York was excruciatingly long.[13]

The tension inside the library was thick[14] as every member of Cornelius's family anxiously awaited Fate to unfold its designs. Alice, a diminutive woman, surveyed the room from her refectory chair, her face visibly distraught.[15] Reginald, the youngest son at eighteen, paced feverishly while the two daughters, Gladys and Gertrude, sat rigidly upright, seated close together. mirrored by a span of large glass bookshelves. They, too, tensely awaited the final decree. Wrenching his fists tightly, a brooding Neily could hardly conceal his growing concern. The diligent businessman and inventive engineer was undoubtedly the best choice among his siblings to take over the railroad, yet the rift with his father ran painfully deep. Would emotions or pragmatism prevail?

William Kissam was keenly aware of the importance of the moment. Standing in the alcove, he revealed no emotion. Alfred, alone, appeared calm, with the detachment of one who had prior knowledge. Exceedingly dapper in his Bond Street black attire,[16] he looked every inch the fashionable young gentleman recently returned from a luxurious adventure abroad.

His confidence stemmed from a long meeting he had the previous evening with William Kissam in the offices of the New York Central and Hudson River Railroad, where his uncle had secretly revealed the will's profound contents.

All eyes riveted on Chauncey Depew, the family lawyer, as he stood up from the attorney's tables and extracted several sheets of paper from his leather portfolio. Depew began with Cornelius's first request: "I give and devise to my beloved wife, Alice G. Vanderbilt, for and during the term of her natural life, my dwelling house on Fifth Avenue and 57th Street." That bequeathed the family mansion, all artwork, and possessions to Alice. That announcement did not come as a surprise, but tensions continued to escalate as the rest of the family anxiously waited to hear their fortunes. Each of Cornelius's residences, including the Breakers, was listed and calmly assigned to Alice, save for Oakland Estates, which went directly to Alfred. Upon Alice's death, the properties would be passed along to the children in the order of Alfred, Reginald, Gertrude, and Gladys. Neily's name went conspicuously unmentioned. Again and again, Depew read each stipulation of the will, dividing Cornelius's massive estate among his children, and in every case, four descendants were remembered, with one son sorely missing. The gold medal of 1864, a gift of Congress to the great Commodore for his support of the Civil War, and a symbol of passage from one Vanderbilt head of household to the next, ignored Neily as well, falling now, like so much else, to the second in line.[17]

Loudly and decisively, Depew announced to Alice a seven million dollar fund. Then went five million dollars each to Alfred, Reginald, Gertrude, and Gladys. In a shrinking circle sat Neily, grappling with his father's torment, angry beyond his senses, yet even more terrified. Depew continued without mercy. After another lengthy drought, Neily's name finally appeared: he was granted a meager $500,000 inheritance, along with an income from a $1 million dollar trust fund, for which he was allowed to reap only the interest over his lifetime. A pittance — indeed, an insult.

Chauncey Depew was, however, far from finished. All of his lengthy declarations had still not touched upon the bulk of Cornelius's formidable estate. The library grew more hushed — and electric — the sound of Depew's voice punctuated only by the sporadic crackle of the fire or the distant sounds of turgid ocean waves. Neily calculated his fate in desperate silence as Alfred looked on.

Finally, at the end of a long day of tortured revelation, Depew announced the remainder of the estate, approximately forty-two and a half million dollars, entirely, and unrepentantly, bequeathed solely to Alfred.[18]

Alfred Gwynne Vanderbilt, barely in manhood, careless and utterly devoid of his father's devotion to the roads, was now the heir to one of the world's great fortunes!

When Depew read the date of Cornelius's final will and testament, signed the first of June in 1896, Neily must well have understood the final ironic blow — this was the very day he had set to marry Grace Wilson. The gods could not have chosen a more stinging reminder of the rift between father and son, an act of absolute vindictiveness. How could this man, honored in society as a bastion and steward of honor and good conduct,[19] vengefully punish his own son so completely, disinheriting him solely for his earnest love? How could resentment rule over affection, even pragmatism? His father had died leaving behind an undying pronouncement writ by simmering anger and unforgiving spirit. Neily reeled under the news, utterly taken aback to finally grasp his father's intense hatred towards him.

As Depew closed his leather case, William Kissam surveyed the carnage in silence. But his mind was fast at work. His brother had erred miserably — and with consequences nearly immeasurable. Cornelius's only son capable of rising to the throne was now a castaway. Instead, an incapable boy stood gazing into the library's fading fire, pondering a future he well might never understand. The calculation was simple. The fates had chosen. Both the burden of responsibility and the glory of opportunity were now squarely in William Kissam Vanderbilt's hands.

Two

At twenty-one, William Kissam Vanderbilt II, Willie K. or "Two" as he was often known, stood little more than five feet, six inches, but every bit a strapping and handsome young fellow, "sturdily built"[1] with curly black hair,[2] playful green eyes, and an adventurous, exuberant spirit. The eldest son of William Kissam Vanderbilt and his tempestuous wife, Alva, Willie K. was, as his sister Consuelo (who knew him well) often remarked, "sweet-tempered"[3] and slightly mischievous. He was a master of play, and little else concerned him.

From his birth on October 26, 1878, Willie was a mama's boy through and through, a curious and kindly lad who "resembled his father in temperament."[4] For her part, Alva, a powerful and passionate woman, had dominated Willie's father and controlled every aspect of her children's lives. Yet she was also an attentive mother, unlike other women from wealthy families of the north that relegated their offspring to unseen corners under the care of governesses and nurses.

The daughter of a plantation owner from Mobile, Alabama, who fled the ravages of the post-war carpetbaggers, Alva knew her fortunes lay in the money-eyed Hamptons. As ambitious as she was a consummate flirt, the girl was introduced to the young Vanderbilt by her friend, Consuelo Yznaga,[5] and married him within a year. Everyone, including Alva, appreciated Mr. Vanderbilt both for his cheerful demeanor and, of course, the fact that he was an heir in the richest family in the world.

Two years later, she bore her first child, a daughter, whom she named after her good friend, the woman who arranged Alva's most fateful and propitious meeting. Young Willie arrived barely twelve months later, adding legacy to Alva's grand aspirations.

At the age of eight, Willie K. traveled aboard his father's new yacht, a two hundred and eighty-five foot ship,[6] the largest of its time, and so aptly named, the *Alva*. His travelling companions included his parents, his doting sister Consuelo, and his one-year-old brother Harold. Here, Willie first developed his immense and life-long love of the sea.

Despite family efforts to the contrary, it eventually became public knowl-

Sporting a moustache, Willie posed for this regal portrait. The days of obscene wealth were now falling to a populist America. Willie K.'s grandfather, William Henry, had said more than he intended in the public relations gaffe heard around the world, "The public be damned." Willie, now four generations from the Commodore, shouldered the burden an angry public brought on by the flaunting of pretentious wealth (courtesy Suffolk County Vanderbilt Museum).

edge that a rift had formed between Willie's parents. It was on another yacht, the *Valiant*, which William Kissam acquired several years later (in 1894) after the *Alva* sank accidentally off the coast of Cape Cod, where the rift between his parents grew all too obvious. Meanwhile, Alva had grown obsessed with promoting Consuelo's fortunes through marriage and presented her "La belle Mlle. Vanderbilt au long cou"[7] to European society. In an effort to further Consuelo's interests on a trip aboard the *Valiant*, Alva brought along a hand-picked trio of suitable bachelors. Among them was O.H.P. Harry Belmont, an ambassador to Spain and a former congressman, as well as Winthrop Rutherford, a twenty-nine-year-old bachelor considered one of the handsomest and most eligible young men of New York.

Apparently, the entourage was not meant exclusively for Consuelo. Immediately upon returning to New York, Alva initiated a divorce. The first woman of stature to ever do so, Alva shook up Victorian society by her bold move and the sensational accusation that her husband had committed adultery, a surprising charge considering her own behavior. Yet, the accusations were seemingly true. Evidence was loud and clear that William Kissam was involved with an attractive young blonde named Nellie Neustretter.[8] Whether it was a scheme to extricate himself from his troublesome marriage or if he had truly been involved with the young woman remains unanswered, but the effects at the time were instantaneous. As the press ate up the details, Alva traded in her Vanderbilt name for the new title of "Mrs. Ollie," as the wife of O.H.P. Belmont.

Yet while Alva busied herself with Harry on the *Valiant*, Consuelo began

It was the style in great society in 1887 to visit the wonders of Egypt, and the best way was to cruise the Nile, in this case on the *Prince Abbas*, chartered by WKV I from Thomas Cook & Son. Alva and her husband found family cruises much to their preference. Willie and Consuelo were not as enamored since they were required to keep daily journals, a practice that stood them well, however, in the future. *Left to right:* Oliver Hazard Perry Belmont (OHP; family friend and second husband of Alva Vanderbilt); William Kissam Vanderbilt I (Willie K's father); Willie's older sister Consuelo; M. Kulp (standing); Captain Henry Morrison (background); F.D. Beach (front and center); WKV II (age 9); Dr. Francis Johnson; a servant (background); Alva Vanderbilt; and William S. Hoyt (courtesy Suffolk County Vanderbilt Museum).

a passionate romance with one of Alva's other bachelors: Winthrop Rutherford. Unfortunately, by the time they returned home to Newport, Alva had conspired a new campaign, planning to marry her daughter off to the Duke of Marlborough. Marriage by Alva's schemes was an alliance of wealth and power, and Alva

Opposite: William Kissam Vanderbilt II at approximately age 5 in a classicly styled portrait (ca. 1883). Willie would straddle the transition years from the family of pretentious riches through populism and the New Deal. His mother, Alva, ambitious to a fault, must have played a hand in this imagery frozen on canvas (courtesy Suffolk County Vanderbilt Museum).

had slowly become obsessed with the notion that her daughter would marry royalty and gain ascendancy into the higher echelons of European society — even if the Duke was a well-known womanizer who barely had a penny to his name. While Alva intervened on behalf of her daughter, planning to marry her off to the Duke of Marlborough, Consuelo resisted, secretly trying to keep up her romance with Winthrop.

But against Alva, love was hardly a match. In a long and exhausting battle, including a feigned heart attack after a magnificent ball hosted in her daughter's honor, Alva emerged victorious.[9] By 1895, Consuelo surrendered and married the Duke of Marlborough in an opulent, high society wedding befitting her mother's grandiose tastes.[10] Such familial drama and pageantry, fast becoming a trademark of the Vanderbilt clan, could not have been lost upon Willie.

Willie usually sported a twinkle in his eye and this photograph is no exception (ca. 1897). The nineteen-year-old was a new entrant to Harvard, but was better off in Boston where he would not suffer competition from Uncle Cornelius's oldest (Cornelius III), a superior engineering student, or Alfred Gwynne, whose prowess with the ladies was legendary (courtesy Suffolk County Vanderbilt Museum).

Unlike his diligent cousin Neily, who thrived in the intellectual atmosphere of Yale, Willie K. lacked a predilection for academics. While academics were not his forte, the young man loved competitive sports, excelling as a bantamweight. He was capable of sudden bursts of speed quickly resolved by a rock-hard right hook. After private tutoring and two years of struggle at the prestigious St. Mark's, an affluent boarding school in Southborough, Massachusetts, a generous financial contribution orchestrated by his mother and paid for by his father allowed him escape to Harvard in 1897.

Competitive yet gregarious, Willie was also known as a democratic young man. The Vanderbilt scion, handsome and generous as he strolled the Yard, had natural social graces that easily won him the support of his peers. Soon enough he joined the Alpha Delta Phi fraternity and

Considered by many to be a democratic youth, Willie entered Harvard in 1897, only to leave in his second year. Here, seated at the bottom right, he appears as a member of Alpha Delta Phi fraternity. As might be expected of a Vanderbilt heir, he was welcomed to the Institute of 1770, which purported to identify the top one hundred of Harvard's future entrants into society. Equally fitting for a young man forced to keep journals by his mother, he participated in Harvard's literary magazine, the *Advocate*, as its business manager (courtesy Suffolk County Vanderbilt Museum).

became manager of the literary magazine, *Advocate*, for undergraduates.[11] Though of necessity, business depended upon continued stability from a pro-commerce administration and, appropriately, Willie's father leaned Republican, providing substantial financial support to President McKinley. In cheerful contrast, Willie K. spent his Harvard years as a registered Democrat.

Receiving a stipend of only one thousand, five hundred dollars a year for school-related expenses, Willie K. did not indulge in the extravagant social expenditures of others in his class, either in dress or entertainment. He ignored the traditional conservative garb of Bond Street black so popular to businessmen and the sons of businessmen. Instead, his collar appeared often frayed, his pants loose and "bagged at the knee."[12] Willie impetuously exuded exactly who he was, an independent spirit.

While Willie seemed to care little for what the press had to say about his attire, it was a different matter when it came to his reputation. After an article appeared in the *Boston Herald* claiming that Willie K. was occupied with golfing at Lexington[13] as the college's richest student, Willie charged into the newspaper's office and demanded a rebuttal:

I am Mr. Vanderbilt, and I have come here for the purpose of denying a story that you published about me this morning. I want you to make a denial of it in your next issue. I never played golf in my life, and I hope that I never will. That account in your paper is simply rot, and I wish it denied."[14]

Regardless of his politics or sporting conventions, Willie K. was a young man with big dreams, with unlimited ambition and passion for nearly everything in the world around him. Without a doubt, sailing was his first love, automobiles a close second — and now at Harvard — he'd found a third: a certain young woman by the name of Virginia Fair.[15]

His life radically transformed in 1898, his twentieth year, as he courted Virginia, known to all affectionately as "Birdie." From the moment Willie met her, a petite and attractive brunette[16] three years his senior, with beautiful hair and eyes, a remarkable wit, and vivacious personality,[17] the young Vanderbilt was instantly smitten. He abandoned his trademark rumpled clothes for finer attire and dramatically improved his living quarters, becoming a "man of the world."[18] Tearing out the walls of his old apartment, he added fireplaces, "green Japanese cloth,"[19] and wood beams reminiscent of an "old feudal castle."[20] The sudden and dramatic cause for these rich improvements (or "this splurge of worldliness") was simple, ecstatic love.[21]

Virginia had not been without assiduous attentions showered upon her by other eligible bachelors. She quickly rose as a popular young woman after the ball her sister Tessie Oelrichs threw five years earlier to announce Virginia to New York society.[22] Raised in San

As Willie K. peered through the eyepiece of a microscope in October 1898 as part of a laboratory exercise in science class at Harvard, he saw the word "hi" become transformed. "The microscope revolves the image through an arc of 180°" (courtesy Suffolk County Vanderbilt Museum).

Francisco, Virginia had accompanied her sister, Tessie, when the elder sister moved with her husband, Hermann Oelrichs, to New York.

While his father rattled Wall Street with fellow giants J.P. Morgan and James Hill during the summer of 1898, Willie raced along the sands of Bailey's Beach in Newport with his darling Virginia. The pair was inseparable, enjoying the seclusion of the private strip of sand and sea. Both naturally athletic, they shared a love of sports and competition. Days on the shore were a tangle of play and caresses—the perfect atmosphere for romance to flower into love. But in other respects, the two made an unusual match. In many ways they were an attraction of opposites. Willie was fast, fun loving, spontaneous, and warmhearted. Though he maintained a nod to social decorum, K. inevitably followed his own heart and took many a reckless turn. Virginia, on the other hand, carried a more serious bent: devoutly pious in her Catholic faith, and a social belle who followed — and invariably met — the highest expectations. Her impeccable stature as a lady was beyond reproach, exactly as it should be for one of her social status.

Willie's courtship was entirely fortuitous, for it was here in the social arena as a young man still in waiting to the family throne that Willie could make his first contribution to the Vanderbilt name and coffers. Virginia was a wealthy woman in her own right. She came to her wealth by way of the famed Comstock Lode, a burgeoning vein of Nevada silver that made her father, James Fair, one of the wealthiest men west of the Mississippi. With her father's passing in 1894, the result largely of his penchant for whiskey, Virginia was already endowed with —*and in full control of*— a massive inheritance.

The importance of marrying well was not lost on young Willie. It was imperative to his clan that he forge an alliance that would strengthen Vanderbilt interests, while important to him was the fact that such ties provided an inroad of independence from familial purse strings. Virginia offered both. While he might not gain the immediate recognition his cousin acquired through intellectual pursuits, Willie was nonetheless delighted to make a move that so easily won the approval of both of his parents, a catapult into the realm of wealth and prestige with a simple certificate of marriage. Under such propitious circumstances, leaving Harvard early would be of little matter.

For the elder William Kissam Vanderbilt, Willie's tie to Virginia also offered an opportunity far more important than even her family wealth; for now he had in hand an inextricable link between a railroad legacy and a shipping dynasty. Virginia's elder sister Tessie was married to Hermann Oelrichs, the manager and owner of the American branch of the transatlantic shipping giant, Norddeutsche Lloyd. Between the two circuits, Oelrichs' ships arriving in New York Harbor and Vanderbilt trains meeting those ships and spreading west, the two powers could enforce a near stranglehold on the world's busiest port. Marriage between Birdie and Willie meant an alliance between Vanderbilt railroading and German Lloyd shipping. Though unplanned at the start, William

Kissam would have certainly made the calculation early on and, thus, his approval proved ebullient. Willie had done very well for his family.

Being close friends with Tessie,[23] Alva, too, strongly approved of Willie's matrimonial choice, and with such encouragement, it was not surprising that the young infatuation quickly blossomed into an ardent courtship and engagement soon after. By January of 1899, Willie K. was engaged to Virginia with plans underway for a wedding only six months hence.

Virginia came to marriage with her own unfortunate share of familial strife and tragedy. Her father, James G. Fair, infamously known as "Slippery Jim,"[24] had abandoned his wife and family upon his election to the U.S. Senate. Fair, an Irish immigrant of swarthy good looks and feisty temperament, had succeeded as a mill and mine owner for several years before striking the Comstock Lode. At a time when many investors hesitated to take risks, Fair boldly stepped forward. He was a "nonconformist"[25] who argued that despite popular belief, the lode's reserves were not only far from failing, but had barely been touched. Rising quickly within society, Fair joined three others and together quietly bought the silver stock early on. Though he couldn't know it when he made his declaration, the Comstock gave of itself for another twenty years, making it one of the richest silver deposits in U.S. history.[26]

After twenty-one years of marriage, his wife, Theresa, shocked society by suing Fair for divorce on the grounds of "habitual adultery."[27] Winning a settlement of five million dollars, she also gained custody of both of their daughters, Tessie and Virginia, while the senator was appointed guardian of their two sons, James and Charley.[28]

Separated through the divorce, the sisters had a markedly different upbringing from that of their brothers. Their mother was a devout Catholic and the two sisters were brought up in a religious manner. Both of the young women were well mannered, gracious, and genteel, their youth marked by traditional balls to announce their debut to society. The boys, on the other hand, had "too much time on their hands and too much money in their pockets."[29] Following their father's lecherous lead, they graduated from innocent pranks to drunken bouts and had serious trysts with alcoholism.

In 1891, their mother died and her estate was split among the daughters, while one million dollars was placed in trust for the two sons, each receiving a stipend of one thousand dollars in the interim. Unfortunately, for the elder son, Jimmy, he died of alcohol poisoning five months later.

Charley, then only twenty-four years old, became eligible to inherit the entire million in six years. However, the pursuit of pleasure had left him not only penniless, but also heavily in debt with creditors knocking daily on his door. After his brother's death, Charley tried to mend his ways, but his father had recently bought him a "string of horses,"[30] which won few races, but succeeded easily in coaxing Charley back to his gambling and bourbon. Now, Charley also took up the company of a young "handsome blonde,"[31] Caroline

Decker Smith, a woman best known for her numerous pseudonyms, the best known being "Maud." Hailing from New Jersey, she had relocated to San Francisco where she ran a house of questionable reputation. In October 1893, the pair wed, enraging the elder Fair who immediately drew up a new will, disinheriting his son.

While the couple was away in Europe on their honeymoon, the senator fell sick. Reporters in the east next cornered Hermann Oelrichs, the husband of Charley's sister Tessie, who was asked if he would provide the newlyweds home and hospitality since Charley had lost the favor of his father. With the full support of both Virginia and Tessie, Oelrichs did not hesitate in replying, "I do not care to have my name connected with the Fairs in any way,"[32] he commented.

Yet the prodigal son did return home, just in time to reconcile with the father who once again changed his will, reinstating Charley to equal stature with his sisters. When the senator died on December 29, 1894, Charley was at his bedside. Despite being one of the most prominent men along the western coast, Jim Fair died with few mourners. Most townspeople remembered him as a "greedy, grasping, mean, and malignant"[33] man, a man who had sacrificed his family and honor to make money. Ironically, so profoundly was he detested that Senator James Fair was also grudgingly admired as a "stout warrior"[34] and a "cool man"[35] who had "no conscience to trouble him."[36]

Upon his death, Senator James Fair bequeathed a fortune of forty-five million dollars, the largest fortune in the western United States at the time, split equally among his three surviving offspring, Charley, Virginia, and Tessie.

While Tessie was "tall and reserved"[37] and known for her queenly presence, Virginia was vivacious and short at sixteen when she moved to be with her newlywed sister and brother-in-law to New York in 1890. The son of a German financier and shipping magnate, Hermann Oelrichs had been educated in London and Bremen in the family business of commercial shipping.[38] A powerful amateur pugilist and swimmer, Oelrichs enjoyed a good joust or two with fellow boxer William Waldorf Astor and others. Deeply admired and envied at work and leisure, Oelrichs was the subject of numerous tales, including a wildly renowned story that he was once found swimming in the ocean by one of his own skippers. The veteran captain, spotting him far from the ship, mistook Oelrichs as struggling for his life and rushed to his aid. He offered the twenty-six year old a proper rescue, which Oelrichs coolly refused, preferring instead to swim back. The skipper declared, "Dot tam Hermann; I schtop no more annuder times for him."[39]

Over the next nine years, every social event the young silver heiress attended was followed with avid interest by the press. When Virginia coyly announced her engagement to the public,[46] the newspapers spilled over with accounts of her charming ways and the ease with which she commanded attention. The result was a flood of new suitors, but Birdie remained steadfastly attached to Willie K. While the engagement was public knowledge, it came as a sudden surprise when the wedding was announced for April of 1898. Willie would leave Harvard[41] to marry his fiancée before completing his education.

In a move befitting an alliance of baronial stature, but intensely eschewing the press, the wedding was held at the home of Tessie and Hermann Oelrichs, a white marble mansion on Fifth Avenue and 57th Street. No less than two hundred guests, New York society's finest, attended the event.

Elegant yet understated, the wedding was marked foremost by piety. Virginia was a devout Roman Catholic,[42] as her mother had been, and requested that a Roman Catholic priest conduct the ceremony.[43] Though born Episcopalian, Willie cared little for the obligations of faith, professing no denominational preference and never attending church.[44] He would certainly accept his love's desire for ceremony, but as décor, not devotion. Faith would, unfortunately, never be something the two would share.

Fueling rumors and speculations, stories of wedding preparations and guests filled the newspapers. By the morning of the wedding, a large and boisterous crowd appeared outside the Oelrichs' residence, stretching up and down Fifth Avenue even before sunrise. Some even waited patiently overnight, eager to be the first to see the wedding between the country's most eligible bachelor and his heiress bride. With the curious crowd pushing and heaving against a band of police spread out to enforce control, squeals of delight and shouts of surprise burst out when Willie K. emerged from the Oelrichs' front door early in the morning. It was obvious he had spent the night there, making a most unconventional visit to his betrothed. By eleven o'clock in the morning, as the first guests arrived, the street was impassable. They, too, could not escape the scrutiny of staring onlookers.

Mobs surrounded the elder Vanderbilt's mansion down the road and an unprepared father of the groom was soon surrounded. Police had to escort him the short distance up Fifth Avenue. Soon after, Alva arrived with Harry, making a grand entrance as Mrs. O.H.P. Belmont. Soon after appeared Willie's aging uncle, Cornelius Vanderbilt, and his wife (and Alva's long-time rival) Alice. The myriad of women gathered in throngs along the street, eagerly anticipating jewels, silk, and satin, were not disappointed.

Despite the cloak of privacy, reports of the ceremony ran rampant. The wedding took place in the Oelrichs' gleaming glass conservatory and adjoining ballroom, decorated in resplendent white and gold.[45] Delicate blossoms and large rosebushes filled the rooms, casting a soft glow upon the radiant bride. Standing below a bower of peach blossoms, the young couple faced the altar in the center of the room.[46] The bride wore a gown "of soft ivory satin trimmed with Irish point lace."[47] Her ornaments were simple yet exquisite. The only jewels she wore included the diamond clasps of her veil, a pear-shaped pearl pendant surrounded by rubies, and a pearl necklace.[48] Earlier, Willie K.

had presented his new bride with a pearl necklace of suitably Vanderbilt proportions—valued at seventy thousand dollars.[49]

Hermann Oelrichs gave Birdie away, as Charley did not attend.[50] Virginia's
five-year-old nephew, Hermann Oelrichs, Jr., performed the duties of page.
The ceremony was followed by breakfast, after which Willie and Virginia
changed into their travelling clothes. Guests gathered to say goodbye, each
holding a box of cake embossed with the Vanderbilt seal.

As a carriage pulled into view the guests threw rice. The crowd, which had
been lulled into complacency, burst its restraints to get a good look at Virginia's
going-away gown, made of black Italian cloth and a long close-fitting tunic
skirt. Ladies swooned and police displayed their clubs to quiet and warn the
women back. Virginia fretted that she would never be able to get into the carriage, and the freshly married Willie K., helpless to improve the situation, could
only grow more impatient and frustrated by the minute. America's royal sweet-
hearts had now made it official.[51]

CHAPTER 3

Trial by Fire

Thank God for the Pinkerton man who first caught scent of smoke as it lazily began to layer the first floor in a stratified blue haze. Shouting, "Fire! Fire! The house is afire,"[1] he immediately woke the young Mr. and Mrs. Vanderbilt. But by then Idle Hour, the gorgeous country house of Willie's father at Oakdale in Long Island, overlooking the Great South Bay,[2] was choking with smoke. Willie and Virginia struggled to throw on a few clothes. With seconds dwindling, but keeping a cool head, Willie soaked towels and draped them around Virginia's head and then his own, making it better to breathe through soaked cotton.

The smoke was dark and thick. The manse was completely made of wood except for two chimneys and a ribbon of stone serving as foundation. Willie could sense the rising tension and the sweltering urgency of the moment. Flames had not yet begun to break through the first floor before unpleasant warmth invaded the blackness. The vast pavilion and marble staircase below Dutch gables[3] was completely obscured from view. Willie and his new bride, Virginia, ran down the stairs and burst out the front door to the chill of a mid–April morning and into the immediate attendance of Mr. P.J. Premm, the estate's superintendent.

Out of concern, Virginia screamed at Premm, "Go rouse the girls at once. Hurry up, there's no time to lose!"[4]

Premm shouted immediately, his voice hoarse, "Get up! Get up! The house is afire!"[5] But the servant girls who domiciled in the top floors of the house were already stirring, and "they came hurriedly down the stairs, half clad and full of sleepy terror, and groped their way through thick, dark smoke to safety. A few minutes more, and the flames burst through the first floor and began to eat their way toward the top of the house. With amazing speed, they spread to all parts of the main building.[6]

Yet things outside were put in order. A servant brought a chair for Virginia's comfort. Between the stream and the flaming mansion, the "mistress of millions" settled in for quite a night. She did not run away nor did she spend time comforting the frightened servants. Instead, she sat down on a chair and watched the mansion go up in flames. A fur-trimmed opera cloak was draped about her shoulders, "a soft black hat on her head, and a silk quilt covering her knees and feet."[7] Remarkably calm, she insisted on staying despite Willie's plea that she move farther out of harm's way. Entranced, Virginia held her ground; there was nothing her husband could do to move her.

Some five hundred yards to the northeast stood a fire tower. Willie directed a young man to ring the bell. Of the thirty servants at his disposal, two were sent by bicycle to East Islip and the Oakdale Station. At Oakdale, the bicyclist roused the stationmaster, Mr. L'Hommadieu, who could do nothing to help. At four o'clock in the morning, the telephone operators were asleep. In consolation, he suggested that the cyclist pursue help from neighboring Sayville. The stationmaster would go to the fire on his own in hopes of lending a hand.

When L'Hommadieu arrived, neither the fire nor its opponents had made headway. Willie K. and his band of amateur firemen struggled to activate a movable steam engine, a pumper that would draw water from the river. A team of servants carefully moved the cumbersome engine to the shoreline, then inserted the hollow shaft into the shallows. The rusty glow of the fire must have hidden the dusky murk just below the thin surface. No sooner had they started the engine than it promptly clogged: "Instead of the waters of the blue Connetquot, a thick stream of mud was rapidly drawn into the pipes, and in a few seconds the engine was *hors de combat*."[8]

Meanwhile, the countryside roused to the now-numerous alarms, and a crowd soon surrounded the brilliant spectacle. The employee sent to East Islip galloped into town crying, "Fire! Fire! Mr. Vanderbilt's place is on fire!"[9] In a world of volunteer firemen, there was no one at home when the galloping messenger pounded at the door of the firehouse.

He hurried on and soon found Isaac Conklin, a blacksmith. Isaac awoke Oscar Conklin, who had the firehouse key, and while Isaac was opening the stall for the gathering firemen, Sidney Conklin gathered a team of horses. The village postmaster and Fire Chief J.W. Frazer managed to gather a crew of some twenty men, who piled into a farm wagon and were off to the scene. There was no need to delay by loading the fire hose since Frazer knew the Vanderbilts kept a thousand feet or so in storage. Others, intent on helping (or gawking), followed in an eclectic assortment of buggies. A ringing fire bell provided little more than musical accompaniment.

They arrived at 5:30 A.M. only to find themselves locked out at the west gate, having to wait as Thompson, the keeper, let them in. As the sun crept over the horizon, they reached the house to find the main building in ruins and the annex now consumed by the fast-spreading flames. Heat from the expensive bonfire kept all but the foolish from getting close enough to throw a bucket of water on the hungry blaze.

Despite Willie's, the servants', and the gathered crowd's best efforts, by 6:30

A.M. on April 12, 1899, the elegant mansion was reduced to smoldering bricks[10] and two lonely chimneys. A few brass bedstands and some mattresses were the only possessions saved.

Two theories circulated as to the cause of the fire. Most of the employees, including Mr. Premm declared it a defective fireplace flue.

The staff had history to support their theory as a flue fire had disrupted a dinner party held by William Kissam seven years prior. Not much damage had occurred, but by implication, someone was at fault for poor maintenance. Willie K. could not be held accountable. Idle Hour had a staff for that purpose. Still, he felt pangs of responsibility, the complete destruction having occurred on his watch.

Willie K. and Virginia discerned a far more sinister cause — arson.[11] Mr. Frazer, a veteran of the New York City Fire Department, described the furnace arrangements in Idle Hour as "old-fashioned.... The cellar was not high, and the hot air pipes ran a long distance along the cellar ceiling."[12] However, when Frazer asked Willie how the fire had started, he replied, "Well, I know that the night watchman and I drove a man out of the cellar a few hours ago. He escaped by way of a window. I think he may have set fire to that kindling wood in the cellar."[13] So much the better, for arson made Vanderbilt a victim, rather than just the proponent of "old fashioned"[14] ductwork.

Though Willie and his new wife suffered the terrifying blaze, William Kissam was the bigger loser. Of the three houses once owned by him and Alva, he had chosen to keep only Idle Hour. This exquisite mansion styled by architect William Morris Hunt, set on a sprawling nine-hundred-acre lot, featured no less than one hundred and ten wooden rooms, all of which now lay in cinders. Countless oil paintings and exquisite furnishings which the elder William had acquired in Europe were now gone. Even worse, three safes were never recovered. Of most importance, however, was a private collection that William Kissam had at his Long Island mansion of "one of the largest and most interesting collection[s] of heads of deer and elk in this country. A large proportion of these heads were trophies of his prowess as a huntsman, and they represented species of animals in Europe as well as in this country."[15]

Houses, and even mansions, could be replaced. Everyone had escaped safely, and no one was apparently hurt by the fire. Yet Willie's pleasant memories of childhood were gone, burned away by a sense of guilt. No solace for Willie could be gleaned from his father; the elder Vanderbilt was already at sea on his way back to France. The wedding a week ago was unforgettable, but now the honeymoon would be a dark stain on that memory. The "dainty, picturesque"[16] home by the sea overlooking the bay lay in ashes. They would build again, from the proceeds of insurance, and this time out of stone, but Willie's past was torn asunder.

No doubt inspired, at least in part, by his fiery honeymoon, Willie found a new way to feed his passion for risking his life. Willie and his friends Payne

Whitney and R.T. Wilson became volunteer firemen. Among other triumphs, Willie and his company later helped save Manhasset from a blaze that leveled seven cottages:

> Then came Mr. Vanderbilt's company from Thomaston Station. They had had a long and hard run of it, but once at the fire, they seemed to know what to do. There was no use in attempting to save the burning hotel and the seven cottages. All of them were doomed and the millionaire fire-fighters turned water on the neighboring cottages, and they were saved.[17]

Willie K. even served as the peacemaker between the Vigilant Hose Company of Thomaston and the Alert Hose Company of Great Neck.

> The Vigilants have claimed for months that the Alerts always got the alarms first and so beat the Vigilants to fires. Finally the Vigilants swore they would not "run wid de masheen" any more; would retire from the Great Neck Fire Department. Learning this, the diplomatic Mr. Vanderbilt invited all of the "boys" of both companies to come to his place ... on the Fourth of July and they have accepted.
> In the afternoon there will be competitions for prizes at laying hose and squirting streams. Mrs. Vanderbilt, Mrs. Harry Payne Whitney and other women of the Meadow brook and Great Neck colonies will be hostesses at a luncheon to the firemen; there will be a fine display of fireworks. Thus the politic Mr. Vanderbilt will quench the hostile fire and lead the Alerts and Vigilants together as a string.[18]

Willie's derring-do was a bit distant from the demands of grand society, but he managed to impress them a few years later by bringing the concept of a Millionaire Fire Department to Bellevue Avenue in Newport. If the locals were going to tax the rich, the latter were going to get services commensurate with their fiscal contributions. They wanted the road properly oiled, and they demanded their own fire department.

Of course, Willie K., with his extensive experience in Great Neck, was a natural to lead the men in red, and he was duly chosen as captain. The townies would have to survive with their bare bones equipment and a volunteer force led by the gardeners of the cottages up the lane. By contrast, the millionaire volunteers went for the highest technologies in their fire trucks and chemical apparatus. The hooks and ladders had brass fittings and were kept at an appropriate shine. No gardeners were these; the firemen of Bellevue Avenue boasted the likes of Payne Whitney, O.H.P. Belmont, Stuyvesant Fish, Henry Clews, E.H. Harriman, Harold Vanderbilt, George B. DeForest and a host of others sufficient to intimidate any fire caring to lick their golden columns. The ladies managed to bring some precious metal to the fore by promising gold cups as prizes in summer tournaments where brave firemen could rescue dummies from sheer terror.

CHAPTER 4

Meeting of Giants

Step back two years, just a few months before Cornelius Vanderbilt's demise. The summer of 1898 held New York in a grip of wicked, sweltering heat. Manhattan endured wave upon wave of temperatures above one hundred degrees.[1] As the mercury rose, so did the tempers of local residents, turning on the latest political stooge, city mayor Robert Van Wyck.[2] Small demonstrations grew to larger protests as citizens rallied for greater self-government. New York strained with another generation of growing pains, struggling under the constant deluge of new immigrants; emerging as a world capital; the financial engine of a nation. President William McKinley had freshly led the United States into war with Cuba. William Randolph Hearst, the loud-spoken publisher of the *New York Journal*, who had clamored for war for no less than five years, still ridiculed McKinley for his slow pace. War sold papers. Despite stunning victories on both land and sea, Hearst charged in late May, "A whole month gone and nothing done!" and demanded, "Wake up Mr. McKinley. Wake Up!"[3] Strife was rampant. The city was too wrapped up in its own woes and political fracas to pay much attention to a meeting of a few millionaires.

In a pristine law office off lower Broadway, two formidable railroad financiers met in secret one hot and sultry July afternoon. While the city hummed outside with its daily barrage of pedestrians rushing through streets, horse-drawn carriages clattering by, and vendors hawking their wares on sidewalks, James J. Hill methodically and precisely pulled out his papers to begin.

Stocky of frame but impeccably dressed, James J. Hill carried a refined air behind his thick, well-trimmed beard. He was neither good looking nor fierce, but exceedingly hardworking and visionary in a way that left his competitors often breathless. Known for his tenacity, Hill had built a 1,700-mile railroad from St. Paul to Seattle, the Great Northern Railway Company. Despite abundant criticism from opponents who called his efforts "Hill's Folly," he bullied and blasted his way across both the Rockies and Cascades. The satisfaction was all his.

Reorganizing and expanding the railroad line, Hill worked carefully, laying out small tracks of up to two hundred miles in length, and bit by bit, attracted settlers along the way. Every new farming community ensured another success for the line.[4]

Yet, like all the other great railroad men of his time, sixty-year-old James J. Hill was only half satisfied. A static empire meant nothing in this cutthroat competitive business. Territory was only good if its boundaries constantly expanded. In the late 1890s, the railroad business was made of a web of powerful competitors, namely J.P. Morgan, Jay Gould, E.H. Harriman, and William Kissam Vanderbilt. Each of these men had substantial holdings and none of them would relinquish control without a fight. The only way that Hill could extend his reach would be to join forces with one or more of his fellow giants.

Unlike the simple mergers that so often happened among faltering lines, Hill's plan of action was decidedly different, his course far more bold and daring. That afternoon, Hill set out to seek nothing less than the grand possibility of a transportation empire, rails stretching across the nation, control of all strategic ports east and west, and shipping across both the Atlantic and Pacific. To this end, James J. Hill had gained water rights in Puget Sound.[5] By controlling all ports of entry and exit, the syndicate would capture all trade in and out of the United States, extending its power into Europe, Japan, and China. They would form a global conglomerate, an alliance whose power would extend far beyond that of any nation — one that would reach deep into the pockets of every merchant and traveler alike. Uniting a transatlantic railroad empire that spanned the entire country with a mercantile fleet offered unprecedented power, privilege, and wealth. Government under McKinley, already severely indebted to the likes of Vanderbilt, Hill, Harriman, and Morgan, would now buckle at its knees. The ebb and flow of all trade would belong to no more than a few men.

One of those men in particular was most eager to forge this strategic alliance: none other than J. Pierpont Morgan, banker, financier, railroad owner, and, most recently, owner of a fleet of British liners.[6]

Now he sat across the table from Hill, massive and broad shouldered, his fierce gaze a persistent symbol of a reputation for building monopolies and crushing foes. While Morgan had been afflicted with a severe case of rosacea since childhood, leaving him physically deformed, with an enormous nose, his unfortunate appearance only added to his seeming prowess. Few could withstand his gaze — so square and belligerent that they, rather than him, turned away, shrinking from his intensity.[7] When others might have been ashamed of this deformity (and certainly Morgan hated photographers), he used it as a weapon.

Morgan was a complex man, known for his rough manner, his cigar-smoking habit,[8] and his indomitable, competitive ferocity, but also for his love of the arts, and steady generosity, including enthusiastic patronage of the Metropolitan Museum of Art.

In all things, however, J. Pierpont Morgan refused to cede authority, especially in business. This meeting was not his, but this time, begrudgingly — and out of some necessity — he accepted the invitation.

The two men had known each other for a good twenty years, but Morgan's experience in railroads was at least double that. Under his father's tutelage at J.S. Morgan & Co., he developed the skills of buying, beating, and monopolizing against his foes, talents that would become his trademark as a pioneering corporate raider. Unlike Hill, who was largely self-taught, Morgan was the son of a banker and had an extensive education from fine academies in Switzerland and Germany.

Morgan ran his business like a country newly asserting its own nationality: He forged new alliances, pecked at enemies, created communities of interest among his erstwhile rivals, and avoided bloody conflict. His rule, while not completely tyrannical, was decidedly and unabashedly authoritarian — monarch of his own ambition.

In the succeeding twenty years, Morgan thoroughly reorganized the railroads, buying large controlling stock shares and using his clout to pressure governing boards. By the time Morgan sat down across from Hill, he had amassed a sizeable share of the eastern railroad market. He was also now in direct control of his father's company, renamed J.P. Morgan & Company.

Hill controlled that vast northwest market through the Great Northern line. What remained of the region belonged to the Northern Pacific. Morgan had recently gained control of the N.P., and the two men shared the territory in a carefully structured collusion. Now, the time had come to consider the rest of the national map. Yet their railroad stock combined was still not enough. They needed to bring in more influence. An incursion from Chicago to the east was almost unthinkable. Every inch would mean all-out war. Defeating the New York Central might destroy them all. But, if not defeat, then perhaps partnership.

Easygoing and affable,[9] William Kissam Vanderbilt I was known more for his good nature and charms, distinguished tastes, and a love of all things equestrian. The grandson of the Commodore was hardly recognized for his business acumen, at least while in his elder brother's shadow. A dutiful son, William Kissam had returned from his private schooling in Europe to study under his father's wing at the young age of twenty-three.[10]

Upon the death of his father in 1885, William's brother Cornelius II managed the family affairs, in charge of the main road, the New York Central, while William, who oversaw the "Nickel Plate" line of New York, Chicago, and St. Louis,[11] now took over as chairman of the Lake Shore and Michigan Southern lines. As time passed, William Kissam found his own voice, but never sought at the limelight. William preferred the role of an investment banker from a distance, spending most of his time in Europe and aboard his pleasure yachts.[12] On one hand, he was a man well aware that wealth did not promise happiness[13] and was determined to enjoy his life fully; on the other, he understood finance and power of empire building.

Over the past three generations, Vanderbilt railroad leadership had become diluted through a combination of divestiture of railroad stock and subdivision through inheritance. The roads were subject to fierce competition and survival demanded a good offensive strategy. Now, forty-nine-year-old William Kissam was cognizant of the murmurings to the west. Indeed, the family banker, James Pierpont Morgan, kept him well apprised of events. This was too tempting a tale to ignore.

It would be a shipping alliance of hemispheric proportions. Certainly this was an opportunity his grandfather would have admired — far more than mere stewardship of the family inheritance. This was something important, something new, something that would belong to William Kissam Vanderbilt.

Hill and Morgan would combine to form one spoke of the wheel, Vanderbilt and Jay Gould (alone controlling 15 percent of the market) representing the other two.

Thus, as this summer day turned to evening on lower Broadway, Hill and Morgan convened, Gould and Vanderbilt in absentia — their holdings speaking for themselves. The goal: to obtain an alliance on equal terms.[14] From this evening of furious discussion and negotiation, a plan would take shape for the allied group to build their own steamships, manufacture their own cars and rails, and operate their own smelters.[15] In this endeavor, dominion would be complete. The reach of four men would span half the globe.

CHAPTER 5

Autofat

Idle Hour may have disappeared in flames but Willie K. was still determined to enjoy his honeymoon. After fleeing to New York and staying temporarily at Belvoir, a cottage overlooking Newport harbor, the young husband ordered his yacht *Carmita* to be readied and brought down from Boston.

Entirely refitted and overhauled, the forty-five-foot racing sailboat, black in color with a gleaming gold stripe,[1] had a beam of twelve feet and a draught of eleven feet.[2] Within two days of arriving in Newport, the *Carmita* was prepared for the young Vanderbilt and his bride. Simply adorned, the craft was a sailor's boat, with hardwoods and leather furnishings throughout. Virginia had softened its appearance by adding light blue velvet drapes, seat covers, and additional comforts.

Virginia was not entirely new to sailing. She had spent a large part of the previous summer sailing on the *Carmita* with Willie along Narragansett Bay. The water held a particular fascination for Willie, and yachting appeared to hold "first place in his heart."[3] It was on the sea that the young Vanderbilt conjured his fondest memories of early childhood adventures and time that he shared with his beloved parents. His first craft, learning under the tutelage of Captain Tom Shea,[4] master of considerable reputation, was the *Osprey*, a small keelboat. There he discovered all the skills he would need to take a voyage across the Atlantic.

The *Osprey* was small enough for Willie to handle himself as he maneuvered adroitly away from docks and out into open waters of the bay. Yet she was big enough for him to fully indulge in a sailing experience akin to grand forty-footers, with a comfortable keel for stability. While Willie ignored his studies and eschewed the boardroom, he spent many a breezy summer day in the place he loved more than any other, the sea. His independent spirit easily surfaced on the waters, and yet it was in handling the *Osprey* (and myriad craft to follow) that he experienced the strength that comes from self-control as master of his own ship. Quickly switching from tilting forward or leaning backward as he pulled the tiller and adjusted the sails, Willie K. was a natural sailor, always in tune with his environment, alive to the ever-changing winds and

Willie would have one consistent love in his life — yachting. Here, in 1898 at age twenty, he appears as the proud master of his second yacht, the *Carmita.* He would never stray far from his love of the sea. As a young man he wished to be so engaged in business as to stay in touch by wireless from his yacht. In his later years he spoke of how he had dreamed of building the ultimate yacht while a boy on his half rigger, the *Osprey* (courtesy Suffolk County Vanderbilt Museum).

waves. His restless spirit and often feisty temperament found immediate release in the calming effects of sailing when the waves were gentle "with occasional whitecaps"[5] or buoyed up by the excitement of a turbulent sea.

His father acquired *Carmita* for Willie when he was seventeen years old. Willie was now captain of his own boat, with his own crew of three sailors (in addition to Virginia, who acted as his first mate). Spacious and elegant, the sailboat was an "excellent sea boat"[6] that had raced in New York waters in previous summers.

It was on a sailboat that Willie K. also developed the habit of writing down his experiences in his private journals. From the time he was a little boy, Willie had been schooled in the fine art of journaling. His parents were dogged in their belief that writing about one's life was an exercise in self-improvement. And though he often balked at laboriously penning the day's exploits, be they a tour on his parent's yacht or a trip through the backyard garden to collect butterflies, journaling came to serve him well — his books became a place of peace.

Whether on the ocean or later motoring over countless country roads, Willie grew into an avid documentarian, his eye for detail vivid and meticulous. One volume in particular provided a host of personal insight and minutia. Chapter titles in *The Log of My Motor (1899–1908)*[7] were simple and to the point: "Monte Carlo to Paris,"[8] "Paris to Madrid,"[9] and "A Short Run Through the Alps Maritimes."[10] Yet each journey carried with it a flood of detail and vivid memories.

Not content to merely document his travels through words, Willie added countless photographs as well. Most were simple in their approach and not the least bit ironic, at least to their photographer, who thought little of snapping half-naked villagers going about their daily tasks, their earnings in a week not equal to the cost of one gallon of Mr. Vanderbilt's precious gasoline. The photo credits reveal the sumptuousness of Willie's adventures, as well as the pleasures of simple tourism. "Chateau de Fontainebleau"[11] reads one, while "View of Harbor of Villefranche, taken from Upper Corniche"[12] is another. Others bordered on the mundane, "Repairing a punctured Tire,"[13] the humble, "An example of how the Spaniards till their soil,"[14] and the self-indulgent, "Mrs. Vanderbilt in Automobile Attire."[15]

All the while, Willie meticulously recorded what he saw, where he went, who he met, where he slept, and even what he ate. Though few could stomach all three volumes, no one could deny that his work revealed an intimate knowledge with often intriguing and fascinating details about both European life and the workings of the motorcar at the turn of the twentieth century.

With the avid interest of the racing enthusiast, Willie faithfully reported the mileage covered on each jaunt, noting his average speed for the day, which often ranged from twenty-seven to twenty-eight miles per hour,[16] although his desire to go up to forty miles an hour,[17] a feat for its time, was something he eagerly pushed for whenever able.

And the stories certainly had their share of adventure. Constant altercations with the police, spending the occasional night in jail, receiving numerous speeding tickets, getting into accidents, and being chased by "a howling mob,"[18] Willie K. had a true knack for stirring up more than mere dust. Eight months into the marriage, Virginia had, by default, experienced more car trouble than she could ever have imagined as she witnessed her new husband get arrested,[19] fight with his mechanics, constantly swap out new vehicles,[20] puncture tires,[21] run out of gasoline,[22] and be accosted by outraged local citizens. She displayed a good sense of humor despite being hit by a chicken that flew up and struck her in the head on a trip to St. Etienne in France that December in 1899.[23] Whether he was burning books to stay warm during a blizzard in the Alps[24] or narrowly evading his car sliding into water as it careened down towards a dock,[25] Willie undoubtedly offered more adventure than most men of his day.

Just like his love of sailboats, Willie's desire for speed along the road was something he had developed early in life. He was only ten years old when he had his first automobile ride. While vacationing with his family in 1888 on the Riviera, Count de Dion invited him to drive his steam tricycle from Beaulieu to Monte Carlo. Willie responded with an enthusiastic acceptance. He held on securely as the Count "steered with one hand and regulated the steam pressure with the other."[26] Willie was astonished by the "extreme speed"[27] they traveled, saying, "Count de Dion was a courageous man."[28] From that day on, Willie K.'s pursuit of wheeled freedom was unquenchable. He soon returned home to spend his time riding steam tricycles of his own and attempting various tricks. Unwittingly, a railroad heir turned out to be a pioneer of the machines that would spell eventual ruin for the lines.

As an adolescent, Willie purchased a steady succession of automobiles, beginning with an electric car, which he quickly traded in for a Stanley Steamer, a true teakettle on four wheels. He later sardonically described the boiler as "more thirsty than a shipwrecked sailor,"[29] as they constantly had to refill it with water. When the steam would sometimes escape, those curiously watching, would rush for "shelter until the excitement subsided."[30] He was soon arrested on Manhattan's Fifth Avenue for the charge of not having a "steam engineer's license."[31] Even as a boy, Willie was breaking new ground.

In 1899, he purchased his first gasoline-powered vehicle, a British tricycle. Willie was soon thrown from the vehicle, but true to his indomitable ways, he brushed himself off and went straight back to kicking up dust. Next came a Mors whose single headlight gave it the appearance of a Cyclops. Willie was pleased, recalling, "It went ripping along at the astonishing rate of twenty miles an hour providing, of course the wind was not blowing. This retarded hindered progress to an alarming extent."[32]

By the end of 1900, only 13,824 automobiles traveled the American roads.[33] Most wealthy Americans who could afford the new toy bought several, thus making car ownership an even more narrowly class-based practice. Like many new technologies, and well before Mr. Ford's Model T, the automobile served as a symbol of status, increasing the ever-widening gulf between the haves and the have-nots. A good horse cost three hundred dollars, a tremendous expense for many, but of little concern for men like Willie K. In addition, the cars frequently broke down and required constant repair, making their acquisition a prohibitive purchase for most. Willie could not only afford a car, but had the money to travel with a chauffeur and a mechanic.

Soon Willie heard that Phoenix-Daimler had come out with a new line of faster machines, inspired by the auto racer Emil Jellinek. Emil would paint his daughter's name, Mercedes, on the side of his cars for good luck. Years later, the Daimler dealership would be renamed after her. Ever taken by the promise of greater speed, Willie immediately purchased one of the new Daimlers for himself — in June of 1900, for the sum of ten thousand dollars.[34] He named his new twenty-eight-horsepower steed the *White Ghost*. Willie K. could barely contain his excitement: "On a good smooth road, with everyone hanging tight, [it's] possible to travel sixty miles an hour."[35] Willie and the *White Ghost* did just that, covering the distance between Newport and Boston in two hours and forty-seven minutes. In a sign of times to come, Willie matched the locomotive record, and beat the electric car time with ease.

Willie's impressive achievement was halted abruptly in its tracks as he was pulled over for speeding, declaring, "Otherwise I would have beaten the railroad [too]."[36] Despite the incident, where he was fined for "scorching" by a Boston policeman who insisted that Willie was going forty miles an hour, while Willie declared that he was going at four miles an hour, saying adamantly, "How could the policeman have overtaken me otherwise?"[37] Willie also set a new record from Boston to New York. He drove without stopping and arrived at his father's house, announcing loudly, "Here I am."[38] The *White Ghost* was undoubtedly one of the greatest loves of his life.

On September 6 of that year, Willie gathered with friends at the Aquidneck Park, a half-mile racetrack in Newport, Rhode Island, to compete in a series of short races. Averaging 33.7 miles per hour, Willie K. won three of thirteen races.[39] "Automobilers," as they were known at the time, became the new scourge of the landscape. Those atop horse and buggy, forced to share the road, detested the new machines, which were not only bulky, dangerous, and prone to breakdown, but loud as well. Startled horses and overturned carriages were becoming a norm, left in the wake of one of these newfangled gadgets roaring through town on unpaved roads and uneven tires.

When Willie and Virginia returned to Newport from their honeymoon, he took her for a spin in the *White Ghost*, kicking up dust down Bellevue Avenue. Willie was, of course, stretching the limit of anything close to a safe speed. And before the dust cleared, he found himself in a confrontation with a horse-drawn wagon. The horses reared, threatening to crush the young speedster and his wife. Virginia could not recall the details of Willie backing out from under the hooves because she had fainted.[40]

With such a fright, many women might have sworn off the dreaded machines. But instead of abandoning motor vehicles—and her husband of a few months, Virginia encouraged Willie to teach her how to drive the electric. She took to the little machine quite readily and was credited with handling her new steed "very cleverly."[41] Newport citizenry complained of the dust trails he left as he sped through the village. The Vanderbilt name, however, stood him well, and Virginia and Willie K. were widely well liked.

Despite the admiration he drew and the occasional infamy of a speeding ticket, Willie's thirst for speed often put him foolishly close to a dangerous edge. On July 5, 1899, around ten o'clock at night, when the streets of Newport were quiet, young Vanderbilt took his car out, followed closely by his friend Arthur Kemp in another vehicle.[42] He raced backwards at dangerous speeds

Top: September 6, 1900, at the races. Driving number 14, Willie is at the starting line in Aquidneck Park, a horse racing track in the vicinity of Newport, Rhode Island. Willie won three of the thirteen five-mile races that day (courtesy Suffolk County Vanderbilt Museum). *Bottom:* On the road from "Nice to Pau and return" in December 1899, Virginia is appropriately bundled as she sits exposed in Willie's six horsepower Panhard-Levassor. The young Mrs. Vanderbilt would not tolerate Willie's automotive adventures for long, but in December of '99 she was still game (courtesy Suffolk County Vanderbilt Museum).

along Ocean Drive, and mistakenly pressing the wrong levers, sent the vehicle careening over sideways. Thrown a good fifteen feet from the carriage, Vanderbilt escaped injury, but was knocked unconscious. By the next day, he was back in another automobile.

Numerous arrests, flat tires, and confrontations with angry pedestrians failed to quench Willie's insatiable driving thirst. Many assumed the cars to be but a passing fad. Others, like Willie and the New York *World*, considered it sport. Claiming that Vanderbilt and other well-to-do automobile owners had given up tennis, walking, golf, and even polo in favor of "a sport that didn't require one to work up a sweat,"[43] reporters sarcastically named this syndrome "Autofat."[44] In a 1903 article, reporters claimed Vanderbilt had gained ten pounds since the purchase of his first automobile. Sport indeed.

In Europe, Willie dared to speed down open country roads without restriction. By May 2, 1902, he had set a new world kilometer record in a forty-horsepower Mercedes, reaching one hundred and ten kilometers per hour. Immediately, he was hailed as "Un Millionaire Recordman" in the popular French magazine, *La Vie au Grand Air*. Willie went on that year to compete successively against the best of the world at the Circuit des Ardennes race in Belgium, placing third in the road race.[45]

He might have been the toast of Europe, but Willie K. did not enjoy the same accolades at home. Racing down country roads invoked not awe but ire from the local citizenry. And farmers and shopkeepers were not going down without a fight. The locals were prepared to go to extreme measures to prevent pampered drivers from running roughshod through the streets of their villages. Passing motorists were often met with glass or tacks strewn across their path, quite enough to tear through the thin-skinned tires of the era. Other times it was upturned rakes and saws. Determined detractors even went so far as to string up rope or barbed wire across the road, a trick that worked best for motorists traveling at night.

The local laws added thick new sections on motoring, often seemingly determined to do away with the motorized beasts, one infraction at a time. One law in Vermont required auto cars to be preceded by someone waving a red flag to alert any possible horses or horse-drawn vehicles.[46] Legislation in Iowa required traveling motorists to alert the next town of their imminent arrival by telephone.[47]

Initially, Willie spoke amiably with policemen after the Newport Chief of Police summoned him to his station for a friendly chat. The young man responded by promising to abide by the laws and be a good citizen, encouraging the police to pull him over if he broke the law. When he came out of the station, his wife, Virginia, carefully drove his buggy outside with her two adorable nephews seated beside her,[48] presenting a charmingly innocent view. Yet that façade did not last very long as Willie K. again itched for speed. He irked his Newport neighbors so that worried citizens persuaded the community leaders to establish the city's first speed limits for automobiles. Not surprisingly, Willie K. scoffed at the ten mile per hour maximum. "Arrest me every day if you want to ... it is nothing to pay fines for such sport."[49] To Willie K., the highest speed allowed to him was nothing short of an insult to the superior craftsmanship, not to mention horsepower, of his imported automobile. Most of his cars could, and regularly did, exceed some sixty-five miles per hour.

Newport mayor Boyle eventually confronted Willie after one of the more prominent neighbors filed a formal complaint against the young Vanderbilt. According to Frederick Sheldon, the complainant, he had narrowly escaped being badly injured.[50] The mayor threatened the youngster with arrest if he did not slow down. That afternoon Willie was once again behind the wheel of a new French automobile along with a party of guests, speeding through Newport at his usual pace. As he was passing Thames Street, a little girl bolted across the street and was struck by one wheel and thrown to the ground. Shaken, Willie stopped the motorcar and ran back to the little girl, holding her in his arms as he waited for her mother to arrive. The child was apparently unhurt, but Willie K. offered to pay all medical expenses if they were required.[51]

In the end, the young Vanderbilts and the rest of Newport could not reach a compromise. Willie and Virginia soon packed their bags in hopes of a warmer reception elsewhere. "Some automobilists such as myself cannot raise dust in the streets without someone complaining,"[52] Vanderbilt called over his shoulder as he and his wife drove from the town.

Willie K.'s next stop was back to his childhood haunts of Long Island. It was a fortuitous return. Back in Rhode Island, most country roads meandered like a wandering hawk, wreaking havoc on unsuspecting drivers with their hairpin turns and doglegs. Motorists frequently found themselves mired in mud thanks to surprise rain showers and loosely packed thoroughfares. At other times, uneven grading or loose rocks gave the vehicle's exposed chassis a run for its money. Willie, on the other hand, was fortunate to motor up and down Long Island's packed-shell pathways.[53] For the turn of the century motorist, no surface could have proved as opportune as the straight white stretches gliding beneath Willie's tires. Though their dry and dusty nature might have proved unfortunate for those riding in his wake, the roads of Long Island were a proving ground for a young man perfecting his love affair with speed.

In addition to the speeding laws, Willie K. also had an apparent disregard for many of the other creatures that crossed his path. Any number of horses, donkeys, chickens, sheep, pigs, squirrels, raccoons, and a seemingly endless stream of stray dogs fell waste at the wheels of this singularly murderous rogue. Regularly, he paid his fines and zoomed off. But it was not merely county clerks and court reporters making a tidy profit off Willie's inability to veer around living creatures:

W.K. Vanderbilt, Jr., was running one of his big automobiles over a road on Long Island a little while ago, and was going a bit over the speed limits, according to reports. The young millionaire was at the wheel, and as he rounded a curve he noticed a man and a dog in the road ahead. He blew his horn, and the dog rushed out in front of the flying machine, and got all that was coming to him quite suddenly. Vanderbilt brought the machine up on its hind legs, jumped out and walked back toward the man, taking out his money as he went. He handed the man $50, and asked him if that was enough to pay for the dog. The man said that it was. As the automobile chugged on its way, the man stood looking at the dog and wondering who it belonged to, anyway.[54]

After Willie started offering to pay for any creature he might accidentally run over, local animal owners started bringing their lame animals onto the road in the hopes that they would be lucky enough to have Willie reimburse them after he had killed their charges. The good people of Long Island were able to profit from Willie's penchant for speed in a way that pointed to their mischievous entrepreneurial spirit:

> The Long Island farmer has been taught by his parents to "do" a New Yorker whenever possible ... [and has] discovered that a horse that isn't worth $6 for glue and fertilizer will bring from $65 to $100 when killed by the Vanderbilt's auto. When Willie K. starts over the Thirty-Fourth Street ferry for a spin on Long Island, news is telephoned along the line. A person unacquainted with the facts would think the cavalcade on the road was a procession. All of them are lying in wait for the young millionaire's motor vehicle. It is said that two fights occurred last week over which man should have the privilege of having his horse killed first. Several farmers who did not own animals have learned that it is profitable to buy streetcar [sic] horses that have been disabled. Recently two near-sighted speculators allowed their horses to be killed by cheap automobiles, and the ventures were a dead loss.[55]

The hardscrabble farmers of Long Island burned up the plough grapevine as accounts of young Willie began circulating from farm to farm. Like children playing telephone, the facts of the matter were somewhat embellished by the time reporters from the Midwest hopped on the story. But if one account is to be believed, the figures are a tad sobering. *The Star* calculated that it cost poor Willie K. "$57.23 a mile to take pleasure jaunts on Long Island, most of that figure being the sum of the damages he paid for horses slain or maimed."[56]

To be fair to Willie, he was not simply a homicidal maniac spraying bone, blood, and feathers across the streets and back roads of rural America. He was, in his eyes, a victim of an overabundant wildlife: "To hear the driver tell it, the roads were aflutter with both man and beast, making a Sunday drive nothing short of the modern equivalent of an African safari. 'Every variety of farm animal,' asserted a common report from that era, 'could be — and usually was — met in the course of a few miles' run. Horses, mules, cows and pigs ... Chickens! They were the bane of the motorist's life.'"[57]

How, then, to calculate the number of maimed, mauled, or murdered chickens, pigs, sheep, or even horses that wound up on the dinner table?

Just as often as his animals fell prey to those motorized wheels, so too did the farmer. "As they dash down the pike, without quaver or hitch," sang a popular ditty for Murine eye drops at the time, "the farmers in front of them take to the ditch."[58] A four-panel cartoon entitled "One Woman Who Did Not Jump"[59] painted an accurate picture of the ongoing feud between pedestrian and motorist. The first panel portrayed a speeding motorist, frenzied behind the wheel, bearing down on a poor old woman in bonnet and full dress. A later panel revealed the car crashing to pieces and the bonnet and bodice falling away to reveal a large rock. Says the farmer in the last frame, "You may remember that you frightened my team last week, and smashed me up, and so I thought I'd rig a little surprise fer ye."[60]

Nonetheless, these perils could not deter Willie's love of imported cars and the speed they delivered. Willie drove his "gasoline tricycle"[61] to victory in the final event of the first automobile race ever held in Newport. Almost ten thousand screaming locals crowded the Aquidneck Trotting Park that afternoon, straining to get the best view of the breakneck exploits of daring drivers. It appeared that the people of Newport, even if they had not completely made peace with the automobile, were at least fascinated by the spectacle of it. The following year, Willie claimed the title.

CHAPTER 6

Commodore

Besides the road, the sea beckoned just as sweetly. His father's example had led the way, forever implanting yachts in his heart. In July of 1900, entered as a stand-in for his father, Willie participated in a well-known yacht race, the America's Cup, in order to build his reputation in the community.[1]

There were four seventy-footers prepared to compete in the seas off Newport: the *Mineola, Yankee, Rainbow* and *Virginia*. Willie's yacht, the *Virginia*, named after his wife, had been launched into the waters just two months prior on her first turn.[2] The amateur captains Herman Duryea of the *Yankee* and Willie K. on the *Virginia* made a good showing against the *Mineola* and Willie's cousin Neily Vanderbilt's *Rainbow*—the latter two captained by professionals.[3]

A battle between cousins arose on the waters with Neily at the helm of the *Rainbow* and Willie K. with the *Virginia*.[4] The two closed in very near to one another getting entangled in a luffing match. The *Virginia* sent up her protest flag. *Rainbow*, however, obtained the best of the contest and Willie K. did not file a formal protest. Cornelius won the race by fifty-five seconds over a thirty-six mile course.[5] Though he lost the day, Willie remained undeterred.

Turning the tables on well-known sailor Duryea aboard the *Yankee*, Willie K. won his first race off Newport the very next day on July 13, 1900, securing the Lipton Cup trophy.[6] Two days later, he repeated the same feat, this time displaying fortitude and a penchant for leading his own way. Instead of tacking in short motions, Willie took his yacht in a sweeping tack that included crossing the Long Island Sound from Connecticut to the shores of Long Island and then back again for a victorious arrival at New London.

Winning against stiff competition on a clear day with a fair wind, Willie K. resoundingly beat the whole fleet in a second race.[7] The *Seventies*, as they were called, beat up and down the coast, and on August 8, arrived in New London, accompanied by the fleet from the New York Yacht Club.[8]

In November of that same year, Virginia and Willie K. welcomed their first child, a healthy baby girl[9] whom they named Muriel. After the holidays, the young family left for Europe to escape the cold winter. The following July, the family returned home on the liner *Oceanic*, Willie reporting that he was tired of his travels and wanted to spend some time at home. Perhaps, in truth, it was his difficulties with local mobs annoyed by his reckless driving or his own numerous small accidents that brought him home.

During a trip to Paris, a lamp fell off his vehicle and exploded as he rushed down a narrow lane, throwing "exploding spirits"[10] in his face and "burning off his eyebrows and lashes." Still, Willie managed to laugh the matter off, claiming that he had temporary dementia for a while from the pain. He also denied that the lamp was affixed to his car or that he was even in motion, saying, "I was standing by an acetylene gas lamp to the left of the car when it exploded right in my face. I shall never know what saved my eyes from destruction. My lashes and eyebrows were burned off, and I couldn't see for a few days. They fixed me up at the hospital, however, and there isn't a scar left to tell the tale."[11] The young Vanderbilt was a lucky sort.

A number of Willie's wealthy young friends shared his passion for breakneck speed. He enjoyed an ongoing competition with his dearest friend, Foxhall Keene, whose love of racing was well known. Keene imported a large Daimler and Willie, forced to up the ante, acquired a custom-made Mercedes that he renamed *The Red Devil* that could tilt the speedometer over seventy miles an hour in a heartbeat.[12] At his first opportunity behind the wheel, Willie rocketed forward, accelerating rapidly to maximum speed as his passengers begged him to let them get out and escape.

Yet no one could convince Willie to slow down, not even the continually growing fines in every town he flew by.[13] Frustrated locals began to complain, "Either the law must take a hand or private citizens must carry guns."[14]

Willie beat Keene soundly in all four championships he entered that year in 1901 at the half-mile track at Aquidneck Park in his *Red Devil* Mercedes.[15] Unfortunately, soon after his victories, the *Red Devil* broke an axle and the sleek *White Ghost*, too, fell out of commission. Suddenly, Willie was forced to travel again by carriage.[16]

Well enough. Foxhall and Willie were satisfied to seek entertainment at Bailey's Beach in Newport. But here, too, danger would pursue young Vanderbilt. One late afternoon in September the two took a frail craft out to ride the waves.[17] Suddenly, it overturned and they were thrown into fifteen feet of water. Though an excellent swimmer, Foxhall developed a painful cramp and began to go under. Willie instantly came to the rescue and was able to pull his friend to a nearby marker barrel. There the two were safe until the swimming master came to the rescue.[18] At least Willie was able to save a human life; perhaps it could make up for all the farm animals he had taken during his Sunday drives.

By the following spring, in April of 1902, Willie returned to automobile racing for one major event in France at Achères, where he reached the fastest official record at 65.79 mph for a gasoline car. However, he experienced considered "agitation indeed"[19] when later that month, another racer by the name

Willie K. in his 40-hp Mercedes Simplex, May 1902, just after making a kilometer in 32⅖ seconds. "A 40 hp Mercedes equipped with racing body was our mode of conveyance," wrote Willie in his *Log of My Motor*, March 18, 1902. In his usual fashion, he wrote of the journey from Paris to Nice, giving excruciating details of distance, travel times, road conditions and accommodations. This *Log* was the likely predecessor of the American Automobile Association tour guides (courtesy Suffolk County Vanderbilt Museum).

of Léon Serpollet bested him in a steam car at 75.06 mph, creating a new land speed record.

But back in the fall of 1901, sailing would come again to the fore as Willie temporarily stepped away from his racing cars. A new craft, the *Tarantula*, soon headed west, towed from London shipyards to Bermuda, where it was decided she would not make the mistake of earlier yachts, making grand entrances by being towed into port. Instead she made it to Newport News, Virginia, and was tied up to the passenger pier of the Chesapeake and Ohio Railroad, where curious onlookers immediately surrounded her.

One hundred and sixty feet in length and sixteen feet in beam, the *Tarantula*, a turbine craft capable of 2,000 horsepower,[20] could make 24 knots. Faster than existing German ships, the *Tarantula* was considered an important strategic vessel in the naval arms race between Germany and Britain. Although it was rumored that Willie's craft had not yet reached that speed, if she did, other turbine yachts could just give up and stay in port.

Her arrival in New York off the New York Yacht Club christened a new

It was a cold Thanksgiving Day in 1903 when Willie, warmed by a fur coat, set a new record for the Eagle Rock hill climb at West Orange, New Jersey. Here he is pictured in his 60-horsepower Mercedes (courtesy Library of Congress).

generation of yachts and a new chapter in the worship of speed. She had the look of a racer, with narrow sleek lines, a black glossy hull, and paired yellow funnels commensurate with her extreme length. The *Tarantula* was the most exciting example of what was termed a "toothpick"[21] or an "ocean greyhound"[22] yet to be found on American shores. It was said that she was so narrow that once one was below decks, a match could not be lit without hitting one's elbow against the opposite wall.[23]

The press tracked the *Tarantula*'s every move north. After replenishing her water and renewing her coal, she made for Newport bellowing her smoke, a black stream visible from a great distance on the horizon. She made the trip leisurely up the coast and proceeded to Tebo's yard, Erie Basin, where she would be overhauled at a cost of some $20,000.[24] Willie sought speed but enjoyed his comforts. The *Tarantula* was luxuriously appointed with a suite of four state-rooms, six bedrooms for guests, and smoking rooms, all exquisitely furnished.

A hundred men worked to get the *Tarantula* fitted to Willie's satisfaction. Changes to the *Tarantula* went beyond the superficial. Willie decided to mix oil with coal to obtain a hotter fire. The oil would be sprayed about twenty inches above the coal fire where the black mix would ignite, increasing the heat. Precautions had been taken to ensure safety but the outcome of the experiment was unclear; the engineer of the *Tarantula* refused to speculate. No one could

Willie (seen above) bought the *Tarantula I* as a racing craft. Built for speed as a naval vessel by the British, the experimental turbine ship had a twin safely ensconced on the Thames. Under the watchful eye of British authorities, a second buyer, purportedly a Vanderbilt, appeared with cash to purchase the second vessel. It made its way down the Thames but fell under the guns of a German cruiser. During the night, it slipped anchor, charging out to sea into the welcoming arms of two Russian cruisers. The ship promptly surrendered into the service of the Czar — who had been the actual purchaser all along. Her prize captain retired a Russian hero (courtesy Suffolk County Vanderbilt Museum).

Willie raced up and down Long Island Sound in the *Tarantula I,* spewing black smoke as he took on challengers. He met his match in a comparable vessel built for speed but lacking in experimental turbine technology (courtesy Suffolk County Vanderbilt Museum).

be sure that the mix would have an impact on speed or if the combination would blow the ship out of the water.[25] Regardless, Willie was primed to race anything that came along. His attitude was much the same that he evidenced with his motorcars: he was the demon of speed and wanted to prove it. He could have no better craft than the sleek steel-hulled *Tarantula.*

Willie K. also plied the waters in his two speedboats, *Mercedes VI* and *Hard Boiled Egg,* so named because it "couldn't be beat," at the Hudson River regatta. Far from a shrinking violet, Virginia was an avid participant, even steering her husband's boat to victory. During the 1904 New Rochelle Yacht Club Regatta, in fact, she jumped into the *Hard Boiled Egg* from the *Tarantula,* wearing a long black cloak and green veil drawn over her face. Willie turned over the wheel and she made the final dash across the finish line.

Appropriately, the Water Boat Committee of the Automobile Club of America consisted of Mr. Peter Cooper Hewitt (chairman), Col. John Jacob Astor, and Mr. William K. Vanderbilt, Jr., who, on March 5, 1904, made a sequence of announcements in reference to the Harnsworth Cup competition: the equivalent of the World Cup of motor boats.[26]

Always to be found at sea, be it by sail or motor yacht, Willie is seen here at the helm of his fast motor boat, the *Hard Boiled Egg*. The name is Willie's tongue-in-cheek statement that, of course, his boat couldn't be beat (courtesy Suffolk County Vanderbilt Museum).

Each country was allowed three entries, all of which were to have been manufactured in the country they represented. Boats could not exceed forty feet but the power plant was unlimited. Robert Jacob of City Island, New York, was the manufacturer of preference for members of the New York Yacht Club, and of course, Willie was first on the list for one of the three in the offing.

The objective was speed, and a light craft with a big engine seemed to be the winning strategy. In this case, keeping within the regulations, Willie's craft had an overall length of forty feet, and a ready sixty-horsepower Mors engine would provide abundant power. However, in deference to the prevailing wisdom, Willie opted for strength in construction to provide resistance to the pounding surf under extreme speed.[27]

The contest was to be held on a one hundred mile round course beginning at Oyster Bay on Long Island, fifty miles up and the same back. Willie, who had been using the *Tarantula* to commute between Great Neck and Manhattan, had been getting ample sea time with her. However, the maximum speed of his yacht was 26.75 nautical mph, while his potential contenders had been known to run at speeds in excess of his top mark. The long course was thought to favor Vanderbilt.

Unfortunately for Willie and his whimsical craft, he would be cheated out of his moment in history. A launch filled with ladies crossed Willie's bow and he was forced to make hard turn on the rudder to avoid upsetting them. Apparently, Willie had neglected to strengthen the rudder blade suitably because it bowed out of shape such that it was useless. The ladies were missed, and sadly so was the race.

The race between turbine and steam yachts that drew public attention stemmed from a somewhat unexpected source. Railroad giant Howard Gould offered his *Niagara IV* traditional steam yacht in competition. Both contenders were stripped of all excess weight. A forty-mile course, from Little Neck Bay and around the Eaton's Neck Buoy and back to the start, was agreed by the challenging parties, with a purse of one thousand dollars for the winner and a silver cup offered to mark the occasion.[28]

The day dawned cloudy but cleared in a timely fashion. When the two yachts were together, Willie hailed Gould and asked, "Mr. Gould, would it be agreeable to go below the line some distance, come up on even terms and cross as nearly together as possible?"[29]

To which Gould replied, "Certainly Mr. Vanderbilt; good idea, and satisfactory."[30]

When the starting gun went off, it took sharp eyes at the stop watches to note that there was a four-second separation between Gould and Vanderbilt, with the former at the advantage.

After five minutes, Willie was a full length in the lead. On the *Niagara,* all hands were lying prone to reduce wind resistance. Gould looked wistfully at the turbine craft and his eyes met his captain with concern. Gould came up even after five minutes and then fell behind a short distance as flames shot out of the turbine's pipes. It was close: the two owners could wave at each other and those in the distance thought the two might collide. Flames shot higher and higher out of the turbine. It was the contest all had hoped to witness.

Twenty-five minutes into the race the turbine crossed the wake of Gould's boat and was following astern. Willie was worried. He consulted with his captain and, at about the twenty-mile turning point, the turbine was a mile in the rear. From a mile behind, she drifted even further until two miles separated the contenders. Gould passed the finish way ahead of Vanderbilt. He continued on a cool-down loop and met the *Tarantula* as she finished. Appropriate salutes were exchanged.

In the annual meeting of the Seawanhaka Corinthian Yacht Club held January 10, 1905, Willie was elected to the exalted position of Commodore of the club. He was without a doubt a favorite choice for his sportsmen-like demeanor. Willie, who had been an active member since September 1895, when he was seventeen, was ushered in without opposition.[31] Given the official title "Commodore" held, of course, a special meaning for the young Vanderbilt — the same name by which Willie's great-grandfather, Cornelius, the original builder of the fortune, had been widely known.

Later that year, a re-match was held between Gould and Willie K. Gold cups abounded and rightfully so, for this was the 75- to 160-foot class: an elite group by any measure. Willie's *Tarantula* defeated the *Niagara IV* in the forty-mile contest, forcing Gould to surrender the much-sought-after $5,000 purse. The ships were besmirched with soot, but no worse for the wear. The dilemma quickly arose: with a one to one tie in the offing, a re-match seemed appropriate.

Vanderbilt was egged on by a story in the *World*, which reported that his prowess was in question. "Gould gave the cup, and both of them have more trophies than they know what to do with: likewise they did not need the money. They had ruined their sweaters and white ducks with smoke and begrimed their yachts for a friendly argument in supremacy."[32] Once again Gould accepted the challenge of a re-match and the sacrifice of yachting sweaters and white ducks to the support. Virginia loved all of it, the epitome of sport and wealth in the grandest tradition.

CHAPTER 7

All Hail the King
of Deepdale

Soon after the birth of his first child, Muriel,[1] in 1900, Willie turned his attention to the hearth. As a new member of the New York Central, he had obligations in addition to his playful pursuits. Thus, true to his obsessive nature, the idea of creating a home began to consume him.

The Vanderbilts as a whole were known for their penchant for building. In fact, followers had a name for it: "Vanderbuilding," the fine art of erecting grand estates and palatial manses like so many million-dollar pushpins on their own personal map of town and country. This was a noble enough cause to which Willie K. could put his shoulder, something ambitious, but not too rigorous; far-reaching, but a sort of sport. Now, as a newly married man with a newborn child, a proper home was an essential rite of passage.

When Willie was forced to take refuge from a thundershower in an old tavern overlooking Great Neck, he spied in the sun's breaking light what seemed an incomparable vista: Lake Success. It was pristine and perfect, known for generations in the environs as "the bottomless lake."[2] From this spot Willie K. could see the city off in the distance: the spires of Fifth Avenue, St. Patrick's Cathedral, and in the foreground, nearby Garden City.

Willie, raised naturally with the sense that everything could be bought, decided immediately that he had found something he wanted, as he gazed upon the fertile land. The bucolic scene lay seductively before him. He decided immediately that he had found his new home. The lake was a perfect setting for him and Virginia to build their grand estate. In the true Vanderbilt fashion, he would construct an edifice that would command the whole of this little lake and leave no question as to the name, and net worth, of its owner.

Yet this lake and the land that surrounded it were no ordinary forces to reckon with as Willie would soon find out. Surrounding the lake were mysterious tales of early inhabitants, including the Secut Indians, a forgotten branch of the Mohawks, who had fought against oppressors, securing — though eventually relinquishing — the shores with their own blood.[3] Another more recent tale belonged to a man who had driven his horse to Lake Success to drink when the animal suddenly grew frightened, dashing forward, with the wagon behind him, and plunged into the lake.[4] Falling out of the carriage, the man swam to shore. Later, he returned with others and grappling irons, but was unable to locate the horse or the carriage, both of which had disappeared entirely from view. No trace of horse or wagon was ever found again. According to popular legend, the lake was not to be owned, not even at the price of blood.

The cold fresh lake was rich in fish and so deep that residents had never been able to touch the bottom.[5] It was undoubtedly a gorgeous spot, alluring for its pristine quality and location, as well as its certain elusive and mysterious essence. Yet, did it have space for the grand estate that young William Kissam Vanderbilt II envisioned?

Willie sped toward his goal with his characteristic reckless abandon, paying no attention to popular folklore or the changing public sentiment towards millionaires. It is possible that if he had a better sense of the mood of the Long Island natives at the time, he might have proceeded in another fashion. But it is equally likely that, raised as he was to expect that the world would comply with his wishes, he would have done nothing differently after all. Regardless, he failed to realize that the world he was so eager to join was instead rapidly altering its attitudes toward wealth and no longer viewed it as evidence of hard work and cleverness but as crass excess handed down from one generation to another. But Willie didn't notice. He had a certain immaturity and obsessive drive that defied comprehension.

The grand estate Willie K. imagined would be named Deepdale. It would perch on the highest point above the lake, possessing a vista that would stretch all the way from the tree-covered dales of Connecticut to the skyscrapers of New York City.

Willie bought four hundred and seventy-four acres of land for three hundred and thirty-four thousand dollars, at the time the highest amount ever paid for farmland in Long Island.[6] As laborers worked hard to ready his fine country estate, Willie's agents gave them strict directions to preserve the British camp tree, a large poplar variety, measuring a good forty feet in its crown width.[7]

While at Deepdale, Willie found a new competition: poultry. Willie K. entered some of his finest chickens into local and regional competitions and was successful in several poultry classes, such as the White Leghorn exhibit.

Willie would pack up his Mercedes and follow the trail of agricultural shows that sprung ephemerally in the rural towns surrounding the New York City hub. His chickens competed mightily in New Jersey, Connecticut, Massachusetts and New York. Under the moniker Deepdale Farms, a truck stuffed with clucking hens and proud roosters followed dutifully behind the Mercedes. While Virginia occupied herself with riding and racehorses, Willie, it seemed, had found an impressive sport in chickens.

Deepdale became "Willie's Folly." The local citizenry was moved beyond expectations when Willie attempted to possess Lake Success. The lake became holy water when he tried to assert exclusive ownership. Each acre became a battleground until only the access roads remained. Willie offered a tidy ransom for privacy, but the local denizens did what Americans sometimes do when pressed — they voted (courtesy Suffolk County Vanderbilt Museum).

Willie's chickens earned their share of ribbons, attesting to his prowess as a breeder. Like everything else he did in his life, Willie was passionate about his fowl, exerting all the energy he could muster. He applied financial resources above the imagination of even the wealthiest of farmers. The conservatories that glassed the breeding quarters of his avian friends were as beautiful as they were functional. Deepdale was outfitted for actual research to develop a better chicken that would feed the masses. Willie could seldom dream small.

As the property took shape, Willie K. soon became swept up in plans of aggrandizement. He loved his new estate so much that he soon decided the land was not enough, and despite the persistent myths, he wanted to own Lake Success. Displaying his Napoleonic streak, the lake had to be completely his. It was all or nothing.

Anticipating a possible public furor, Willie decided to acquire the land around the lake surreptitiously. Quietly but steadily, Willie K.'s agents went about purchasing the land around Lake Success for the reasonable sum of $30 per acre. Using the name "Mr. Smith," they approached the locals to acquire their lots. This unimaginative pseudonym was perhaps Willie's first strategic error. The ploy poisoned public opinion toward Willie from the outset—no doubt fueled by the ill will of those who unwittingly sold when the price was low, for once word got out that a Vanderbilt was in the market, prices leapt higher than a Secut's smoke signal, first to five hundred dollars per acre and then to seven hundred.

In August of 1902, Willie offered the town of North Hempstead fifty thousand dollars for its "right, body and interest"[8] to Lake Success, including ownership of the town's three roads to the lake.[9]

He dreamed of stocking the lake with fish to create his own private sportsman's paradise. At first, certainly through his own cajoling, the newspapers were positive about Willie's endeavor, trumpeting it as a "beautification"[10] project and describing in awestruck terms the numerous employees brought in to dredge the lake and landscape its shores. They praised the architects and grounds experts hired to design the winding driveways, sinuous walkways and hidden grottoes that were to be its hallmark. Rapturous local reporters wrote about deciding upon the ideal spot for a house, to be built as a stone castle. Virginia had "endeared herself to the country folk ... when she presented every Sunday school in the North Hempstead neighborhood with a big Christmas tree."[11]

The Success Lake Hotel served as a familiar attraction and popular destination for locals and tourists alike, and had long been the beloved site of "public entertainment,"[12] the media euphemism for a dozen yearly gatherings from summer refreshments to winter enthusiasms. But here the public turned sour when the announcement arrived that the local landmark, a hotel beloved for its skating parties and cozy evenings by the fireplace, would be leveled.[13]

As public dismay grew, so did a sharp undercurrent of bitterness among the locals no longer awed by the grandeur offered by either the Vanderbilt name or even the tempting fifty thousand dollars bid by Willie.

It was decided that there must be a special election to decide the matter: "Already nearly all the picturesque spots in Nassau County have been purchased by wealthy men, and there is a growing feeling [of distrust] among the small property holders."[14] Naturally, the natives feared that they would be entrapped by the restrictions designed to benefit their richer neighbors. Old-timers began to dread the loss of what had been publicly theirs for generations.

The first round was fired by one Mrs. Abbie Ann Woolley, who staunchly refused to part with the final parcel of acreage Willie needed to encircle the lake. Her property had been in her family since the Revolutionary War. Likewise, George Washington Payne, the wealthy owner of a large tract along Lakeville Road, lived in a colonial-style house that had been occupied by his family for generations and refused to budge. Eventually, Willie's agents gave up pursuit of the Payne purchase and the homeowner himself commented wryly on the outcome in the July 20 edition of the *Brooklyn Eagle*:

Mr. Vanderbilt and myself own a square mile of land hereabouts. I think Mr. Vanderbilt has paid me a great compliment, as he evidently prefers my company to my land. I have come to the conclusion after considering the matter of selling out my home here, that there is nothing to be gained by disposing of your home, even though the price offered is large, and then trotting around looking for some place and buying it, not knowing whether you can live there or not. I am sure I can live here, for I have tried it.[15]

Payne, however, was the exception. Many others did sell. In his endless pursuit for local domination, the persistent Willie purchased and demolished the rustic home of "Aunt Hannah" Chisholm.[16] Chisholm had received the homestead from her employer who had quarreled with her own children on her deathbed and, out of spite, left the land to Hannah. An aging black woman known for her fine cooking and her witchcraft skills,[17] Aunt Hannah stirred up public sentiment against Willie, then made a tidy profit for herself. Although she was relocated, her move was not without some degree of difficulty for Willie, who noted that "she received $10,000 for her acre without the cottage on it. Later she made so much fuss about moving from the house she was paid $3,000 more. Even then she retained the keys until another $200 was paid her."[18]

Descriptions in the press turned as well, adding fuel to the fire. The area surrounding Lake Success transformed from being simply farmland to hallowed ground where George Washington himself had once camped. New legends of disappearing British soldiers crossing the ice sprang up. Suddenly, tiny Lake Success became the very symbol of democracy itself. Suddenly, Willie, the millionaire upstart, was the problem; the man who wanted to steal it right from under them.

Frustrated, Willie responded in *Town Topics*, a paper that had become more associated with spreading public opinion and gossip than real news: "Gentlemen, it is very strange that for two hundred years you have not seen enough beauty in the lake or historic glory around it to clear away the underbrush or exterminate the water-snakes. The meat may be yours, but the coconut is mine; and the first man who attempts to bore holes in it will uncover trouble."[19]

Ever persistent, Willie prevailed in purchasing all the land that surrounded the lake. However, matters became more complicated when the town fathers made it clear that Willie might own all the land surrounding the lake, but *he could never own the lake itself.*

Lake Success, they posited, belonged to the people. It would be fine for Willie to place a sailboat in the middle of Lake Success, but before setting sail he would need the town's permission to use it. He might, if he wished, fill the waters with a billion fingerling trout, but in so doing he would be donating a considerable amount of marine life to the public at large. He might clear the lake's shoreline of its numerous obstructions and even dredge its margins to improve navigation, but he would be entering into the town itself the very moment he ventured into the water.

When the people realized that the invisible and ghostly "Mr. Smith" was, in fact, a very flesh and blood Mr. Vanderbilt, they cried foul at the hands of a scurrilous and deceptive millionaire. The image of Willie tooling around in one of his fast cars, scaring their horses and running down their chickens and dogs, only added to the fire. Finally, the thought that he might actually buy what they had taken for granted for generations and make it into his own personal playground incensed the residents of Lake Success so much that they decided to do what Americans did under only the most extreme of conditions: they voted.

The public defeated the millionaire by a margin of six to one. More people voted that month than had appeared at the polls for the last presidential election. "The fashionables were not in evidence today,"[20] proclaimed one local judge transparently. "You see, most of them are registered in town, and cannot vote here. Why, William K., Jr. himself has not voted on his own proposition."[21] The traditional enmity between "townies" and vacationers was now laid bare clear: "He and his friends did not take their coats off and work for what they wanted, as they should have done, if they meant business. They just said, 'Yes we would like to have Lake Success, and will pay fifty thousand for it.' Then they took automobile rides, and that was the end of it for them."[22]

Although Willie now owned the surrounding land, he had failed to acquire the three access roads that were large enough to allow public use of Lake Success. The press and politicians who had supported the sale to Willie were now confronted with an awakened and angry public. Common men were quoted as saying they wouldn't accept one million dollars for their liquid treasure.[23]

But Willie would not accept defeat. The following day, the *Journal* reported that Vanderbilt had "seized"[24] the lake. Having been refused the vote, he had begun erecting a five-foot wall around the land. He might not own the waters, but no one else could have access to it without wings: "Once on the lake the citizens could paddle about as much as they please, but there was no way to get there. One man suggested in a jocular vein that as the lake was said to be bottomless and to have an outlet somewhere in China, access to it might be gained by going halfway round the world and diving."[25] Willie believed that once the voters recognized that they were not going to have their lake *or* their $50,000, they would naturally accept his victory in the matter.

As if there were insufficient issues to entangle Willie on the front line, he was outflanked by a potentially bigger foe: the City of New York announced an interest in utilizing Lake Success as a water supply. In an effort to measure the efficacy of such a proposal, city engineers were sent to sound the bottom and finally determine its depth, once and for all. Symptomatic of the fervor associated with the future of the lake, the press took umbrage that the mythical idea that the lake was bottomless would be lost if such scientific determinations were carried through.

In a colorful editorial in his spritely *Town Topics*, Ambrose Bierce wrote that it was the Vanderbilt family that needed to be studied rather than their environment as "no naturalist has ever adequately catalogued them."[26] The paper then played with Willie's distinctive stubbornness and his newsworthy obsessions: "If some members of this illustrous and insistent family are distinguished by a conspicuous conformity to the type, one at least is equally noted for talent. He is known as W.K. Vanderbilt, Jr."[27]

Alluding to Vanderbilt's undue influence over the city engineers, Bierge concluded that the millionaire's desire to resolve the bottomless question was frustrated only by his lack of ownership. The writer poked fun at the willingness of town authorities to go along with Vanderbilt's wishes and wrote a fiction in which Willie, in his desperate attempt to plumb the lake's mysteries, convinced them to drain the lake:

> The lake when drained was found to have been a singularly shallow body of water with an uncommonly hard bottom, but that is neither here nor there. What is both here and there and whatever it is needful to prove the superiority of man to the beasts that perish is the amazing fact that the unaided human mind could think out so effective a way to resolve so dark a doubt. Even the highest anthropoid ape would have thought of nothing better than to take soundings with a weighted line.[28]

Willie's building project ground to a halt by May of 1903. The *New York Times* speculated whether or not Willie would ever take possession of the estate, or instead choose to sell it off in parcels. As evidence that the fickle Willie might have lost interest, they noted his increasing enthusiasm for motorcar races in Madrid. The paper's emphasis was clear that Willie had traded in one fad for another. Indeed, he had come out the better, keeping his money and abandoning the residents of Lake Success in his wake, leaving behind a bitter taste for locals to swallow.

But not quite. Later in 1903, the newspapers reported that Willie was sponsoring a bill submitted in the State Legislature by Assemblyman G. Wilbur Doughty of the Third District, Queens. Underneath its arcane language and generalities, the verbose legislation masked a provision that gave more power to the Board of Supervisors, allowing them to lease the rights to Lake Success without public approval.

Not surprisingly, Willie denied, vociferously and indignantly, that he had anything to do with it. The *Brooklyn Eagle* reported Willie's rather long-winded gasp of horror:

> I knew nothing of the Doughty bill until I saw it in a newspaper. I condemn it unequivocally. I made a proposition to the Town of North Hempstead to buy Lake Success which the town refused, and that ends the matter. If, at some future time, the town desires to sell and I desire to buy the inhabitants of the town and myself may come to terms, which shall be mutually satisfactory. In the meantime I shall take no underhanded measures to acquire the lake. If I ever do acquire the lake it will be with the full knowledge and consent of the inhabitants of the town and on terms satisfactory to both of us.[29]

The difficulties that Willie experienced in creating the perfect paradise did not stop the young family from enjoying the summer of 1904 at the Long Island estate. It was idyllic and, despite all of Willie's protests, provided a peaceful oasis from the pressures of the New York Central and the social demands of Newport. Deepdale was akin to Willie's father's estate, Idle Hour, now under reconstruction, hidden away and private.

Despite his rhetoric to the contrary, Willie continued his pursuit for sole possession of the lake.[30] Willie and his lawyers were again standing before the Board of Trustees of North Hempstead, this time petitioning to lease a sliver of land, "the Old Wood Road," which provided right of way to the lake.[31] Willie did not attempt purchase of the access points to the lake, but instead he decided to lease them for 99 years. In October he applied to lease the right of way. The "knotty question"[32] Willie posed forced the board to go back as far as 1684 in their records to find a precedent. No town record of ownership for the right of way could be found, and the opinion was that in order for the town to possess Old Wood Road, the town must prove "usage and occupation."[33] On the advice of counsel that the town had no ownership to the land in the first place, there was no opposition to Willie's request for a lease, given the shaky legal ground upon which the Board found itself standing. Only one "no" vote was voiced on roll call. Perhaps the supervisors were aware that state legislation proposed by Assemblyman Doughty authorized an increase in member salaries from three dollars a day to twelve hundred dollars per year. Republicans were quick to respond to the vote of the nearly all–Democratic board. The only Republican, Monroe Wood, had been the sole naysayer. No terms of the lease were made public at the meeting.[34]

Losing the first round of the battle of Old Wood Road, Mr. John Baker and Mrs. Daniel S. Woolley, both residents of North Hampstead, were unwilling to surrender and took their fight to the courts.[35] The Highway Commission had condemned the old road as useless, but Woolley insisted that it was the best place to cut and load ice and that, as a pleasure drive, it should also qualify as having value. Yet after a number of hearings, the commission determined that the road was, in fact, useless.

Baker and Woolley refused to let go, determined to stop Willie. Represented by Lieutenant Governor–elect M. Linn Bruce,[36] they sought to set aside the decision of the Highway Commission by appealing to higher courts.

In the fall of 1904, Justice Robert Seabury,[37] who had appointed the commission for Willie's land ownership, listened to Bruce's arguments before moving to set aside the decision of the commissioners. Bruce argued that while the road was useless, it still could serve as a pleasure drive, no doubt proven by Willie's own improvements. Willie offered to build another road, but supervisors, feeling the heat of locals who disapproved, declared that the new access road Willie proposed was too remote to be useful.

Judge Seabury listened to the impassioned testimony of over a hundred people who had rallied against Willie. In turn, Willie's lawyers spoke of the mud and the poor condition of the road to demonstrate the uselessness of the passage. The residents insisted that Willie was as responsible for the damage as he was for the improvements. Seabury bent to the crowd; Willie could not have the road for his own.

The war was over. Willie had not realized that the construction of great estates after the turn of the century was not as simple as it had been in his parents' day. In situating his potential Eden on an elusive lake surrounded by existing homes, Willie had staked a claim in a land and at a time when it just was no longer easy to be a millionaire.[38]

The *World* suggested that Willie's defeat arose from a lack of diplomacy, implying that he had lacked finesse and had been too heavy handed in his dealings with the natives. However, the article, which had acknowledged an animosity toward the "encroachments of the rich"[39] who had been "invading"[40] and which pre-dated Willie's arrival, ended with a conciliatory gesture toward him: "In fairness to Mr. Vanderbilt, it is said that whenever he has appeared personally in the fight he has conducted himself so as to win not only the esteem of his opponents but in many instances the friendship of those who from principle are opposed to his plans."[41]

Another factor went unmentioned: as a fourth-generation Vanderbilt, Willie K. was a young man with a big name and a small purse. His offer of fifty thousand dollars, a pittance compared to his wife's fortune, was enough to whet an appetite but not enough to seal the deal. Willie K. did not have a fortune of his own; he was a man living off an allowance, which, as cousin Neily could attest, could be cut off at any time. His father, William Kissam, given the same scenario, would have quietly acquired the land through a team of skillful lawyers and overpowered the town with the weight of his financial prowess; it is unlikely that challenges would have prevailed.

Even in comparison to his cousins, Alfred Gwynne or Reginald Claypoole, Willie did not possess the same clout or financial resources to command the will and attention of his neighbors. The late nineteenth century had witnessed the growth of populism and with it came many new questions. His father, William Kissam, had given his sister, Consuelo, a substantial inheritance when she married the Duke of Marlborough. His cousin Neily, cut off from the family inheritance, was making money from his own inventions. Only Willie K. had no direct source of income or inheritance to call his own and was entirely dependent upon the will of his wife, Virginia, and his parents to provide him with money to fund his projects, whether it was acquiring a new boat, car, or house. The name Vanderbilt still inspired awe, curiosity, and a certain dubious respect, but Willie K., the poorest of the Vanderbilt line, was the least likely to profit from it.

That December, as Willie went whizzing down the Old Wood Road in his gleaming Mercedes, the axle suddenly broke, crashing the vehicle and sending Willie catapulting through the air. He landed on the lake's ice, thin enough to

Willie's defeat on the Lake Success matter was celebrated symbolically when he was thrown into the lake in an automobile accident that broke through thin ice (courtesy Suffolk County Vanderbilt Museum).

shatter under his weight, just about a dozen feet from the shoreline. Willie may not have been physically hurt by this confrontation with the lake, but, soaked through and through, he felt its certain chill.

The lake had won.

CHAPTER 8

The Scapegoat

In the summer of 1902, the *Louisville Herald* announced William K. Vanderbilt's return from France to run his broad railroad holdings because "Alfred cares but for outdoor sports, and Reggie has shown no inclination whatever for business. William K. Vanderbilt Jr., is a regular man of leisure and Harold is too young."[1] The *Herald* did not leave it at that but went much further, quoting a family friend, who had a lot to say about the matter:

> Here is one of the greatest properties in earth without a single one of the younger generation of Vanderbilts to look after it in the future. Here is a great house, akin in this country where money is the power to royalty in another land, without a single descendent of the man who planned it, who saved and worked for it, to keep it on its career.[2]

Willie saved the article, positioning the clipping boldly in the upper left quarter of a page in his scrapbook. The story, despite its terse message, had undoubtedly hit home because soon after its release, the young man went to work at the railroad office as a clerk.

Three other newspaper clippings that announced his employment eventually surrounded the article. The "man of leisure"[3] had become, almost overnight, a man of work.

The press paid heed and took note. In June, the *Times* reported that he was "busily engaged studying electricity and getting informed on the technical points of railroad administration."[4] They further spoke of his hard work and dedication, stating, "He gets to his office every morning before 10 o'clock and leaves about 4 P.M. for his yacht anchored at the foot of east Forty-Second Street."[5] Willie's status as unpaid apprentice made him a living contradiction; a man who earned nothing would typically be at the bottom of the ladder, but he was also a Vanderbilt, the only apprentice who commuted by yacht.

Meanwhile, rumors abounded that Willie's father had fallen for Mrs. Anne Harriman Sands Rutherford, recently widowed for a second time. Known as pleasant, beautiful, and wealthy, Anne suited Kissam. A blonde with a fair complexion, Anne had exquisite taste and a quiet, genteel nature.[6] They had a natural partnership and their wedding announcement bore the approval of

Willie, Consuelo, and Harold. Willie said in defense of his father's new interest, "We are all marrying and leaving my father practically alone and there is no reason why he should not marry."[7] It seemed as though the elder Vanderbilt had a new lease on life.

Within two days of the ceremony, Anne was showing her mettle as a good luck charm: William Kissam's horses won two important races in France. Like Willie, his father had a love for the competition of racing, but he preferred the more traditional pursuits of his own generation, the thoroughbred track and the sea. Horses were Kissam's favorite indulgence, and to Anne's delight they encouraged him to stay in France. He purchased a chateau in Normandy, named *Le Quesnay*, which Anne took charge of furnishing, filling the large estate with comfort and warmth. The agreeable atmosphere offered a sharp contrast to his previous consort Alva, whose décor was inevitably ostentatious and overpowering.

But Anne was much more than just a beautiful widow; she was also financier Oliver Harriman's niece and — more importantly — E.H. Harriman's cousin, the head of both the Union Pacific and Southern Pacific railroads.

Edward Henry Harriman's short stature and unassuming appearance belied his immense cunning and masterful execution. He was a man who, like James J. Hill, had built his entire fortune on his own. He was also one of Hill's greatest rivals, both rulers of western territory, both keen for a transcontinental alliance. With ruthless and speedy efficiency, Harriman had transformed the bankrupt Union Pacific into a prosperous business, all the while rapidly accumulating wider expanses of track and stock. Clearly, Vanderbilt understood an opportunity as grand as this. Harriman had already jammed his foot in the door of Hill's international shipping alliance. Vanderbilt knew that, though detested by Morgan, Harriman would take his place at the table. Now, as love would have it, Vanderbilt, the king of the eastern seaboard, could count on profits from not one, but two suitors from the west.

For Willie K., Harriman was a serious potential threat. Just as he'd entered his father's tutelage as heir to the family lines, the seasoned Harriman may well usurp his future place at the helm. Willie had blessed his father's marriage, but it is unlikely that he sought to turn over his budding railroad career. Of course, if the threat of Harriman domination was not incentive enough, Willie's cousin Alfred occupied (though rarely) a desk in the financial department, and of course, there was always cousin Neily, a trained engineer, waiting hungrily in the wings.[8]

Willie would soon have the opportunity to prove his worth. On January 2, 1902, smoke filling a tunnel in Grand Central station had obscured a commuter train from Danbury, Connecticut. A second train approaching from White Plains barreled in and collided with the first. Fifteen people were killed and scores more injured. William Kissam rushed from his Fifth Avenue mansion to lend aid, but by the time he arrived, the damage had already occurred. In minutes, the press descended, trumpeting death, destruction, and blame.

In response to the obviously unsafe conditions, and the resultant public outcry, the railroads were given until July 1, 1908, to stop using steam locomotives in their tunnels. All railroads entering Manhattan, including the New York Central, had to electrify or cease operations. The loss of the New York terminal, the nexus of so much of the Vanderbilt railroads, was unacceptable.

William Kissam Vanderbilt, William J. Wilgus, chief engineer of the New York Central Railroad, and Willie K. took on the task of rebuilding Grand Central Terminal with unmistakable vigor. At last, the Vanderbilt heir had his chance to shine.

Unequalled for its time, the original Grand Central Terminal opened in 1871. A giant arched shed standing atop massive iron trusses housed the seventeen tracks that received the daily rush of long-haul commuter traffic. The largest enclosed space in America, the shed, resembling a massive half tube interlaced with glass, was colossal to behold. Its central arches soared one hundred feet in height. The canopy stretched six hundred from end to end. The station, a monstrosity in its own right, formed the top of a gigantic "T." The Commodore's personal vision of grandeur followed a classical style, with architectural elements akin to Napoleon's empire: elaborate stone and brick ornamentation, donning a mansard roof with five domes. When he opened Grand Central to an awaiting public, the *New York Times* reported, "New York opened its eyes and gasped."[9] Some present that day thought that the Commodore had gone insane. Yet, given its immensity, the governing sentiment was that the richest man in the world had built "a terminal that would last for all time."[10]

This certainty proved to be short-lived. By the death of William Henry in 1885, the railroad had outgrown the terminal. By 1899 the *New York Times* called the behemoth "inconvenient,"[11] "unpleasant,"[12] and "wretched."[13] Once a source of civic pride, it was now considered ugly, disgraceful, and reeking of gross stenches.[14] The 1902 collision was the final straw. The public demanded change and the responsibility for bringing that change lay with William Kissam, his twenty-four-year-old son, Willie K., and the chief engineer, Wilgus.

At the drafting table stood William J. Wilgus, confident and outspoken. He had immense experience and an inventive, visionary mind. He was the right person for a very difficult problem. The short deadlines that they now faced would require all the genius that Wilgus could muster and all the funding that Vanderbilt could accrue into the new terminal.

Willie K.[15] was immediately assigned as apprentice to Wilgus, with the secondary and clandestine mission of keeping watch on the engineer. William Kissam, though wishing to maintain control over the project, needed to attend to the rest of the business, and more importantly, he deeply yearned to return to France. Willie knew his father's expectations and was ready to faithfully carry out a junior officer's duties. Certainly, some might have viewed mentoring the twenty-five-year-old Vanderbilt an honor and an opportunity. For Wilgus, who had better things to do, the inquiring eyes were sheer annoyance.

Willie occupied the office adjacent to Wilgus. Not everyone was oblivious to the significance of this placement:

> Should you the purlieus of the new Grand Central office tempt,
> Rest sure that from espionage you will not be exempt,
> For in a gilded office tapestried in fashion gay
> You must not interrupt the work of junior Willie K.[16]

Yet in Willie's own eyes, he had far more purpose than that of a mere spy. Electrification would be his key. While Wilgus oversaw the arduous construction of the terminal, Willie would take charge of the electrification process. Every New York Central line coming into the terminal had to turn over to the new source of power—from the center of Manhattan to as far away as Albany. This would be no small undertaking.

In early 1903, Wilgus brought his proposal, based on the concept of "air rights," to Newman, president of the Central at the time. Since Grand Central Terminal extended from 42nd Street to Central Park under Park Avenue, the railroad would achieve a significant stream of income by leasing Park Avenue, the street above the subway which was filled with buildings. But not merely storefronts and offices along the street: Wilgus's proposal suggested the building of track to serve the railroad complex sufficiently below grade to allow for the construction of a colossal planned real estate complex built overhead.[17] Massive high-rise buildings would command the avenue, generating a wealth of income for the railroad and extra space in buildings that could be rented or sold. The terminal itself would be built with office space towering above it. Wilgus offered a plan that far surpassed the demands of the legislature and the traffic needs of the railroad. He brought forth a brilliant strategy for the development of prime real estate in a scale that had never before been conceived.

The underground railway yard began at 56th Street and would extend under the terminal at 42nd Street. Some three million yards of dirt and rock would be removed to create the underground cavern seminal to the plan.[18] Wilgus's proposed electrification of the railroad throughout Manhattan, Bronx and Westchester would require generation plants and a power distribution system on a massive scale. Development of the air rights would require a massive planning effort as well as construction of tens of millions of square feet of revenue-generating space.

Construction posed enormous challenges, exacerbated by the necessary operation of the railroad, which could not abate through the construction. Wilgus would have to build while every line continued to operate.

Delivering the functional aspects of this project would require masterful execution, disciplined organization, and appropriate delegation of responsibilities to talented and capable individuals. Wilgus needed to be more than a visionary, but something of a magician in carrying it out. Given that the project as a whole was perhaps the largest and most complicated construction effort ever undertaken by an American city, it also required a leader. Wilgus never shrank from the task.

After approving Wilgus's plan, the board announced a competition to choose an architect. The contest was by invitation only and attracted the notable firms of McKim, Mead and White of New York, Samuel Huckel, Jr., of Philadelphia, and Reed and Stem of St. Paul, Minnesota. Wilgus was married to Charles Reed's sister and collaborated with him in his original design. By turns of influence, the prestigious contract was, of course, awarded to Reed. Later that year, dissatisfied with the design and perhaps feeling a need to exert his ownership, Kissam demanded a second architectural firm added to the mix. The firm of Warren and Wetmore of New York joined the project design. Whitney Warren, a distant cousin of the senior Vanderbilt, was also a close friend.

An "at will" contract was signed with the two architectural firms, merged for the purposes of this project under the name Associated Architects, that could be canceled at any time. In later years, when Charles Reed died in 1911, the railroad promptly canceled the contract with Reed and Stem, awarding an exclusive design contract to Warren and Wetmore.

All the architects considered were conversant in the architectural style known as *Beaux Arts*. Beaux Arts took the classical grandeur of Greece and Rome and blended it with French influences, particularly of the Napoleonic era. The American translations were not simply copies of the earlier forms but rather they represented a particular infusion of a great American characteristic: energy and vitality, and — some might argue — overbearing grandiosity. While America could not lay claim to the component forms, it had arrived at its own indigenous and stunning version. The Beaux Arts style exuded confidence and grandeur, appropriate for a rising nation whose stature in the world was reaching for the heavens. So too, William Kissam sought to glorify in stone the Vanderbilt dynasty once more. This would be the greatest and grandest of his homes, the home of the railroad itself: a temple to entrepreneurial divinity.

In a celebration of the "brain and brawn,"[19] employed by railroad entrepreneurs for almost a century, William Kissam and Whitney Warren chose Hercules and the Roman gods Mercury and Minerva,[20] representing moral and mental energy, to dominate the summit of their triumphal entrance arch. With one sure stroke, the two men created a lasting monument to four generations of a Vanderbilt legacy.

Willie K. had only been in the railroad office less than half a year, when the media began to focus its attention on him. The *World* asked him to say "something about the advantages of work"[21] to other young men and how to "earn their living day by day."[22] Gasping, Willie laughed and cried out: "Want me to say all that? Why, I'm only a young man myself. You see how it is; what can I say?"[23] And with characteristic forthrightness, he added, "Why say anything you please about it — of course I believe that all young men should do something."[24] Then with a turn to humility: "But I'm too young, I'm afraid, to be able to give much advice."[25]

The birth of Willie's second child, Consuelo, another daughter, was greeted cheerfully enough, but did not assuage his longing for a legacy for himself. Willie hoped for an heir to carry his branch of the family name forward. But it was not in the cards this round.[26]

Construction began expeditiously in 1903. Although Wilgus had provided a compelling argument for the capital value of air rights, he still had to provide cost projections for his project. In 1904 he estimated it would exceed forty million dollars, about half of the revenue the New York Central had generated the prior fiscal year. However, within a year, anticipated costs had skyrocketed to a staggering fifty-nine million and nine hundred thousand dollars[27] and in 1906 to nearly seventy-two million dollars.[28]

William Kissam faced a daunting, and growing, challenge. He would have to not only find the money to fund the endeavor, but also retain enough working capital for the railroad to function as well. Indeed, just twelve months after the start of the project, feeling the weight of responsibility, William Kissam morosely complained about his life and inheritance. In a rare public comment, he declared it "had left me with nothing to hope for, nothing definite to see or strive for."[29] He decried wealth by inheritance a "big handicap to happiness,"[30] dramatically adding, that it "is certain death to ambition as cocaine is morality."[31] Astutely, he observed a great distinction: a man who could find happiness by making money to increase his business and the man who inherits great wealth, and whose labor only added "to what may be an over-sufficiency."[32] But with characteristic lightness, William Kissam ended his diatribe on a more pleasant note, saying, "Oh, I get all the fun I can out of life, and I am quite pleased if other folks get something out of it also."[33] William Kissam had always enjoyed a blend of work and play. The railroad-maritime consortium, under the aegis of a new president, was now focused on survival. Teddy Roosevelt had pursued the railroad magnates through Supreme Court challenges against their new conglomerate Northern Securities. William Kissam found the enmity of the government, enveloping Hill, Morgan and Harriman with the scepter of criminal prosecution, a powerful incentive that made life in France on a horse farm, with his beloved Anne, all the more appealing.

Immediately, people responded with sarcasm that they would willingly take the burden without complaint if Vanderbilt were inclined to relinquish his fortune.[34] The notorious newspaper publisher William Randolph Hearst responded with clear denunciation. While he described the senior Vanderbilt as a pleasant, sympathetic man with friendly, sincere eyes, and "not a bad example of the average American,"[35] he snarled in epithet that "he pities himself publicly because he simply doesn't want to work."[36] Hearst went further by claiming that William Kissam did not have the intelligence or drive to grow a fortune.

What no one knew, not even Hearst, was that Kissam's one glorious dream — a shipping empire from Europe to Asia, and America in between, was slowly falling to pieces. If he could not surpass his father and grandfather before, then William Kissam Vanderbilt was in his own eyes little more than a sorry shepherd.

Without expanding his kingdom, then, was it not consolation for Vanderbilt to build his new castle, a monument to his own name? The costs were growing more astronomical by the day. William Kissam was aware that he would probably not recoup the financial gains from such a large endeavor during his lifetime, but he threw himself whole-heartedly into the project. What was flesh in brilliance of legacy? Ironically, the man chastised just one year prior for being among the idle rich would now push forth the creation of the greatest monument to Vanderbilt achievements.

Building the railroad terminal would also result in the development of a planned city, transforming midtown Manhattan into thirty grand blocks. While he did not construct the high-rise tower Wilgus conceived originally, the new Grand Central Terminal brought organization and "transformed the core of the city into a masterpiece of harmony and planning."[37]

The immediate ramifications of the terminal were an expansion of commuter traffic. As the railroad stretched outward, through the electrification of points north, commuter traffic in the Bronx, Rockland, and Westchester counties swelled inward.[38] It was becoming increasingly possible to live in the suburbs and commute to the city. The city itself was expanding its reach and it was now possible to ride from lower Manhattan to the Bronx for a penny. Commuter traffic exploded from the outset, making New York City the largest suburban metropolis in the world almost overnight.

In 1904, only a year after his arrival, Willie K. Jr. transcended his role as clerk under Wilgus and was given the privilege manning the throttle of a test engine built for the Central by General Electric. The road test of the locomotive was dramatically reported: "Mr. Vanderbilt threw back the controller notch after notch, letting the engine forge ahead at between fifty-five and sixty miles an hour." When pressed by reporters for his reaction, Willie followed his father's lead, "All he would say was: 'I have had a most enjoyable ride.'"

Surely Wilgus would not miss the prying eyes of the young Vanderbilt and must have blessed Willie K.'s ascension in the Central ranks. Electrification of the railroad was a critical element of Wilgus's own design, and who better to speed it along than a Vanderbilt?

Willie was next elected to the Board of Directors of the Lake Shore and Michigan Southern Railroad. The election was broadly interpreted as a strong sign that he would succeed his father in the administration of the family interests: "Vanderbilts take to railroads as naturally as ducks to water, and the election of W.K. Vanderbilt, Jr., as one of the directors of the Lake Shore and Michigan Southern is received with general congratulations."[39]

Willie K. was soon on an inspection trip of the traction lines around Cleveland, where he was the guest of Horace E. Andrews, president of the Cleveland Electric Railway Company. While on tour with his host and an entourage of other company presidents and officials, the automobile caught fire. Willie deftly put it out with a bucket of water and they were once again on their way. When they reached the depot, it was under repair, and the men played baseball instead: "Mr. Vanderbilt is a pitcher and has famous curves. With only a kid glove, he tackled some warm ones."[40]

Willie's star was clearly on the ascent. The speed of his pitches was matched only by the rapidity by which the young Vanderbilt moved toward electrifying the cities of the Mohawk River Valley. He was soon appointed as Director and Vice President of the Utica and Mohawk Valley Railroad Company and of the Syracuse Rapid Transit Company with the intent of electrifying the West Shore between Utica and Syracuse.[41] Nothing could be finer than to be the darling of the press while championing new technology. Willie was in his element as ambassador and developer of the family fortune, with a bit of the sportsman thrown in for good measure.

The June 1, 1905, the *Syracuse Journal* headlined "Vanderbilt Welcome Here."[42] Accordingly, the press followed his every upbeat word. The *Post-Standard* reported that Willie had made a surprise visit, traveling in a day coach as opposed to a private car.[43] Willie freely conveyed that all was well on the Syracuse project and that service should be expected by the next spring. He expounded further that the steam railroad business was in a "healthy state of affairs"[44] and he "was well satisfied with the progress of the terminal work in New York.[45]

Like the Commodore of old, who brought prosperity wherever his trains made station, Willie could see himself bringing electric efficiency to every village deserving of his attention. Towers bearing the sagging weight of electric lines would bring needed power across the land. If there was no town, he could create one, for where his ribbons of wire rolled out, so did commerce. An adoring public would hail the new modernity. His engines could go anywhere without bellowing towers of smoke. Tunnels would not be darkened, and stations were no longer stench-filled pits. The image was seductive: creating an asset for the future, and, best of all, it looked like good business.

Willie soon announced an arrangement to purchase a large block of electrical power from the Ontario Power Company. Headlines read, "25,000 Horse Power to Be Delivered from Niagara Falls to Syracuse for Most Complete Trolley System in the World." Power generated on the Canadian side was to be transported by aluminum wire, from Niagara Falls to Devil's Hole on the American Side. The *Plain Dealer* of Cleveland noted Willie's command of his business approvingly: "Instead of being satisfied with a superficial knowledge of the traction enterprise he has started out to master the general proposition and inform himself so that he may become an active traction official."[46]

Such career focus did not come without a small cost. The *New York American* lamented that "America to Lose One of Its Best Auto Drivers While Millionaire Applies Himself Assiduously to Work."[47] They reported expectantly:

> Mr. Vanderbilt's duties are becoming more complicated daily. When his father dies or retires from the control of the great railroad system, which W.K., Jr., is doing much to expand and strengthen, the young man will find his business responsibility doubled or tripled. For a long time he has spent gradually extending hours of labor at his desk and has acquired a grasp of the affairs of the vast system that has astonished men who have been in the business many years.
>
> Hence W.K. Jr.'s hours of leisure have been slowly shortened, and he is preparing to plunge entirely into the business he will some day control. This does not mean, however, that he will discard motor touring — only that Ormande Beach will know him no more as an active participant in smashing records and guiding lightning-speed machines.[48]

But what had happened to Willie's racing obsession? Fitting to his new direction, Willie refrained from the French circuit in 1905, using his expertise instead on behalf of the Automobile Club of America racing committee to inspect the *Locomobile* intended to represent his country in the French trials. With his blessings and that of the A.C.A., Joe Tracy drove, using custom modifications recommended by Willie. Sadly, the French prevailed, with the American entry placing a dismal 18th.

Willie did not lament. He was now a true "Railroad Man." The excitement generated in western New York about his inter-urban electrification plan and the welcome he received from farmers in Central New York was his new sport. He had the power of Vanderbilt coffers behind him and the demands of the State to encourage him.

Not everyone welcomed his arrival. Some lampooned youthful ways, such as the full-page comic in the *Syracuse Telegram* mocking Willie for his reckless speeding:

MY, OH MY, THERE'LL BE DOINGS WHEN
WILLIE K., JR., COMES TO SYRACUSE

> Just imagine the joy of being pushed off the earth by a real Vanderbilt in a racing "Red Devil." That will top over anything that can be done by any plain, ordinary Syracusan, won't it? Willie K., Jr., plays no favorites. He runs over men, women, children, and policemen without distinction. And imagine the increase in the city's revenues from his fast chauffeuring fines. Pretty soon we will be able to run Syracuse without taxing anybody but Vanderbilt. Oh, joy! Willie K., jr., likes country homes. There are a lot of them around here that he can have for the price. And he has the price. His price is welcome.[49]

Yet Willie wisely did not engage his detractors, and if anything, used his penchant for speed adroitly to his own advantage. Speed was now part of his cause to promote his electrification projects and he traveled with panache:

> All records for fast time on electric roads were broken this afternoon when William K. Vanderbilt experienced a run of fifteen miles in about thirteen minutes, or at

the rate of seventy miles an hour. The trip was made on the Toledo & Detroit
Short Line to enable Mr. Vanderbilt to make connections with the Twentieth Century Limited.[50]

As he toured Indiana, Ohio, and Michigan to inspect inter-urban lines,
Willie also considered the acquisition of the Widener-Elkins syndicate of traction lines. He was no longer the wealthy young socialite mocked in the press,
but now a person of apparent commercial and civic value, who had the ability
to unite not only "New York, but ... Pennsylvania, Ohio, Indiana, and Michigan"[51] in one great traction syndicate.

For the whole next year, Willie continued acquiring electric lines. He
brought the various branches under one central entity called the Central Railway Syndicate. New stock was issued under the Mohawk Valley Company to
assist in recapitalization and immediately the stock value went up from a valuation of one hundred thousand dollars to ten million dollars.[52] Almost con-
currently, Willie announced that his syndicate would soon extend 450 miles of
electrified inter-urban railroad with many of the constituent components purchased.[53]

Even the most miniscule detail about Willie's projects and his own personal life drew instant attention. He had become a celebrity in his own right.
He had invested heavily into the new electric road. The first electric train to
pass through Amsterdam traveled as fast as fifty-five miles an hour. Willie was
on board and "approving at every stage of the trip," passing out cigars.

By September 30, 1906, Wilgus had cause of his own to celebrate as he stood
at the controls of a new General Electric engine, leading the first electric train
into Grand Central Terminal.[54] The short journey was a huge step well celebrated by the press. It had taken four years for G.E., the Electric Traction Commission, and Wilgus to bring electric trains to the subterranean world of Grand
Central Terminal. By December, electric engines were fully employed in regular service. W.J. Wilgus was triumphant, and appropriately rewarded with a
five thousand dollar raise and a richly deserved one-month vacation.

Few would have taken notice of the modifications G.E. felt required to
make to the engine version Willie K. had first ridden. The original design concentrated the weight of the engine in the center, over the driving wheels. In the
engines actually delivered, two-axle guiding trucks were added, front and back,
in an effort to spread the weight over a greater surface. The guiding wheels
were added to reduce the tendency of the engines to "nose," a condition wherein
the mass forward stuck out off to one side of the tracks on a curve, causing a
heavy engine to potentially derail. It had also been noticed that after repeated
running on track surfaces, the weight of the engines would wear at the track
alignments and joints, a condition that could ultimately result in rails being
worked out of place.

Despite these potential issues, the train was operating smoothly. Traffic
increased daily. Within weeks of introducing its first electric line on the Harlem

Division, the New York Central added an additional train, a second express to serve the burgeoning demand from White Plains. What should have been another triumph, however, turned into a sudden and fateful disaster. The new engine on its second run flew off the tracks at Woodlawn, instantly killing twenty people, while injuring another seventy-five passengers.[55]

The public erupted.[56] It was the second railroad catastrophe in no less than four years in the Northeast. Someone had to be blamed, and all fingers pointed at Wilgus. The changes were labeled failed attempts to resolve more serious design flaws where engineering problems had been ignored. The district attorney, President Newman of the New York Central and Vice President A.H. Smith were all quick to accuse Wilgus.[57]

Wilgus justifiably tried to assemble a paper trail, but the legal department commanded him to destroy it. Wilgus had written a letter to President Brown detailing attempts to deal with the nosing problem. However, Wilgus was an engineer accustomed to living with details, and his letter was a condemnation of the Central. If his letter went public, then the world would know that the Central knew the nosing problem posed a danger.[58] His efforts to clear his name had made the district attorney suspicious that the problem might not have been fully resolved.

Though Wilgus had agreed to bury his letter, the pressure on his reputation was intense. On July 11, 1907, Wilgus resigned his position and gave up his historic task. Official blame for the wreck was placed on excessive speed. Design changes were indeed made but escaped public scrutiny. Sending up Wilgus as the scapegoat had narrowly averted a disaster for the New York Central and, perhaps more likely, the Vanderbilts.

CHAPTER 9

The Carnage

Willie preferred to purchase his auto cars overseas and ship them back home, to both the horror and amusement of local Long Islanders. For instance, in a chapter of his journal entitled "Hints to the Motorist,"[1] Willie referenced the *Annuaire de Route de l'Automobile Club de France*, an annual Parisian publication. To obtain the book, it was necessary to apply to the club. The book gave all kinds of practical information as to nearby hotels, garages, tire stations, addresses of doctors, telephone booths, and railroad stations. Willie, ever the visionary, sought to change all that. Every day, Willie duly recorded only that which *he* deemed worth devoting to paper. The result was a staggeringly self-indulgent work that stood as the precursor to those handy little "trip-ticks" for what would eventually become the American Automobile Association, or the AAA.

Despite his hardy work at the Central offices, Willie managed to slip in a few motoring events. Willie K. soon took a leadership position as vice president at the foundling American Automobile Association, a historic concept for a country still clinging to its horses and buggies. If ever there was a symbol for the turn of the century Renaissance man, it would have been Willie K. Vanderbilt.

Proud of his race in Belgium in August of 1902, where he sped along at an average speed of fifty-three miles per hour, Willie shared with reporters how he had defeated some of the best French chauffeurs, but also admitted being unable to maintain top speed, competing against another daredevil, Mr. Jarrot.[2] Nonetheless, he enjoyed his own performance. Willie's interest in auto racing persisted despite the enormous risks and the carnage he witnessed at racing events. In May 1903, Willie participated in the Paris-Madrid auto race. A cracked cylinder in his eighty horsepower Mors forced him to pull out the race. Fortunately for him, he exited early: the event was fraught with heavy casualties, killing even the renowned car maker Marcel Renault.[3] In his journal that night, he dutifully recorded the day's events, with descriptions of his own participation, the surrounding crowds, and even accidents by other motorists: "The poor fellow was killed only a short time afterwards, running into a tree on account of not being able to see, owing to the dust from a car ahead of him. His mechanic was also killed.[4]

Deaths, unfortunately, were commonplace. The gruesome event resulted in eight people fatally injured, earning the ghastly nickname, "Race to Death." Willie had talked with a friend, Lorraine Barrow, who in "trying to avoid a dog, he ran full speed into a tree, his car being split in two, his mechanic killed, and he himself mortally injured. Barrow lived for four days, suffering intense agonies."[5]

In a later race in Bordeaux, fifteen casualties spurred government officials to stop the event, "the sacrifice of life being too great."[6] Experiences like these were very publicly disturbing and in 1903, one of his friends, Mr. Watson, was so "unnerved"[7] by such carnage that he refused to continue and instead went back to Paris on the train.[8]

While Europe continued to allow racecar driving on main roads, back home in the United States such events were limited to the trotting track. Round and round they went at tracks such as the Aquidneck Trotting Park, spinning out and causing casualties to both drivers and fans. Where Europeans had grown accustomed to carnage and dodging the speeding vehicles, Americans were not only inexperienced at watching a racing event, but far less adept in getting out of the way.

Despite their name, trotting tracks were still little more than hard-packed earth and smooth concrete. Endless laps loosened the earth and sprayed it into the faces of other drivers, not to mention fans. Steam, smoke, oil, and grease filled the air in a haze that only worsened with each passing mile, and often the worst accidents occurred simply because following drivers could no longer tell where the track ended and the audience began.

At the turn of the century, a pit crew was a single mechanic who, in addition to continually oiling the hulking beasts, had to be just as ready to jump out at a moment's notice and fix a flat tire or loose lug-nut. This, in spite of the looming cars that zoomed by at breakneck speed often on the verge of hurtling into the assembled crowd as a result of a broken axle or burst tire.[9]

Despite their reputed modernity, the autos of that era were unsteady and haphazard affairs in varying stages of repair. Most were prototypes available in short supply. Automobiles in general, and automobile racing in particular, were both so new that supply simply could not keep up with demand.

Through the haze of smoke, dust, and grit, some of the ten thousand spectators, aching for a better look, often crossed the track, finding themselves in the path of an oncoming car. With bulky, half-ton automobiles to the left and right and nowhere else to turn, a doomed driver had little to do but stay the course and hope for the best.

Onlooking fans found it difficult to distinguish between drivers and autos alike. This was long before sponsors painted modern racecars to the point of distraction. Turn of the century autos were quite the opposite. Racers owned their cars, and as yet there was no standard model. The early days of racing lacked the well-known celebrities of, say, the cycling or even the boxing world, and although many fans knew Vanderbilt by name, few could place his face, especially once he had squeezed into his protective goggles and trademark fur-lined racing jacket. Patriotism was as important to these races as petrol, and woe to the fervent fan that too late discovered he had been cheering on a Frenchman for two or three dozen laps!

Given such a fledgling state in the early 1900s, Willie had to import not only foreign cars, but also foreign car racing. He began, slowly at first, testing the waters. When he found them not quite warm enough for his taste, he simply began heating things up, ignoring his detractors and forging full speed ahead into his brand new passion.

The Atlantic coast had long been a playground for the rich and glamorous, and Florida was a natural choice to revive their energies and indulge their hobbies. The beach sand was, in fact, hospitable for auto racing. At the right time of day, with the tide out to the left and the stacked dunes to the right, the seemingly endless strip of Atlantic coastline just south of Daytona Beach was a perfect racetrack to Willie and his boys.

On January 27, 1904, a special race was held in Ormond Beach for gentlemen drivers only.[10] Willie won the ten-mile race in a special ninety-horsepower Mors with a time of six minutes and fifty seconds. More important than the win, Willie covered a mile in thirty-nine seconds, beating a recent mark set by Henry Ford of thirty-nine and two-thirds seconds. Willie's managed an astounding 92.3 miles per hour — a new world record for an automobile. Willie K. Vanderbilt became the fastest man in the world.[11]

This accomplishment was no mean feat. To straddle an iron beast without benefit of roll bar, air bags, helmet, or even guardrails was akin to literally flying by the seat of one's pants. At that speed, a blown tire or punctured hose meant more than just a nasty spill; it meant being thrown from the speeding vehicle onto the hard-packed sand at nearly one hundred miles per hour or being pinned under the nearby ocean by the hulking vehicle.

Many might have considered him more playboy than daredevil, but this singular feat proved beyond anyone's doubt that Willie K. Vanderbilt certainly had nerve.

Willie's generosity and love of the sport was also evident immediately before the race, when he handed over his expensive sports watch to a timer, Col. W.A. Thompson of New York. After the race, Willie K. insisted that the man keep the watch as a gift.[12]

Walking away with nine victories out of ten, Willie K. was the toast of the town, the star of the four-day event. Records, however, seldom live long. Shortly after Willie sped his way into the record books, a daredevil named Barney Oldfield, the nation's first major professional racecar driver, beat him by nearly one mph when he raced Henry Ford's Ford 999 at a dizzying 91.37 mph on a bone-crushingly frigid day in Detroit. Willie's only loss in Ormond had been to Oldfield.

Willie K. must have felt unconquerable that year. Some time later, at Palm Beach, Willie displayed his gymnastic skill at trick bicycle riding. In front of the Hotel Poinciana, he hurdled over his bicycle's handlebars, and bucked up onto its hind wheel while riding backwards. He jumped with it in his "white flannels shimmering against his legs, small dark mustache standing starkly against tanned skin. He was a handsome devil, twenty-six years old, athletic and strong — every inch the sportsman."[13]

They were a rough and tumble group of men, yet fashion seemed as important, if not more so, as it did to their wives. Driving caps perched aloft, goggles pressed firm to driven eyes, leather gloves affixed just so, the proper driving jacket and just the right size handlebar moustache: the dandy, dapper images of the drivers were in sharp contrast with their stripped-down, beat-up automobiles, many of them with hand-painted numbers and grills that had seen better days. To drive so fast without a single hair out of place took some doing, but such was the moxie and dedication of men who took their driving as seriously as they took their money. Such fascinating and eccentric characters captured the attention of newspaper reporters and the imaginations of readers, and lent authenticity to the rumors that racers lived as hard and fast as the cars they drove.

In his time at the races, Willie had become famous for something more than just his millions. The racing circuit took Willie and his boys up and down the Atlantic Coast, from Ormond Beach to Long Island and back again. Along the way he shed the spoiled little rich boy image and emerged as something quite different. Suddenly, he was known not only for his charm, good looks, and jovial demeanor, but now for his daring. The combination impressed everyone. He brought his own panache to a rich man's race.

Willie returned to Ormond Beach for another racing season, but events quickly turned dismal. The beach was the same, the speeds a tad faster, and he had acquired another new car. But Frank Croker, a good friend of Willie, had died as a result of racing injuries sustained earlier in the week.[14] Willie's performance and his enthusiasm suffered as his spirits were dampened by Croker's death. He failed to win a single race and his racing record for the one-mile event was shattered by another contestant, Louis S. Ross driving a Stanley Steamer.[15]

Perhaps Croker's death gave Willie pause. He had certainly seen his share of fatalities in the name of sport. Nor was Virginia enthusiastic over his high-speed exploits. Not long after returning from Ormond, he turned his interest to sponsoring a race of his own. He received permission from the Nassau County supervisors to hold the first Vanderbilt Cup car race on public roads that October. Willie's days of recklessness behind the wheel were not entirely over, but they were about to take a turn.

Putting his name to an exciting new event, a symbol of progress and modernity, would be another sign of Willie K.'s ascension, and certainly an excellent statement that this Vanderbilt had plenty of backbone. Hearst might scoff at Willie's father, but not this young man, unless he wanted trouble — and perhaps one of Willie's famous right hooks.

The American Automobile Association would handle the management of the event; Willie would provide the leadership — and the Vanderbilt name, as well as the silver cup. The race was intended as an international affair, pitting the best of America with the best of other countries, particularly the French with their well-establish racing pedigree. Thus, the William K. Vanderbilt, Jr., Cup would soon bring serious racing to America.[16]

CHAPTER 10

The Vanderbilt Cup

Willie K. was no longer thinking in small terms when it came to racing. He had sped along with great enthusiasm all over Long Island and throughout Europe, competed at Ormond Beach and Aquidneck Park in New York, and added his name to the record books. Still, he thirsted for more, something that would put him, and the automobile, on the national map. Willie later recounted, "I felt that the United States was far behind other nations in the automotive industry and I wanted the country to catch up. I wanted to bring foreign drivers and their cars over here in the hope that America would wake up."[1] At the age of twenty-six, young William Kissam Vanderbilt II, Jr., proposed to the AAA that the Vanderbilt Cup be held on his home turf, Long Island, organized under his watchful, detailed eye. One of the first formally recognized and legitimately sponsored races ever to be held in the United States, the Vanderbilt Cup would give American automobiling the spark it needed.

The race was to be held on public roads, while following safety precautions for both public spectators and participants. Cars had to be manufactured in the country they represented, as it was an international competition intended to bring honor to the winning nation. There were also weight restrictions of between eight hundred to two thousand two hundred and four pounds. Two passengers were required in the vehicle, the driver and the mechanic, neither of whom could weigh less than one hundred and thirty-two pounds.

The cup itself was beautiful, designed by Tiffany's of New York, weighing thirty pounds and made entirely of silver. The magnificent award also bore the symbol of Willie's finest achievement — his victory at Ormond Beach — embossed in an image of him driving his Mercedes.

However, the peculiar history of events prior to the launch of the Vanderbilt Cup deserves particular attention: Why would Willie want to forgo his spot behind the wheel, tearing up the countryside, for a role behind the scenes, serving as sponsor, but playing the part of the observer? What had changed?

Two close associates of Willie K. had died behind the wheel, his friend Croker and his brother-in-law Charley. The death of the latter had invoked a particular bitterness between Willie and Virginia. Despite their amorous interest in each other at the onset of their courtship, the young married couple soon found that their interests were quite different. While Virginia initially supported her husband's auto racing and sailing endeavors, she began to display a certain distance from Willie K. over time.

Maybe the seeds of that discontent began at the wedding itself when Willie had failed to show enough decorum to avoid public scrutiny by staying at the Oelrichs' mansion the night of the wedding, or perhaps it lay in the unfortunate accident that destroyed Idle Hour. Their union was shaky right from the start.

On one motoring trip outside Florence, Italy, on a dusty country road, Willie and Virginia had a terrible driving accident, where a small six-year-old boy by the name of Adolpho Battini "ran out from behind a cart directly in front of the machine and just cleared the front wheel."[2] The citizens of the little town were furious. Seized by a mob,[3] Willie K. was yanked out of his seat. Wresting himself loose from their angry hands, he ran as fast as his legs could carry him and took refuge in a shop. The mob of locals swelled to four hundred and began to pound on the doors. As Willie K. later recounted:

The Vanderbilt Cup, a giant 10.5 gallon, thirty-pound specimen, was worthy of the family and the race that bore its name. The cup, created by Tiffany & Co., now resides in the Smithsonian. On the front, Willie's name appears, on the reverse, Willie is seen driving his Mercedes at Ormond Beach, where he set the world land speed record (courtesy Suffolk County Vanderbilt Museum).

> Two or three men seized me by the throat and others drew knives.... I managed to beat off two attacks successfully when the crowd approached for the third time, most of them with knives drawn. Noting this, I seized my revolver, but some one from behind me wrenched it from me.[4]

Fleeing down a hallway and up a staircase, he rushed through an open door into an apartment. The women occupants, unaware of his crime, welcomed him. He barricaded the doorway. Willie suddenly realized he had left Virginia and the mechanic to their own devices:

> It then occurred to me that perhaps the same attack I had endured might be brought against Mrs. Vanderbilt and the mechanic, and although I did not know where they had disappeared to, I decided to go back, face the enemy and see if I could find them. I thereupon rushed out and started to descend the stairs, but to my great relief met the police [who were] coming up. They arrested me and put on the handcuffs.[5]

It would take the efforts of the town mayor to calm the brewing lynch mob, who argued vociferously to protect Willie, Vir-

MÉSAVENTURE D'UN CHAUFFEUR MILLIARDAIRE
M. William Vanderbilt, aux prises avec les paysans de Pontedera

Virginia's patience for Willie's auto car exploits was worn thin by his many misadventures. Most notably, Virginia's brother Charley had bet Willie $50 that he could beat Vanderbilt's personal record to Paris. It was a fatal mistake, ending in death for Charles and his wife. On a motoring trip from Florence, Italy, February 1906, Willie struck a six-year-old-boy, Adolpho Battini. The citizens of Pontedera were furious and a lynch mob gathered. He wrestled himself free and ran from the angry mob. Willie was saved from the knives of his pursuers only to realize that he was doomed to face a deadly trial by fire: he had abandoned Virginia in the process (courtesy Suffolk County Vanderbilt Museum).

ginia, and their mechanic. The chief of police hid Willie and Virginia in the police headquarters. Immediately, Willie's lawyers were summoned and they came along with the American consul. Willie declared that "it was an accident pure and simple, and no one regretted it more than I."[6]

In a torrential rain, the court building was opened to hear the case, where carabinières, police, and detectives escorted Willie to a room to sign "about a hundred documents."[7] Under heavy escort, he was driven to the railway station where Virginia awaited his arrival. She would never sit in a motor vehicle with her husband behind the wheel again.

Willie soon found, too, he did not have much in common with his sister-in-law, Tessie. Tessie was very similar to Virginia, especially in her devout Catholicism. Willie was aware of his wife's upbringing, but could not help himself when the issue became a powerful force in his own marriage. Instead, he withdrew and refused to participate. Sunday services at St. Joseph's in Newport came and went, just as Virginia came and went, but Willie attended only

Virginia, a devout Catholic, attended St. Mary's in Newport. Willie never attended church services, preferring instead a trip to the casino. Here, in an undated photograph, Willie is wagering a bet on a polo pony (courtesy Suffolk County Vanderbilt Museum).

the first Mass. When Virginia changed to another church in Newport, St. Mary's, their separation became obvious to the public. While Virginia was a member of St. Mary's parish and "a most devout Catholic,"[8] Willie never attended church services. To add insult, while she was at church, he was at the casino, dropping her off and picking her up after the service.[9]

Willie instead found that he had more in common with his Protestant brother-in-law, Charley. Estranged from Virginia, Charley took up quite a friendship with Willie. The pair shared the same boyish enthusiasm for speeding motor cars, and with each new model, Charley rushed to have it shipped to San Francisco. Like Willie K., he used chauffeurs largely as companions, often trading places with them to take over the driver's seat. Unlike Virginia, Willie K. understood his new brother-in-law. They were kindred spirits.

In 1902, Charley traveled with Maud (Caroline) to France where he acquired a Mercedes Special capable of eighty-five miles an hour. Willie K. and Charley met in Trouville, where Virginia and Willie took up residence in a villa they had acquired for the season. When Charley and Maud headed back to Paris, he was intent on beating Willie's speed record of two and a half hours back to the capital. The two men wagered a small bet of fifty dollars. Instead of allowing his chauffeur, Louis Bretry, to take the wheel, Charley took command.

On August 14, 1902, Charley set off from Evreux, racing along small dirt roads in the French countryside, with his wife and chauffeur at his side.[10] The miles rushed by and all seemed well. At the top of a long hill, leading down from a plateau from Evreux, they approached the village of Pacy-sur-Eure, about four kilometers ahead.[11] Bretry noticed that one of the left tires was becoming soft. Suddenly, just as the chauffer leaned over to point out the problem, the tire burst to pieces. Charley applied the brakes too fast, swerving to the left,[12] sending the Mercedes spinning out of control.

A woman gatekeeper witnessed the accident. The Mercedes plowed into a tree right in front of the entrance to the Château Buisson-du-Mai. Two objects that looked to the woman to be bundles of clothing flew from the vehicle and hit the tree hard before crashing to the ground. Bretry, the chauffeur, was thrown out of the Mercedes some fifteen meters, suffering bruises and cuts, lucky to survive.[13] However, the force of impact for both Charles and Caroline, catapulting them with enormous velocity, caused instantaneous death. Their bodies were recovered "badly mutilated"[14] with their faces "atrociously cut and bruised."[15]

It was a horrible accident and, despite Virginia's alienation from her brother, his death affected her deeply. Resentment against her husband for encouraging her brother in such folly added another weighty stone to the already sinking marriage.

Since Charley and Maud had named each other heirs with rights of survival, not anticipating they might die at the same moment, a fierce debate of inheritance spanning two continents suddenly erupted. At its morbid core, the issue hinged on whose blood spilled the longest and which body pulsated last. Someone had to die first, leaving the other inheritor — however briefly. A gruesome question: the answer worth a fortune to one family or the other. Charley had an estate of some ten million dollars and Maud the significant but lesser sum of three hundred and fifty thousand dollars.[16] Of course, the press had a field day.

The sordid battle went on in the courts for two entire years. Willie was among the most determined to have Charles declared survivor, thus retaining Virginia's share of the seven million dollar inheritance. Finally, a settlement was made with Caroline's relatives totaling two million dollars.[17]

The corpus of the estate that had passed to Charles from his father, Senator James G. Fair, now passed on to his two sisters, Tessie and Virginia, with Hermann Oelrichs appointed executor of the Fair Estate.

Thus, understandably, by the time Willie embarked upon his plan for the Vanderbilt Cup, Virginia had had her fill. From then on she steadfastly refused to accompany him on his jaunts through Long Island. (Still, she could not be kept from the track once race day arrived.)

Her absence at his side and the unfortunate deaths of his brother-in-law and his friend Croker undoubtedly caused both regret and anxiety for Willie, as well as dampening his enthusiasm for getting behind the racing wheel to some degree. The somber memory of death left a bitter aftertaste.

So, too, Willie quietly mourned the loss of his fellow racing enthusiasts and withdrew from Ormond Beach after the death of Croker. Willie had not lost his passion for the sport but understood the need to overcome its deadly reputation. He sought the approval of a wider audience. Perhaps, in beginning the Vanderbilt Cup, he could bring a certain dignity to the sport.

Despite protests from local Long Island farmers who viewed racing as an idle sport of the rich, local authorities were enthusiastic about an opportunity to profit from such a promising event and garnering a reputation as an international host. Preparations increased their pace with each passing week. Warnings consisted of signs nailed to telegraph poles and trees, outlining local rules, including a demand that farmers "chain your dogs and lock up your fowls!"[18]

Willie felt a rush of pride. The race was his first public business venture, and it was of grand proportions. European mud could not hold a candle to firm Long Island shell, as he boasted, "I have driven in five races abroad, and not one of the courses compares with the present thirty-mile stretch on Long Island."[19] Moreover, true to Willie's ambition, others in the new American auto industry were catching his enthusiasm to take on the Europeans. By lending the Vanderbilt name to a race featuring cars from this side of the pond, they were sure that they could turn the tide and convince the nation to buy American.[20]

While Willie K. had still not promised to abstain from driving by any measure, he became increasingly occupied with promoting and pushing the race forward. Little time was left to spend behind the wheel. He had far more important tasks to attend to. His presence, sponsorship, and demeanor indicated that it would be a great social event, as well as a prestigious race to win. This was Willie K. Vanderbilt's party indeed, and the world would come to his doorstep. He could lay claim as a true pioneer of the American auto industry, and in a sense, the father of American automobile racing. Grand achievements indeed.

The Garden City Hotel became the focus of attention as the headquarters of the AAA board. Visiting dignitaries found themselves bunking together because the demand for vacant rooms fast outstripped availability. The venue also lay in the center of the course, which began in Westbury, with two controlled stops at Hicksville and Hempstead, two towns that had not granted permission for the race to proceed at speed.

A lacework of country roads, the course was 28.44 miles long. The circuit would be traversed ten times. Using Hicksville's and Hempstead's denial as speedways to his advantage, he made them safety checkpoints, called controls, where each vehicle was reviewed for condition and compliance with the regulations. To moderate their speed, another nod at Willie's apparent desire for safety on his track, the drivers would have to follow bicycles. There were telephones along the route for constant communication, and over a hundred safety officials, more if needed, would be stationed along potentially dangerous spots.

The people and the press speculated feverishly about the speeds that might be achieved, particularly since the man behind the race had himself made the record books as one of the fastest drivers on the planet. Never before had a single affair, let alone an automobile race, galvanized all of New York City with such excitement.

Finally, the sun rose over race day, October 8, 1904, clear and bright.

For Willie, there had been little time for sleep. He anticipated the rising sun and arrived thirty minutes prior to the 6:00 A.M. start, in his splendid *White Ghost*. He soon took his official position as the master at hand and authoritatively conferred with the officials in charge of the adventure about to unfold.

Anticipation was high. Spectators vied for the best view. The previous night local roadhouses had been packed full with curious visitors. Thousands kept pouring in overnight. The elegant women clutched parasols in one hand and the train of their best dresses with the other. Men greeted the day in their Sunday best, shoes shined, moustaches waxed, and clasping timepieces tightly in their fists, ready to play amateur officials. The city's most prominent figures, including the Astor family, waited expectantly.

Some of the finest automobiles from America and Europe had been entered into the race, including an eighty horse power De Dietrich. A ninety-horse-power Fiat, driven by Paul Sartori, represented Italy and its sponsor, Alfred Gwynne Vanderbilt, Willie K.'s cousin.[21]

The cars lined up with drivers seated at the ready, their goggles affixed and racing gloves squarely gripping the wheel. In the stands along the roadside for miles in either direction, everyone waited for the race to begin. The roads were choked with dust and crowded with spectators. Over one hundred thousand people lined the course, straining to witness the spectacle of speed.

The American Mutoscope and Biograph, a small company experimenting in the new technology of film, turned on its camera as the race began.[22] The first full two minutes of the race from the grandstand was captured, just as Willie K. stepped off the wooden plank that served as podium, giving the wave for the race to commence.

Immediately, the cars took off, hurtling down the dusty shell road. Alfred Campbell shot to the lead in his sixty-horsepower Mercedes. Numerous spectators had gathered at the first turn of the race in Jericho, waiting at the Jericho Hotel, which offered an excellent view of the notorious "Curve of Death," a dizzying turn by the Jericho General Store and the hotel.[23]

Excitement soon turned to confusion. Despite all the precautions, the road checks, the speed limits, and the pacing bikes, the casualties hurtled forward, fast, furious, and fatal.

Top: Bert Dingley makes a hard turn in the 1905 race in American built Pope-Toledo. No American was to win that year. Dingley placed twelfth (courtesy Suffolk County Vanderbilt Museum). *Above:* Driving a powerful French 130 hp Hotchkiss, Elliot F. Shepard would become a thorn in Willie's side during the 1906 race when Shepard killed a careless spectator, Curt Gruner. Shepard, Willie K.'s cousin, was quite flamboyant (courtesy Suffolk County Vanderbilt Museum).

Louis Wagner's Darracq Juggernaut led the 1906 race throughout. He would be waved in by a checkered flag, believed to be the first in history used to celebrate the winner at the completion of an automobile race (courtesy Suffolk County Vanderbilt Museum).

On the Hempstead-Jamaica road, the No. 5 Mercedes driven by George Arents, Jr., blew out a tire. Instantly, as the rim hit the track of the trolley line, the car ricocheted and overturned on its side, catapulting Arents out of the vehicle while pinning his mechanic underneath.[24] Arents suffered a serious injury to his head, but eventually recovered. His mechanic would not be so lucky.

Despite his best efforts to minimize accidents and address concerns, Willie K. was helpless to stem the deluge of trouble. In the end, he was a spectator and observer, engulfed as events unfolded on their own. Yet, though the fate of each driver was his own responsibility, every accident belonged to Willie. Though a spectator might foolishly and dangerously step into the road on his own, he was inevitably one of Vanderbilt's liabilities. The thought brought a terse knot in the young man's stomach. He no longer just participated in races, he was responsible for them.

Pulsing forward with a momentum akin to the speeding cars, spectators gathered in conversation in the road, carelessly leaning in as the speeding vehicles rush by. With every oncoming car, they would repeat the cycle. When minutes passed without a car in sight, the well-heeled chatted about this stock tip or that social fete, until at last a man with a megaphone would call out an

Tire failure was a big factor in racing outcome and safety. Various manufacturers showcased their wares. Michelin tires were supported by a crew distributed around the course shown here wearing sweaters emblazoned with "MICHELIN" during the 1906 race (courtesy Suffolk County Vanderbilt Museum).

approaching car. Immediately, the crowd would fall silent, listening raptly as a low rumble in the distance quickly became a roar. In a matter of seconds it was over, the crowd shifting back to the sidewalk to resume their idle chatter.[25]

In the end, the first running of the Vanderbilt Cup had as much to do with politics as precision; flat tires had more of an influence on who won than skill. Saboteurs had spread glass and nails over various sections of the road in protest of the race. After one hundred and seventy-five miles, only nine cars were still running the circuit, including three Americans, spread over a distance of some thirty miles. As the finale approached, the race boiled down to a battle between two French cars, a Panhard driven by George Heath and a Clement-Bayard by Albert Clement.[26] Round and round the pair went, with Clement in the lead for the eighth and ninth laps after a tire puncture for the Panhard, but Heath recovered to take the lead and secure a dazzling first-place finish.

By early afternoon, it was all over. Willie was glad to call an end, avoiding further injuries to either drivers or innocent spectators. Overrun by the crowd, the track's finish line was obscured from view.

Despite the fact that a French vehicle had won, the driver was an American, a point of pride the newspapers and public did not overlook. Indeed, the

Announcer Peter Prunty kept the crowd at the start-finish line informed. He received his progress reports via telephone from strategic points along the race course. At times he was called to use his large megaphone and piercing voice to warn of incoming race vehicles. But there was little that Prunty or Vanderbilt could do to clear the path. Race watchers would stream onto the course at the passing of each vehicle, seemingly oblivious to the dangers of speeding cars approaching from behind (courtesy Suffolk County Vanderbilt Museum).

fact that three Americans were still in motion when the race ended was certainly a hopeful sign. What it lacked in patriotism, the race nonetheless provided newfound dignity for the fledgling American automobile industry, spurring many forward in pursuit of better-built machines, or at least faster ones.

The next day, the Vanderbilt Cup took front and center of the *New York Times.* The paper summarized the race in a flurry of headlines that read much like a stock market ticker of fatalities and triumphs: "HEATH AUTO WINS: ONE MAN KILLED *George Arents, Jr., Unconscious, Mechanician Dead,* CLEMENTS SECOND IN RACE *Mrs. W.K. Vanderbilt Jr., Leads Grand Stand Cheering,* A GREAT DAY FOR NASSAU *The course of 284.4 Miles Covered by the Winner in 5 Hours, 29 Minutes and 45 Seconds.*"[27]

Nevertheless, the editorial comments provided a less enthusiastic account: THE "GREAT" RACE.

The great automobile race is over. Who won the Vanderbilt Cup is of little consequence. Those for whom its news aspects have interest will find the story fully told elsewhere in these columns. However regarded, the race was utterly futile, proving nothing of interest and value to any one concerned in promoting "sport" or the mechanical development of the practical and useful motor vehicle.[28]

"Not a great Spectacle," one spoiler *Times*' headline claimed, continuing: "The contest was not as exciting as a horse race. The course was not visible, the accident marked by fatality was far from the crowd, and there was no straining of nerve, no wild contest for supremacy within sight of the spectators."[29]

In truth, no matter where one stood, only a small portion of the track was visible. Vehicles were started on a staggered basis, and unless one was keeping a detailed record, it would be impossible to know the lap count. Spectators must have felt awkward when a speeding juggernaut barreled by, not knowing whether it was ahead or a few laps behind or, for that matter, a countryman or foreigner. Only at the starting grandstand was a public scoreboard available for view. The event was so new, the crowds so naïve, and the track so fragmented, that few of the spectators knew how the race was truly progressing.

Yet some in the press offered up praise for Willie's muster: "There is no more intrepid automobilist than Mr. Vanderbilt, and he is constantly taking his life in his hands, in his racing machine, as well as his motor boat. If we had a few more men like him, who have the means and the enthusiasm, every branch of sport in America would be the best in the world."[30]

Willie, however, was ecstatic, sharing his enthusiasm with the *New York Journal-American*: "I consider the event a very successful one in every way. The race proved that the automobile is a wonderful piece of mechanism, capable of carrying people over long distances."[31]

In October 1905, Willie prepared for the second running of the Vanderbilt Cup. Through an American Elimination Trial race, twelve U.S. entrants had been reduced to five. Out of the five, two were stock entrees, lacking the power of the racecar factories and their latest technology. To enhance American chances, the Cup Commission, under Willie's dominion, opted to eliminate the three slowest vehicles and replace them with choices of their own. The Commission took a bombardment of bad press and protest in the wake of the announcement, of course, but held their ground. Unfortunately, their decision represented a choice between speed for its own sake and the health of the automotive industry. It became painfully clear that this was a sporting event.

Rural roads became masses of excitement, as some one hundred fifty thousand spectators descended on Long Island; two-thirds came from New York City alone.[32] Even the locals, who had plenty to complain about, could not whine about the potential for profit. They knew big city equaled big pocketbooks, and with inflated prices and race-oriented goods, they were determined get their share.

Contestants complained the previous year about the two controls at Hempstead and Hicksville as too long.[33] The 1905 race eliminated both, though enhanced other safeties by reducing the number of sharp turns. For the sake of entertainment, the course retained its ten laps, but the length was reduced to 28.3 miles. Westbury was replaced by the Mineola grandstand at Jericho Turnpike, four miles away, as the new location for beginning and ending the race.

Willie was so absorbed in the process of running the event that he found difficulty in delegating. Instead, every detail became his personal duty, including the safety of the drivers. In practice, he and Virginia administered first aid for Louis Chevrolet when he crashed his 110 Fiat.

Against five American entries, Germany, Italy, and France assembled fourteen contestants. Competition would be fierce. Among the drivers were two men who would later go on to start their own car companies: Vincenzo Lancia, a favorite among the crowds, and Louis Chevrolet, born in Switzerland. Willie's friend Foxhall Keene, who lived just a few miles from the race's starting point, drove a No. 5 Mercedes. George Heath, the 1904 Vanderbilt Cup winner, was back again, this time driving a larger one hundred and twenty horsepower No. 14 Panhard.

The race began promptly at six A.M. with Willie K. announcing the start with a charismatic flourish.

Almost immediately, casualties and unexpected crashes littered the raceway. While the White Steamer sputtered, Louis Chevrolet crashed his Fiat into a telegraph pole, and Foxhall Keene's Mercedes collapsed as he broke a wheel along the S curve in Albertson.[34] Lancia gained the lead, ripping ahead at seventy-two miles per hour. But soon he, too, was forced to stop for repairs for forty minutes while two French cars rushed past.

In a repeat of the previous year, two French cars battled for victory. In the end, a Darracq, the lightest vehicle in the event, captured the finish line, averaging 61.5 miles per hour.[35] Much to Willie's frustration, the placing of other racers will never be known. Once victory was signaled, bedlam ensued; the crowd jumped over the Mineola grandstand and swarmed the track just as the winner was crowned. Over one hundred thousand spectators filled the course. For safety's sake, Willie had to stop the other racers before they could finish. The October 1905 papers were full of pages of Vanderbilt's apparent failure.

Although the auto races may have seemed like expensive hobbies of the idle rich, they were, in fact, Willie's first attempts at individuality, maturity, and that rarest of all Vanderbilt commodities, an identity of his own.

That same year, the show *The Vanderbilt Cup*[36] hit Broadway with seventeen-year-old Elsie Janis leading the cast. The headlines proclaimed Janis a star, and Willie's race joined the ranks of popular theater. Also gracing the stage on opening night was Barney Oldfield, the famous cigar-smoking auto-racer who had beat Willie's record as the world's fastest man. Oldfield was truly a racing star by this point, as big a name in the sport as Vanderbilt.

Much to the audience's amusement, at the end of the race segment of the play, Oldfield emerged from one of the cars and removed his goggles to reveal himself as one of the contestants. A racecar on stage was, at that time, an incredible feat of theatrical technology. Rather than some cardboard cutout, two real cars were brought onto the stage on a treadmill-like track. Behind them scenic drops scrolled by to show the passage of landscape. Another even more revolutionary prop was the use of motion pictures at the beginning of the play, showing the main character, poor farm girl Dorothy Willetts, as she traveled to New York from the country.[37]

The actual play seemed to fade into the background behind all the gimmickry. The music was considered weak and the plot, although entertaining, was not altogether sparkling with originality. Dorothy, played by Janis, moves to New York to join her brother, who has made himself a fortune in the great city. After a string of social and romantic intrigues, a villainous woman rival bribes the driver of the Willetts' car to lose the Vanderbilt Cup. Dorothy disposes of the conspirator and places her own love interest behind the wheel. Her man, of course, wins the race, and everyone lives happily ever after.

After two fledgling years, the Vanderbilt Cup had finally come into its own. Although the 1904 race had been tragic and the next blasé by the somewhat critical standards of race reporters, there were nonetheless high hopes that, for the 1906 running, the third time would indeed be the charm.

The course again was redesigned, this time due to construction of a trolley line from Queens to Mineola and the desire to create more challenging sections such as a hairpin turn in Westbury. The event's new course ran 29.7 miles, with the start-finish line returned again to Westbury along the Jericho Turnpike. Refreshments were now offered behind the grandstand. A new color-coded map, albeit difficult to follow since it was printed backwards, was also posted. As in the 1905 race, a large scoreboard was positioned by the grandstand to help spectators follow the action.

As race day approached, excitement reached new heights, with spectators arriving from greater distances than ever before. By now, word had spread beyond New York. With the event reaching spectacle status, more and more fans sought to become a part of racing history. "The Cup," as it was fast becoming known, had brought a tinny sparkle to Long Island and with it, the allure of fast cars and even faster money.

The Garden City Hotel, ground zero for the inaugural race, was a large part of the frenetic festivities, but by now, other hotels, drug stores, taverns, restaurants and other retailers were determined to benefit from the event. Some local hotels took the Garden City's cue and sponsored "Vanderbilt Breakfasts," while the Long Island Railroad offered "Vanderbilt Specials" that carried the engorged ferry and bridge traffic from the city.

Manhattan became a ghost town as its race-crazed residents made their pilgrimage to the dusty, naked racetrack on Long Island. The highways were crammed with anxious observers, and the night before the race bonfires gave the impression of a giant army at bivouac, restlessly wiling away the sleepless hours before the next day's battle royal. Over the days before and after the race, the untold masses surged in varying stages of dress, refinery, and sobriety. There was a festival feel in the air. Every pool table, picnic bench, or dry floor brought an unheard of tariff, as price gouging became the norm. Vendors lined up to provide food, pennants, spyglasses, and race programs.

As Henry Austin Clark, Jr., wrote in his article "Vanderbilt Cup Races 1904–1937":

> By this time, The Vanderbilt was not only one of the most important racing events in the world; it was also the leading automotive social outing in the country. Since the races started at the crack of dawn, and the scene was some distance out from New York, overnight race parties were the rule. After a champagne breakfast at some hotel such as the old Waldorf, the celebrants would pile into the faithful Lozier or Pierce Great Arrow and head for the 34th Street ferry. Sometime in the wee hours by gas headlights they would edge their way up to the parking spots they had received from some farmer-highwayman along the right of way, preferably near a dangerous spot. Then they would either nap or sample more bubbly until the starting gun went off.[38]

Tourists and locals alike milled about in the middle of traffic and all rules of propriety and good manners were duly ignored — along with street signs and race officials. The tension was palpable as Willie realized that his handpicked staff was not up to the task of clearing the roads for the start of the race.

Poor traction on the track gave a pronounced advantage to the foreign drivers equipped with Michelin tires, dubbed "non-skids." Unfortunately, the American counterpart could not provide a comparable grip. Despite the lower quality of U.S. wheels, American tolerance for safety problems was far less than their European counterparts. But for Willie, the inadequate tires kept him on edge.

Members of the racing board were most concerned about boisterous crowds.[39] The fans indeed proved one of the greatest hazards. As word of the great race spread, so did the crowds, fueling its magnificent and malevolent swell. Racing might have been a gentleman's game but it was a bawdy sport, and attracted an equally rowdy fan.

Hardly the well-behaved crowd of a Broadway play, this was the biggest party of its day. Willie presided over it all with trepidation. What Willie had envisioned as a dignified achievement, a crowning cap of glory to his regal head, had, instead, in its three inaugural years, somehow descended into controlled chaos.

The crowd swelled beyond expectations and beyond enforceable control. Spectators clamored, climbing telephone poles or standing on roofs for a better look, renting spaces for unheard of sums and then cramming in their friends and family like sardines. Upwards of two hundred and fifty thousand spectators lined the track, either unaware or unheeding of the danger they faced as they stretched for a better look while the cars zoomed by — often in excess of sixty miles per hour. The question was never *if* any fans would get hurt, but how many.

Hoping to make liars of the reporters, Willie threw himself into every aspect of the event. The public became his and he was theirs. In their minds, in the minds of the press, and perhaps even in his own, the two were inescapably linked. And for twenty-four hours in October, he was at their mercy. Whatever they did, he alone took the blame.

In a very real and tragic sense, the race was only in his name. The crowd owned it; they trampled and defiled it, pissing on the streets and spitting tobacco in the ruts behind his tires.

Yet the Cup had become Willie's obsession, his chance to prove his name and his worth, to prove that America could rival Europe, even a chance to prove to America that this fledgling industry could be a contender.

What glory or shame lay ahead would come only after the roar of the engines had ended.

Rumors floated in the advancing days that Willie would join the race himself. He had not been in a race since the winter of 1904. Everyone knew he had recently acquired a new Mercedes; the press seemed determined to enter him.[40] And so he did.

Yet within twenty-four hours he backed down, turned back by the anger of several American manufacturers. Contrite in his withdrawal, he wrote to the race board:

> Being that I only entered in the spirit of the sport and not wishing to take any part that would not be agreeable to all contestants, I beg to withdraw my entry. I remain yours very truly,
>
> W.K. Vanderbilt Jr.[41]

The race began with its usual cacophony of roaring engines and smoking oil. At the main grandstand on the Jericho Turnpike, gentlemen and ladies in their finery waited anxiously, while William K. Vanderbilt in racing togs stepped down from his own Mercedes and prepared to signal the beginning of the race. Applause from the swollen crowd equaled the pitch of the roaring pistons.

Eighteen drivers from around the world quickly gathered speed as they fought for the lead, dodging each other *and* the fans. As smoke billowed and dust flew, obscuring both car and driver from the curious, crowds crept perilously closer.

Louis Wagner, a professional driver in a Darracq, bolted quickly to the head of the pack. Again and again he battled for first place, maintaining consistent speeds of sixty-three miles per hour and slogging through some ten laps—two hundred and eighty-three miles of track. Mechanical failure, unfortunately, dogged the racers from start to finish, especially car tires, which would get so hot they had to be sprayed with water at intervals. Sprinkling, however, rendered the rubber tires brittle, and tubes often ripped apart after less than 100 miles of driving.

One of the most thrilling — and terrifying — moments in the race occurred at the hairpin turn by Old Westbury, when a spare tire and rim loose from the Lorraine-Dietrich, driven by Arthur Duray, began to thrash against the engine. As the mechanic, Franville, grabbed the loose part, he lost his balance. While the car skidded through the turn, Duray drove with one hand while grabbing Franville by the shirt and yanking him back from certain demise.[42]

Hampered by these frequent delays, the racers grew frustrated, and many Europeans were flabbergasted by the demand that, prior to passing intersections, everybody had to come to a full stop, which put the driver's nerves on edge about once every five minutes.

Willie's cousin, Elliot F. Shepard, Jr., drove the fastest vehicle, a French Hotchkiss capable of one hundred and thirty horsepower.[43] Unknowingly, Shepard hit a spectator, Curt Gruner, who had stepped too far into the course. Shepard continued on, battling the Lorraine-Dietrich. However, when stopping to fix a crankshaft, he was finally informed of the casualty. Shephard immediately withdrew, distraught by the unfortunate accident.

Once again, Americans showed poorly, none reaching any closer than seventh place at any point in the course. In the end, the victory went to Wagner — another victory for France. Second place went to Lancia from Italy.

Wagner, clearly shaken and purely frustrated, trashed the event and helped seal the race's already uncertain future with a well-quoted epitaph, describing the race as "five hours of unbroken nightmare." He shot on, "It would not be possible ... for eighteen racing cars to negotiate nearly three hundred miles without killing or maiming one, a dozen, a score, a hundred reckless onlookers among these hundreds of thousands."[44]

Unfortunately, Wagner's estimate was not, in fact, far off. Two fans were killed in the 1906 race, resounding in morbid and lasting echoes. Once the casualty count made the press, the name or nationality of the winner was of little interest. The horror of tragedy, not the spectacle of victory, would become the Cup's unhappy legacy. The debacle brought an immediate end to racing on public roadways.

While the American press interviewed Wagner, Willie hastened again to damage control. His efforts were fruitless, barely diminishing the growing concern. Meanwhile, an American was officially credited with third place; driving car No. 6, a bulky Pope mobile from Toledo, Ohio. But the victory was only symbolic. Few on hand that day noticed that, after the crowds spilled onto the raceway consuming the first and second place winners, the driver and mechanic of the Pope vehicle simply got out and pushed the American car across the finish line, all its tires long shredded to pieces.

Good stories did not sell papers, but criticism did, and they had plenty of it to go around. The newspapers trounced Willie over the deaths. There would have to be a scapegoat and once again it was Willie. The *Chicago Tribune* prophesied, "The trail of dead and maimed left in their smoke makes it almost certain that the mad exhibition of speed will be the last of its kind that the country will ever witness."[45]

Despite his best efforts and a cascade of warnings, Willie never really had control of his race. But though the blame would be Willie's, this time he surprised them all with his reply.

The day after the 1906 race, the *New York Times* quoted an apologetic Willie, who said, "I am deeply ashamed."[46] The apology was extraordinary for a Vanderbilt, indeed, perhaps for American royalty of any kind.

It was obvious that the young man had reached a turning point in his life. With those four words, "I am deeply ashamed," Willie not only owned his decision, but also took public responsibility for his actions. The daredevil showed a sudden maturity.

Humbled by his experience at Deepdale, Willie K. was well aware of the power of the populace. He was a fourth generation Vanderbilt, living in a time where money and privilege no longer held complete sway over the public. He was being held accountable and, unlike his father or grandfather who often paid little attention or offered no reply, Willie K. responded. The young man had a conscience.

Still, despite the tragic consequences, the public derision, the shame, and the lingering infamy, Willie realized he had, in fact, achieved something special. Never before in the history of United States had so many thousands gathered for a sporting event. Never had such enthusiasm surrounded men behind the wheel. Never, on either side of the world, had the automobile achieved such public fascination. This was no time to give up; he would not abandon the Cup, but only relocate it.[47]

Willie knew he had achieved a victory after all.

CHAPTER 11

An Empire Implodes

While Willie K. divided his attentions between the Vanderbilt Cup and electrification across the rail network, trouble was brewing in the railroad offices back on 42nd Street. His father, William Kissam, nervously surveyed the scene as the New York Central was visited by a ghost from its past, the Interstate Commerce Commission, or I.C.C., created in 1887 after the Supreme Court ruled that states could not control interstate commerce.[1] The I.C.C. gave the federal government the power to regulate instead. Railroad barons never took the organization seriously because it lacked the teeth of Supreme Court rulings and hemmed itself with a jungle of confusing regulations.

However, with a new administration in the White House under the ambitious populist Teddy Roosevelt, regulation became more assertive. Under the Elkins Act, passed in 1903, the lines began to pay closer attention. The Elkins Act allowed the I.C.C. to issue maximum freight rates and increased the penalties for those railroads that did not comply. At the time, most of the railroads were actually grateful: in a sense, rate control now allowed them to put the days of rampant competition and price gouging behind them.

However, three years later, another piece of legislation passed, this one with more aggressive repercussions. The Hepburn Act of 1906 marked the end of government compliance and the beginning of an onslaught of regulation and intrusion. The Hepburn rule gave the I.C.C. both greater investigative and regulatory powers, throwing open the doors of railroad management.[2] The I.C.C. could now enforce the maximum railroad rates it set,[3] leaving it to the lines to challenge its rulings in the courts. Moreover, the powerful Hepburn Act gave the I.C.C. power to demand standardization of all railroad ledgers. The I.C.C. also created an annual report that summarized the books, explicitly listing ownership of railroads. The incursion pulled the velvet curtains from the railroad boardrooms, allowing in the glare of public light for the very first time. No longer could acquisitions, trades, and sales simply go unmentioned under the table.

Armed with its new investigative powers, the I.C.C. pursued "The Consolidation and Combination of Carriers,"[4] the long history of collusion among railroad leaders to protect their own markets and, more importantly, control the rates. For the past twenty years, J.P. Morgan led a loose alliance among the eastern carriers to carefully avoid bloody rate wars. His success was exceptional, keeping battles among giants to a relative few. In turn, rates could be set at will, keeping farmer and manufacturers at their mercy.

The target of the investigation was anything associated with E.H. Harriman. His ownership of the Union Pacific and Southern Pacific gave him a big piece of the transcontinental pie, and made him an easy target for inquiry. In a time when regulatory control was in vogue, suddenly "being everywhere" had become synonymous with being in the wrong place. Harriman was in for a rough ride and the president was not going to let him go that easily. He was a marked man. President Theodore Roosevelt was in his second term and out the door of the interim elections. He was in the business of legacy building. Attacking monopolies— and the wealthy barons who ran them — would not only be popular, it might put him in the history books. Roosevelt's move would be the Sherman Anti-Trust Act.

By virtue of the Sherman Anti-Trust Act, which hoped to prevent the artificial raising of prices by monopolies, the commission concluded it was illegal and against the public interest for a railroad to purchase parallel or competing lines. While the first statement was true, the latter was debatable. In a logical corollary, they deduced that a railroad should not own stock in a competing and parallel line nor should directors serve on both of the lines in question. Harriman and most of his colleagues, including William Kissam Vanderbilt, were clearly guilty of nepotistic and clandestine stock ownership as well as interlocking directorships.

Roosevelt pushed his assault across the web of roads. His most direct, and press-worthy, attack took aim at Northern Securities, Morgan and Hill's cornerstone of the transcontinental shipping alliance.

With every month of court battle, William Kissam could read the handwriting on the wall. His hopes of building an international shipping dominion were dashed. The Roosevelt regime did not hesitate to take rabid advantage of the situation, whipping the public, the press, and the courts to war against the railroad titans. Achieving a decisive blow from the Supreme Court against Northern Securities, the populists thought that they would have their victory within the Hepburn Act.

The senior Vanderbilt understood well that the pendulum was swinging hard against him. Within an extraordinarily short time, Vanderbilt's retreat into his own shadows brought about severe splintering in upper management, and the myriad lines he had acquired were left reeling with a lack of direction. No longer could any policy decisions previously managed by one of his many captains be conducted without him. His operating officers were now stripped of their powers, acting more like clerks, while all decisions were swathed in layers of red tape.[5]

The fault is in the administration.... The man who is in actual control is not on the lines. His men do not know him. A Pennsylvania man is a Cassatt man. A Lack-awanna man is a Truesdale man. An Erie man has come to be an Underwood man. Presidents Truesdale, of the Lackawanna, and Underwood, of the Erie, lead their railways. But a Vanderbilt man is for himself. It will be so until there arises a Van-derbilt strong enough to impress his personality on the system, able enough to administer it, active enough to participate in it.[6]

The time of mergers, cooperation, and acquisitions was now in rapid decline. Vanderbilt found himself alone, except for A.J. Cassatt with his Penn-sylvania road, which offered some stability and price regulation.[7]

For an exhausted William Kissam, even government controls were far bet-ter than rebates and competition. The worker wanted more pay while the pub-lic wanted to pay less, demanding cheaper transportation. Rates dropped as the I.C.C. used its powers under the 1906 Hepburn Act to set railroad rates.[8] The public wanted cheap transportation. Politicians, so used to pandering to the interests of stockholders, were now giving away their assets, and were worried about keeping the vote of a much more powerful political force: the traveling public, which was now more organized and vocal.

It was the end of an era: the beginning of a downhill journey for the rail-roads from which they could not recover.

With J.P. Morgan's reluctant consent, Vanderbilt and Cassatt decided to have the latter pen an amendment to the Interstate Commerce Act to end rebat-ing. Rebating was the process that enabled big traffickers to obtain price con-cessions from the railroads by forcing competition between them and thereby getting a discount in the process. State regulatory agencies were unpredictable and capricious; they couldn't be trusted to maintain agreeable terms, and there-fore, reasonable profits.[9] Without the protection of monopolies, railroad lead-ers sought stable rates and freedom from rebate policies.[10] It was a historic step for the railroads. But by seeking protection from competition under the aegis of the Interstate Commerce Act, the railroads also had moved one step closer to becoming quasi-public utilities.

In one fell swoop, business in the railroads changed irrevocably. William Kissam Vanderbilt no longer focused on expanding and developing the empire; instead, the railroad strictly became the avenue for reaping maximum divi-dends. The pillaging of the railroads for profit had begun. Once the opportu-nity for building their own cartel of power and pooling of resources was slowly torn apart in wave after wave of regulation, the railroad barons immediately turned insular, preoccupied solely with increasing their own riches. In essence, they gave up on building the business of railroading, instead handing over the lines to the government in exchange for a 6-percent payout. With that, they focused solely on squeezing for themselves and their stockholders as much money as they could. Thus, dollars were quickly siphoned away from infrastruc-ture, such as repairs and improvements. The logical outcome was a total undermining of capitalization and investment. The railroads were being crushed from the outside and gutted from within.

Though the I.C.C. convened investigations into the railroad's financial practices, it could do little to gain control. The power to strip the roads of their assets was the final entrepreneurial right that the railroad owners reserved for themselves. No large railroad suffered more than the New York Central. Given her riches, she was robbed the most. Bankers and investors did not comprehend the traffic demands of a railroad, certainly not one with the complexities of a giant system like the Central, nor could they keep up with the condition of her track age, rolling stock, and power plants.

While the government pressed from one direction, Vanderbilt and Cassatt suddenly had to face two more old enemies on another front. George Gould and Andrew Carnegie sought to create a new trunk line to the east.[11] Their railroad would pass through both the Pennsylvania and Central territory. But if Vanderbilt and Cassatt were not going to profit, they were not going to allow other railroad magnates to prosper either. Immediately in response, both the Pennsylvania and the Central presented a unified front, insisting that they would not carry Gould's traffic. The Central then instituted a ban on the Gould-owned Western Union telegraph poles along its mainline, costing Gould a fortune by breaking the integrity of his system. Gould was made to pay exorbitant sums for each mile of trackage. Furious, Gould took his protest to the courts, employing his lobbying clout to force a federal investigation of the Pennsylvania/New York Central Community of interest.

The Interstate Commerce Commission took up the charge, holding investigative hearings in 1906. There was nothing left to do but turn to defense. William Kissam's dream to surpass his legacy and reach beyond the towering achievements of his father and grandfather quickly evaporated. Instead, Vanderbilt became trapped in the growing maelstrom of government attacks and the seemingly endless campaign to complete Grand Central Terminal. The future of the railroad would have to rest in the hands of Willie K.

CHAPTER 12

The Speedway

All eyes turned towards the evening's keynote speaker for the American Automobile Association (AAA) meeting at the Sherry Hotel in Manhattan. More than five hundred guests of the "most prestigious and powerful automobile organization in the United States"[1] had gathered to listen to Willie K. Vanderbilt II, who had been rumored to be working on a private parkway only for automobiles.

The fact that public roads could no longer be used for automobile racing had forced his hand. "It has been the dream of every motorist," Vanderbilt said that chilly night in December 1906, "to own a perfect car and to have a road where he may drive unhampered by speed limits."[2] After describing his proposal for a new motorway one hundred feet in width and about sixty miles in length, where one could drive unhampered by policemen and pedestrians, Willie elicited guffaws and bursts of laughter when he declared most solemnly, "The automobile and women — God bless them! — are the dearest things on earth."[3] Then he grabbed the room by its collective ear when he described his latest great idea, the Long Island Motor Parkway.

While the exact course still remained to be determined,[4] the Parkway's scope would be much larger than a mere race, as were its costs. Willie would need considerably more than what his annual fifty thousand dollar allowance could afford. Akin to a real highway, the proposed motorway, open to all "pleasure motors,"[5] would be free of regular traffic and pedestrians, enabling races to be held without risking life or limb. The Board of the AAA favored the continuation of road racing if a private course could be found.[6] Duly noted, they appointed Willie as chairman of a committee to secure an appropriate course. The members included Jefferson De Mont Thompson and A.R. Pardington,[7] two men who would become pivotal in the Parkway's progress. Two days after the 1906 Vanderbilt Cup race, John Farson, the AAA president, appointed a special committee to consider the development of a new motor speedway.

The fate of road racing seemed entirely uncertain. Despite its apparent decline, the *Times* suggested that the speedway was still necessary:

It is conceded that a private motor speedway is an actual necessity, for as long as high-powered cars are made and used there will be a constant desire to test them in runs and record-breaking contests for short distances.[8]

Willie's plan relied on a toll road concept, accessible to all who paid access tolls at tollgates constructed as English inns. The "inns" would offer sleeping accommodations for travelers, refreshments, and a garage to supply gasoline and offer repairs if necessary.[9] Costing approximately two million dollars to construct, the parkway soon received pledges for four hundred thousand dollars.[10]

Under the committee's planning, the concept of a racetrack had rapidly been transformed into a highway for public use.[11] If Willie felt disappointed about the quick turnaround, he remained mum on the subject, preferring to let others do the talking for him. At one point, Pardington announced, "The racing features will be purely incidental."[12] After the tragic events of the Cup, Willie, Thompson and Pardington were covering all their bases, lest the slightest hint of bad press squash their larger vision.

An article in the November issue of *Motor-Print* did not shy away from comparisons, immediately referencing the Vanderbilt Cup as a "veritable slaughter of the innocents,"[13] and that organizers of the race would want to avoid shouldering again "so great and so grave a responsibility."[14] Public road racing on a highway, it seemed, would have to be abandoned.

A.R. Pardington made special efforts to reassure the public and guarantee the highway, saying, "The success of the proposed motor highway is assured. It will be built. It will be on Long Island and will be open to all drivers of pleasure cars."[15] With the seeming success of the motor parkway nearly assured (and accepted by the public), members of the Plan and Scope Committee unanimously called upon Willie K. to serve as next president of the AAA.[16] Willie agreed, certainly recognizing redemption in the offer and a chance to even grow his stature as a leader in the fast-growing automotive world.

Rather than the private speedway Willie had first envisioned, access would be granted to anyone able to pay the toll. A municipality could provide the right to exceed normally posted road speeds, but permission to use a highway could not "be exclusive in the parties to whom the permission was granted."[17] The public roads were to remain in public hands and no special interest group, even the AAA, could have it for their limited use.

Of course, in 1906 the price of a car was still well beyond the regular citizen's means, and he was as likely to get stopped for speeding in his horse and buggy as he was to win a Vanderbilt Cup race. Speed remained an underlying draw for the "pleasure" driver, but received only limited play as the process moved along. The proposed direction was well received by the powers that be: "The committee desires to have it understood that the company promoting the highway is not building a race track. They are planning a highway intended for the use of motor cars at all times, on which unlimited speed may be possible, presenting grades, turns, etc."[18]

That was not to say that Willie did not hope that it might still serve that function. He was still considered the "Apostle of High Speed,"[19] caricatured as a "begoggled"[20] and "bemasked"[21] racing enthusiast who introduced a "superlative thrill"[22] that could be "reproduced ad infinitum."[23] From the "flame-breathing monster"[24] of the *White Ghost* to his even faster *Red Devil*, and countless other fierce machines of superior horsepower, Willie K. had history of terrorizing the sleepy roads of Newport, and now the newspapers again revived old stories of his stunts, accidents, and reckless speeding.

Immediately, Pardington ran damage control and adroitly positioned himself on the more genteel side of the plan, changing Vanderbilt's more exuberant designation of "Speedway" to the more subdued "Parkway."

Nevertheless, under Willie's design, his penchant for leaving a cloud of feathers where a chicken once stood was readily apparent; the parkway's smooth straight-aways, banked curves, and wild hairpins, were tailored perfectly to match Willie's bad behaviors. For once, Willie would be hurtling at the *right* speed, no matter how fast he might be going.

Though its board of directors was aggressive in touting the Parkway's many advantages, the planners had not quite absorbed the fiscal realities of the unopened road. While newspaper reports of the time almost daily calculated the rising costs, Pardington continued to paint a romantic picture of the quaint Long Island countryside and destinations that held tremendous allure. Pardington projected that construction would begin by April 1907 and that by October the roadway would be ready for the next Vanderbilt Cup Race.

In the meantime, plans for the Parkway changed constantly. Funding realities were now continual problems, and breaking new ground meant estimates that evaporated into fiction, often recounted column-by-column, figure-by-figure, in the local press. News stories fluttered like so many construction permits that awaited approval, and with it came weekly updates for the residents of Long Island.

If the roadway needed to perpetuate the races, it was suffering an identity crisis. Someone, probably an investor, concluded that the race lasted part of a day, but for the road to survive, it had to be viable for the rest of the year. Even the smallest details were debated. For example, the name "toll lodge"[25] took up considerable debate; first called gateways, then tollgates, then gatehouses, and finally toll lodges in early 1908.[26]

Willie did not help matters much by getting himself arrested for speeding. The trial was an appeal of sorts. In special session, Willie had already appeared before a magistrate in a rather cordial encounter more akin to a meeting of old friends than a legal confrontation. Willie walked up grinning and announced, "Hullo, Freddie."[27] The response was an equally friendly "Hullo, Willie."[28] The charges were dropped, but the locals would remember.

The first shovelful is turned from the Long Island (Vanderbilt) Motor Parkway. A.R. Pardington does the honors while Willie is away at his stepfather's bedside. Willie's parkway was a technological triumph. It was the first considerable stretch of macadam road, complete with limited access. There were no intersections to create safety hazards. The road passed under and over intersecting roadways and railroads by overpass and underpass (courtesy Suffolk County Vanderbilt Museum).

In May of 1908, the construction of the Long Island Parkway commenced. The original width of fifteen feet was soon found to be too narrow so a three-foot shoulder was added as an extra safety precaution. Along the outside, spike fences were put in place. The purpose of these fences was to keep pedestrians and animals out of the roadway in order to limit the number of casualties.[29] Pulled away at the last moment because of the illness of his stepfather, O.H.P. Belmont, Willie could not deliver his carefully prepared speech. Instead on June 6th, A.R. Pardington read his eloquent words:

> We are here today to celebrate the commencement of work on a road which, when complete, will give to the world one more mode of transportation. There have been in the past highways for all kinds of vehicular traffic, canals for the movement of freight, railroads for the transportation of passengers, and trolleys for the convenience of those living in the suburbs of our large cities, but in no case has the motorist been considered.... And now the day of the automobile has come. A highway is about to be constructed for its use, free from all grade crossings, dust and police surveillance, and a country opened up whose variegated charms are hard to equal in any part of the world.[30]

With those auspicious words, the real work of building the Parkway began in earnest. The automobile parkway varied in width along its course. Despite his grand plan for a "magnificent pleasure boulevard"[31] bordered by quaint inns

Work began in earnest after Pardington's symbolic shovelful. Willie may be best known for the Vanderbilt Cup, but his most significant moment must be considered this day in June 1908. On that day, ribbons of highway began their triumphant voyage around the world. Strangely, a railroad man had set the demise for his own business. It would not be long before the nation's goods and populace would be carried by auto car and truck. Pictured here, an inspection tour of a bridge being constructed over Newbridge Road in 1908 as part of the construction of the Vanderbilt Motor Parkway (courtesy Suffolk County Vanderbilt Museum).

and cafes, three years of construction later, Willie's "Appian Way" had become merely a Parkway, and his English tollhouses little more than gates with tollbooths. Willie's grand vision involving vast lodges featuring dozens of rooms and twice as many amenities had shrunk to something far less impressive.

Willie had envisioned a Parkway that was at once innovative and impossible. Without masterful planning, his visionary designs could not succeed. While the Parkway possessed features present in other landscaped roads, it was unique in combining different aesthetic elements together. His initial plan of a course one hundred feet wide had been reduced to twenty-two feet, and the course shortened from eleven to eight miles. Nonetheless, Willie's enthusiasm could not be abated. Fueled by his relentless energy, Willie K. managed to lay more concrete road than existed in the entire country at the time.

As promised, access was controlled by tollhouse. At the Ronkonkoma end, an inn designed by John Russell Pope to reflect the appearance of the Petit Trianon in Versailles, was constructed to receive thirty guests, with leisure activities nearby including boating and tennis.

Despite its historic and progressive impact, the Parkway still failed to reach its target destination of Riverhead and, since the parkway was linear, did not provide a return loop. The absence of a return made the highway difficult to use as a racetrack and was only partially employed for that purpose during the 1908, 1909, and 1910 running of the Vanderbilt Cup Race.

The Parkway's opening was commemorated by a special race titled the Motor Parkway Sweepstakes on September 10, 1908. American Herb Lytle won the event, driving an Italian Isotta at an average speed of 64.25 miles per hour.[32]

Four years after its inception, the Cup was no longer the only game in town. New races were popping up everywhere: the Brighton 24-Hour Contest, the Jamaica Speed Trials, and the Bridgeport Hill Climb, to name just a few. With their rapid growth came considerable strife for Willie. In the summer of 1908, the two leading automotive organizations in the country, the American Automobile Association (AAA) and the Automobile Club of America (ACA), had a very public falling out.[33]

For Willie, the rift between the two automotive superpowers meant little beyond more bad press. What did matter was the fine print still drying on the hasty agreement between the AAA and the ACA, elevating a new upstart race held in Savannah to the same status as the Vanderbilt Cup. Willie was once again steaming over the failure of Americans to organize races as sophisticated as those in Europe. Not only was his prestigious race linked with some lesser Savannah contest, but the very organization to which he had achieved a leadership role was now pledged to make his racing rival a success. The most obvious outcome of the rift was that the available foreign entrants were split between the two races, with the new and shiny Savannah race getting the lion's share.

For the first time, Willie was forced to do the unthinkable; he had to scramble to find entrants for his race. The 1904 cup had boasted eighteen cars, the 1905 Cup had twenty-seven, and in 1906 the number spiked at twenty-nine cars. As the day of the 1908 race drew near, less than half a dozen were slated to appear in that year's contest. Willie, who was in Europe at the time, struggled to increase the number of foreign entrants; he was only able to scare up five by race time, mostly from his American friends. A banner headline trumpeted Willie's defeat: "VANDERBILT BACK WITHOUT ENTRIES. Has Brought No Additional European Competitors for the Cup Race."[34]

Pardington saw the need to beat the Parkway's detractors to the punch, bragging, "I wish to say, too, that the Motor Parkway will positively be ready for the race in plenty of time. It will be opened before Oct. 10. Mr. Vanderbilt and I spent six hours on the course today, inspecting every foot of it, and he is more than pleased with the progress made. There is not the slightest doubt that we will be ready in plenty of time."[35]

For once, the *Times* concurred, saying, "Whatever uncertainty is felt by the members of the Vanderbilt Cup Commission as to the success of the cup race from the standpoint of entries, there is no diminution in the efforts to complete the parkway course in plenty of time to allow the drivers thoroughly to try out the course prior to the race."[36]

By the day of the race, however, only nine out of the proposed eleven miles of cement road were available to serve as part of the proposed track. An additional fourteen miles of country roads would have to supplement the parkway proper. Still worse, the parkway stretch was in rural land too remote to draw a huge crowd, and was guarded by a wire fence with only a few openings. However, the public roads went through the usually more densely populated areas along Jericho Turnpike. With a year off from the races, and a general public confused by all the pre-race publicity, the Vanderbilt Cup seemed in danger of falling on deaf ears for perhaps the first time.

During the Motor Parkway Sweepstakes prior to the 1908 race, Herb Lytle is seen driving his Italian No. P42 Isotta over an open straightaway on the newly constructed Vanderbilt Motor Parkway. He finished in second place in 1908 (courtesy Suffolk County Vanderbilt Museum).

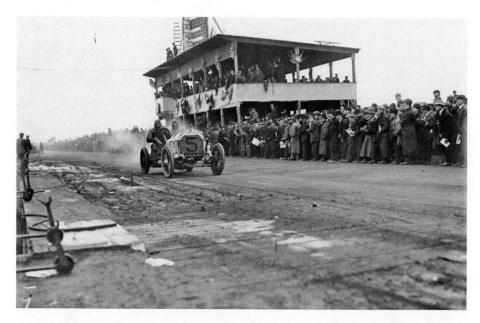

At the start-finish line during the 1908 race, driver William Luttgen speeds by in Mercedes No. 5, entered by Willie K. Likely because of a shortage of entrants, Vanderbilt entered his own vehicle but did not drive, instead serving as referee. George Robertson, an American, won the race in a locomobile (courtesy Suffolk County Vanderbilt Museum).

To draw attention to the race, Willie made the startling announcement that he was finished with racing and would never even speed again. Willie's stepbrother, Northrop Sands, had been killed that summer in an automobile accident. Willie used this as leverage, claiming that Virginia was against the races in light of the recent tragedy and that of her brother Charley years before, and he wished to respect her views.[37] Willie even claimed that he would use a taxi to go to work. It became a national story.

Virginia's absence during the 1908 race[38] indeed gave rise to the suspicion that the death of Willie's brother-in-law and then stepbrother might have been at the source of his very public withdrawal from the race. But the public was still unsatisfied: "Men who know Mr. Vanderbilt well, will not take stock in this theory. No one loves the motor car better than he, and its fascination for him increases in direct proportion to the speed."[39]

Shortly before race day, the *New York Times* offered readers a special view right from the driver's seat. The *Times* sent a reporter to ride shotgun during the test run of American favorite George Robertson. The reporter was kitted out in the proper gear: "a sort of rubber bag, with holes for arms and head, was slipped on and fasted with difficulty between his legs"[40] and they leapt into the seat of Robertson's locomobile, number 16.

Promotional ad for the 1910 Vanderbilt Cup Race (courtesy Suffolk County Vanderbilt Museum).

Few of the paper's readers had ever had the experience of driving, let alone topping speeds of sixty to seventy miles per hours. Indeed even the reporter "had practically no experience in automobiles and had never in his life so much as touched any of their mechanism."[41] Though the test drive was de rigueur for an old pro like Robertson, "To the reporter, the speed seemed terrific. He started with fear in his heart, but this was soon displaced by a sensation of exhilaration."[42] The twenty-three-and-a-half-mile course was driven in just over twenty minutes, with an average speed of 70 mph. In so doing, Robertson barely missed tying the record for one lap by a mere thirty seconds.

The *New York Times* article succeeded in whetting the public appetite for the Cup. Thus the stage was set for another exciting race day. For once Americans were not to be disappointed. Willie did not drive. Instead an American driver drove Vanderbilt's Mercedes, and whatever the reasons for dropping out of racing, the ploy proved a good one evidenced by the large turnout.

Willie still faced some of his old and painfully familiar issues as spectators again rambunctiously burst through rails, lined steep embankments along the course of the road,[43] and foolishly stood again in the way of speeding vehicles. This time, however, he had a large security force of thirteen hundred men ready to hose down some two hundred thousand spectators in order to control the crowd.

Nonetheless, the race offered Americans an opportunity for celebration since one of their own had finally won a race in an American automobile. George Robertson's victory was met with a "great cheer as he came up to the line, his face set in a head-gear and training veil that made him look the image of an Egyptian mummy."[44] However, the playing field had been almost completely American, with only one French vehicle driven by a Frenchman and a handful of other foreign cars driven by Americans. It was entirely expected that an American would win. Regardless, patriotism ran rampant.

The event itself lost most of the carnival feeling that had so characterized earlier races as "The day was very cold, and possibly chilled what little enthusiasm might have been let loose."[45] The size of the crowd was a fraction of prior years, with "25 percent"[46] of the last year's attendance. The excitement level seemed diminished. Unruly crowds, unnecessary accidents, and incomplete races had been the bane of Willie's existence from the very first Cup in 1904. That year the crowds were under control simply because of their absence.

Willie simply couldn't win. First his event had been deemed incompetent and reckless, and now, it was being criticized for its poor turnout: "The contest lacked the spectacular sprint," crowed the *Times*, "and reckless driving that appeals so strongly to the motorist, although the event itself was admirably conducted and the management in every way satisfactory."[47]

Yet the races served as an impetus to stop importing foreign cars and to put more money and effort into American vehicles. Willie had repeatedly expressed that his primary goal in both starting the Vanderbilt Cup and the Long Island Motor Parkway was to wake up the American automotive industry. At least in one sense, it appeared that Willie had achieved his goal.

The following season, Willie redoubled his public relations efforts, and the press responded in kind, drumming up ecstatic pre-race headlines and wild public enthusiasm. The Vanderbilt Cup had suddenly acquired classic status as America's race where "the general public throughout the country takes unlimited interest and the prestige of which is bigger than any other road or motordrome race. It is the greatest event on motordrome's calendar, has meant much to the automobile industry, and this season's cup race, with its daybreak start, bids fair to outshine all the contests of the past, both in speed and public interest."[48] Spectators included Sir Thomas Lipton, host of the Lipton Cup, and Dave H. Morris, president of the AAA and husband to Alice Vanderbilt, Willie's cousin. Wintry conditions prompted his wealthy guests to don thick ankle-length fur coats and indulge in hot coffee delivered in thermoses obligingly by the American Thermos Bottle Company.

The crowds returned for the 1910 Vanderbilt Cup stronger than ever, numbering over two hundred and seventy-five thousand.[49] Local hotels swelled and burst beyond capacity. Revelry began early in the afternoon of the previous day and continued into race day and beyond. There were thirty entries this time around, making the 1910 race the largest event in the history of the Vanderbilt Cup. Each lap measured 12.64 miles and with twenty-two laps, the entire course now ran 278.08 miles. New pit crews were assembled, ready to assist vehicles at periodic intervals. Spectators lined bridges for good vantage points.

The last leg of the race became a fierce competition between Harry Grant driving his Alco against new upstart Joe Dawson, a twenty-one year old daredevil with a spirit akin to the cup's founder. Dawson had the lead but, unfortunately, a spectator jumped in front of his vehicle. Dawson stopped immediately to check on the man who had injured both of his legs, and then jumped back into his vehicle, accelerating rapidly as he tried to catch up to Grant. Grant barely placed first, with Dawson just twenty-five seconds behind.[50]

Unfortunately, the excitement was matched again by tragedy. Despite assertions that no accidents were caused by spectators crowding the course,[51] accidents still plagued the Parkway with four dead and twenty people hurt, with injuries ranging from contusions to fractures and shock from impact with "flying tires."[52] Among the injured were Louis Chevrolet of the famous automobile family and Charles Miller, who were trapped at the helm of their speeding Marquette-Buick when its steering gear broke at seventy miles per hour. Helpless, they plowed into the car of a spectator parked by the side of the road and went straight through it, with "almost no diminution of speed ... through a paling fence and uprooting a cedar tree." Chevrolet was thrown twenty feet, while his mechanic, Miller, was pinned under the wreckage and died.[53]

After the race, Willie K. reluctantly agreed to move the Grand Prize race to Savannah in a move the *Club Journal* called the "little slip between the Cup."[54]

As the first decade of the new century drew to a close, Willie reflected that his life until then had been a swirl of fortune: victories, yes, but failures dogging him all along the way. Willie's vision for the race had finally captured the public. American manufacturers had their proving ground. At the same time, the Long Island Motor Parkway finally ground to an expensive halt by 1911, never coming close to Willie's grand vision. But, despite its flaws and crumbling concrete, Willie's fantastical idea was ahead of its time, proven decades later as toll highways sprang up across the country.

After leaving its island home, the Vanderbilt Cup wandered like a prodigal child all over the country, from Savannah to Milwaukee, Santa Monica, and San Francisco for the next five years. After the Santa Monica race in 1916, the Cup was formally withdrawn. When asked by a reporter: "It just didn't seem like the Vanderbilt Cup Race when it was taken away from Long Island, did it, Mr. Vanderbilt?" Willie replied: "No. And it did seem that all that could be hoped for had been accomplished, so it was a fitting moment to end the races."[55]

Willie had his legacy, bittersweet though it might have been:

> Results far surpassed anything I had anticipated in my most imaginative moments. Ten years ago the cup went on the shelf. It had served its purpose."[56]

CHAPTER 13

Bailout

In the autumn of 1906, President Theodore Roosevelt looked forward to announcing an initiative to regulate interstate traffic by inland waterways.[1] It was one more legislative victory against the transportation syndicates. Indeed, it may have been the final blow to the great London-to-Tokyo scheme. Morgan, Hill, Gould, and Vanderbilt could only look on while a steady stream of populist backlash pecked away at their grand design. This time, Roosevelt and his band of angry Midwestern farmers dismantled a well-crafted Morgan ploy at generous federal maritime subsidies.

Accepting an invitation to cruise the Mississippi aboard a paddle steamer, Roosevelt was eager to cement his regional support and reward his backers who helped him vanquish J.P. Morgan.[2] Aboard the boat, the president made his announcement.

The news, unfortunately, was overshadowed by economic clouds rising from Wall Street. But instead of rushing to face the rising tide of economic bad news, Roosevelt went hunting.

The Northern Securities pact had been beheaded by the Supreme Court in October of 1904. Since then, government and the railroads pursued a careful dance of daggers through the courts, splintering monopolies while locking in flat rates. The Hepburn Act was directed towards price control, which in turn, reduced competition. As the practice of rebating was dealt a fatal blow, the railroads actually stood to make a profit again.

While the railroad giants raved and ranted against the imposition of regulations, a prospering nation failed to listen. However, the American treasury had limited means to loosen credit supply without a central bank and the American industrial machine had outrun the ability of its markets to absorb its output. America had been the world's wholesaler, selling its wares from ammunition to grain. Peace had come to the Russo-Japanese and Boer War theaters, slackening foreign demand. Meanwhile, U.S. consumers tightened their purse strings. American business thrived on the liquidity of bank offerings and, as peacetime ushered in a reduction in demand for American munitions and supplied, excess capacity began to flood marketplaces.

Woodrow Wilson, then president of Princeton University, warned that the economic troubles gathering in 1906 were a by-product of government interference in the railroad's ability to borrow. Immediately, Roosevelt reacted by threatening to place all railroads under government control. Unfortunately, this saber rattling only served to increase his image as a demagogue fighting the past, pitted against the railroad barons while failing to grasp the realities of a changing economic climate.

While Roosevelt went in search of big game, the bulls lay on Wall Street bleeding from mortal wounds. For J.P. Morgan, the decision was a call to arms. Staring ahead at telegrams from 23 Wall Street that mounted up before him, Pierpont Morgan resolutely decided, "They do not know what to do, and I don't know what to do, but I am going back."[3] A lot was at stake. Morgan met with the president. He then followed by convening the railroad leaders.

By now, public fears were showing in the market. Corporate earnings crashed to a record low on March 14, 1907. As the prices plummeted, brokerage houses evaporated. The Dow lost 25 percent in value. A crisis of confidence ran rampant.

Roosevelt's hands were tied. Without a central bank to provide relief, and regulatory bodies that only offered rules but no protection, Roosevelt had little choice but to turn to the investment bankers to bail out the nation. Just as panic broke, Roosevelt met with bankers E.H. Harriman, Henry C. Frick, Jacob H. Schiff, William Rockefeller, H.H. Rogers, Abraham Kuhn and Morgan to create a twenty-five million dollar bailout fund.[4] Immediately, as the cash was released and news of the bailout became public, the panic began to subside.

Despite the turnabout, investors remained wary, continuing to sell stocks and hoard gold. Cash became an increasingly dear commodity. The market remained fragile as the months passed. Banks diminished reserves as many businesses and brokerages continued to collapse. J.P. Morgan went abroad, taking respite in Europe where he stayed for five months.

With stunning similarities to the debacle of 2008, the breakdown of finance in 1907 was a disaster of worldwide proportions. Repercussions of the market tumult reverberated globally. First, the Egyptian Stock Exchange crashed. Then, the Bank of England suddenly found itself suffering a lack of liquidity. One by one, stock markets around the world fell like dominoes. The Japanese suffered, followed by the French, and then back home again in New York. An earthquake had ravaged San Francisco the year before, leaving the west without a stable financial center. New York City attempted to float a general obligation bond, but failed to interest sufficient subscribers. By August 10, 1907, the stock market in New York had collapsed again, with losses this time plummeting to an unprecedented one billion dollars.

Just as J.P. Morgan sailed home, a group of some of the most powerful bankers convened to decide which trust companies should be allowed to fail and which to live.[5] With a vote of no confidence, the formerly blue chip

Knickerbocker Trust was let go. Considered a safe investment, the Knicker-bocker Trust had built highly leveraged credit on packaged securities of ever-decreasing value. Every loophole had been employed to feed corporate greed.

The lines that formed outside of the Knickerbocker Trust at Fifth Avenue and 34th Street grew long and winding during the late-night hours. By the middle of the following day, the trust had paid out eight million dollars, and at two P.M., she closed her doors. Depositors petitioned the other trusts in droves. Tellers counted the money at a snail's pace, just to slow the process. The Morgan bankers pondered feeding cash into the system to avoid further closings, hoping the panic might subside.

The deluge continued. Next in line was the Trust Company of America, with assets of one hundred million dollars. George Courtelyou, the secretary of the treasury, announced that the trust would be supported. It was a mistake. There was a rush across the board. Government arrived too late with too little — and too loud with the wrong message. Trading was virtually halted and the system neared total meltdown. Frustrated beyond belief, the president of the New York Stock Exchange wanted to shut down the market. He implored Morgan for relief liquidity to prevent the brokerage houses from falling down like a deck of cards.[6]

All power lay in the hands of Morgan, to whom everyone looked for guidance and support. With currency at a dire shortage, Morgan had script issued to take its place. Morgan summoned the banks to his offices and demanded they come up with a plan. Morgan, Baker, and Stillman agreed that the Trust Company of America was the place to stop the trouble.

He even sought assistance from church preachers to gather their flocks and urge calm. John D. Rockefeller agreed to surrender half his fortune to support the American markets.

The Trust Company of America still had one hundred million dollars in resources though she was nearly cash dry. It was a liquidity problem. Early that day, TCA was down to one hundred and eighty thousand dollars in cash to fulfill the demands of anxious depositors. Boxes of securities were retrieved from the trust vaults and Morgan orchestrated the liquidation of select assets to capitalize the tellers. First National, National City, the Hanover National, and J.P. Morgan and Co. all purchased securities to keep TCA afloat.

The Trust Company of America made it through the day, but the Pittsburgh exchange had suspended trading. Call money had reached 90 percent interest. They had to stop the effects from reaching New York.

J.P. Morgan fell asleep in his chair, suffering from an intense cold that left him blurry-eyed and more cantankerous than usual. Awakening suddenly, he immediately took action, pressuring the assembled bankers into surrendering yet another eight and a quarter million dollars, making up the difference from his own coffers.[7] Ordered by Roosevelt to New York, Cortelyou arrived seeking cooperation with the bankers and brought twenty-five million in government funds. Cash, a limited commodity, now flowed from government coffers to the hands of private bankers.

When Morgan walked outside, humped over from his illness, shouts of, "There goes the old man!" and "There goes the big chief!" greeted him, as a cheering populace called out its gratitude. It was his greatest hurrah. He had prevented a global collapse and humbled a president.

Unfortunately, the panic in the stock exchange was endemic. European money flooded back to take advantage of cheap market conditions. Morgan again took decisive action, leading a syndicate to purchase thirty million dollars in municipal general obligation bonds, thereby saving the City of New York.[8]

Confidence began to seep back into the markets as United States Steel issued a strong fiscal report. Not all fires could be put out and some companies became casualties. Morgan's men repeatedly issued pleas for people to leave their money in the banks. The country was poised to herald J.P. Morgan a hero and Roosevelt a misguided failure.

However, greed would soon prevent such laurels. Obtaining a concession from Roosevelt that no antitrust action would be taken against the players, including his favorite, U.S. Steel, Morgan acted upon his opportunity, forcing the acquisition of the steel producer Tennessee Coal, Iron and Railroad Company of Birmingham, Alabama. The repercussions of his ploy would forever stain Morgan as a greedy profiteer. He might have saved the world from disaster, but the public, ever wary, preferred to remember him for this.

Just as the first tidings of severe economic storms arrived in J.P. Morgan's Wall Street library, Willie K. was out for a special run with his friends David Barnes and O.H.P. Belmont.[9] On Friday, March 1, 1907, leaving the Hotel de Paris in Monte Carlo in Vanderbilt's 60 horsepower Mercedes, the trio set out on a beautiful day. Roads were clear and in fine shape. Within six hours and six minutes they reached Turin, Italy, a distance of two hundred kilometers.

At Turin, they stopped for the evening and rested. The next day, they set out again and ascended on good roads to tremendous altitudes. However, within four kilometers of the summit, snow became embedded in their tires, and by the time they crawled forward to the mountaintop, they were impossibly stuck in four feet of snow, unable to move forward or back. Fortunately, an Italian barracks was close enough to provide assistance but the troops could not dislodge the vehicle. After four hours, all parties gave up in despair. While Willie took photographs of the troops, Belmont and Barnes were sent to summon mules to do the work at which men had failed.

Nine mules struggled to set the vehicle free. Relief was found at a nearby roadhouse where all of the rescuers were treated to Willie's ample largess. Many of the rescue party drank themselves to sleep. The adventure ended in a room warmed by a fire, smelling of onions and cigars.

While the world plunged off a financial cliff, Willie enjoyed his excursion with warmth and relish. The trip ended back in Monte Carlo at the Hotel Imperial, none the worse for wear.

When the evil days of August resounded through the markets, Willie was once again on the road, this time from Paris to Aix-les-Bains. Another beautiful morning encouraged the travelers to depart early. No news from the States would slow this venture. Their only mishap occurred when the mechanic suffered some bruises as he was thrown from the ninety horsepower Mercedes, landing on his left side. No pharmacy was open at the hour so the injured man had to wait until proper facilities could be located. While the mechanic stayed behind, Willie continued forward from Aix-les-bains to Chamounix, ambling through the countryside, enjoying the views of castles and country homes, and seeing the magnificent Mont Blanc and brilliant white glaciers.

Despite the feverish anxiety surrounding Wall Street, Willie remained unperturbed and unaffected. He did not rush back to New York to attend to business. Thus was Willie's grasp of the events going on around him.

However, later that month, when he finally returned home, he came back to a decidedly rude awakening. Willie K. was a victim of his own overextension. He was involved in too many endeavors to juggle any or all of them through the times at hand. His various businesses had crumbled overnight, unable to handle the pressure. First to go was his Night and Day Bank that depended upon inter-bank loans to float capital. The bank had served primarily as a safe deposit box for jewels, where guests could keep their cherished ornaments after visiting the theater and before returning home in a carriage.

Repercussions of the bank failure were evident in every aspect of his business. His office cleaning business was over-extended and required an influx of resources to gain wider market acceptance. Thus, another business went under.[10] Road building, too, had become a finance-intensive mess. Willie was overextended and could not meet the price to purchase right of ways. The Long Island Motor Parkway spilled into a circuitous path through the countryside. The road would have to be delayed and, with this delay, the race would have to wait as well. Thus, the 1907 running would be lost without a single car hitting the track.

The taxes on Deepdale's vast holdings were considerable, and the maintenance an equal burden. To make matters worse, Willie had no money of his own. His father was not inclined to transfer his bequests prematurely. Surprisingly, even one of the wealthiest men in the world, William Kissam, was feeling a financial pinch that year.

Willie K. was left to his own devices, few that they were. Desperate, he put Deepdale, and even his prize chickens, up for sale. He needed cash.

His wife, Virginia, the heiress to the Comstock Lode, had inherited property in San Francisco from her father. In secret, hiding his efforts from his wife, Willie set about to sell some of the land holdings, as well as selections of Virginia's expensive jewelry. Foolishly, he offered up the ornaments to the notorious gossip Hetty Green:

William K. Vanderbilt, Jr., who had gone in excessively for motoring and other expensive sports, who reported to be in financial straits, from San Francisco information came that some of his wife's extensive real estate there had been offered for sale and it was reported here that he had pledged family possessions, including silver and jewels to Hetty Green, for a loan.[11]

When Virginia found out, she was furious. Hetty Green was an infamous slumlord, having accumulated a giant fortune through "the blind accumulation of money."[12] Her greed and avarice were legend and she was considered "one of the most bizarre figures of her time."[13] Rivaling the Vanderbilts in fortune, she was of a curmudgeonly nature despite sitting atop a fortune amassing one hundred million dollars. Yet it was from her that Willie K. thought he could find financial salvation.[14] Green would take pleasure in making it known that she had been approached for assistance, enjoying the accompanying scandal.

E.V.W. Rossiter, vice president and general manager of the New York Central, published a scathing denial, "The New York Central directors have never applied to Mrs. Green at the Chemical National Bank to my knowledge ... the statement is ridiculous. Neither has the Vanderbilt estate ever applied to her for a loan. I cannot believe that Mrs. Greene was correctly quoted."[15] Soon after, Mrs. Elliot F. Shepard, sister of the late Cornelius Vanderbilt, also came swiftly to Willie's defense, "Mrs. Vanderbilt would never seek such means of obtaining money as Mrs. Green is said to have been described. Her statements are amazing."[16] At the same time, Harry Payne Whitney, married to Willie's cousin, Gertrude, had negotiated a million dollar loan from Mrs. Green for himself, and refused to make any comments.

Willie, meanwhile, was also struggling with the fallout from yet another casualty of the market. The Vacuum Cleaner Company, an investment of Willie K., banker Henry B. Hollins, and others went into receivership with a debt of some $270,000.[17] The company, formerly known as the David T. Kenney Vacuum Sweeping System, based in New Jersey, had a promising beginning in January of 1906, with a capital stock of $1,060,000 for the purposes of manufacturing and selling vacuum cleaning machines for installation in public buildings, hotels, theaters, churches, private houses and railway terminals for cleaning cars.[18]

As the bank crisis burned, the pace of business and luxuries such as soot-free windows, clean walls and rugs were the first to be dropped from needed expenditures. Hence went the vacuum business. The patents that gave Willie protection began to expire. The one million dollar expense of purchasing the patents from inventor David T. Kenney, and the development of prototype equipment and methodologies were of little worth in an empty marketplace. The timing was simply a disaster. Willie, in fact, had found fertile ground. He paved the way and cleaned up some of the doubts that the venture was a good one. But the crash of 1907 would claim many good ideas, and even Willie would not go unscathed. Kenney was one of the first to bail out of the floundering venture, stepping down as president in November 1907, leaving behind forty cleaning contracts expected to yield twenty-five thousand dollars in future profits.[19] A debt of one hundred and fifty-two thousand dollars, however, remained for funds borrowed, and Willie, it seemed, was left holding the empty bag.

Back in New York and with Deepdale behind him, Willie began building a new house at 666 Fifth Avenue. It stood next to his childhood home, now one of Alva's spoils of divorce. The new structure was out of place from its surroundings, squeezed in next to its neighbor, crammed into a fifty-by-ninety-foot parcel. One of its most distinctive features, separating it from all the other fabulous mansions on Vanderbilt row, was a complex of playrooms for little Muriel and Consuelo.

Despite the pleasure Alva must have experienced in having her son so close by, she also knew troubles were brewing next door. Willie and Virginia were on rocky shoals. The idyllic days on Newport's beaches, where they had raced on the sand together, playing like children, had been replaced by cooler and more formal ties.[20] Virginia was too religious for Willie, and Willie, in the end, too much of a daredevil even for spunky Birdie. Virginia had matured, and perhaps desired her husband to do the same, but Willie was simply not ready to give up his youthful dreams. After drifting apart for several years, the two were now on decidedly different paths.

CHAPTER 14

Overextended

In 1907, as the nation grappled with the effects of the stock market failure, Willie K. struggled with his own adversities. Energetic and charismatic, Vanderbilt had started myriad endeavors—from working in the Central offices to planning construction of the Long Island Motor Parkway, managing the Vanderbilt Cup and running a vacuum cleaning business and personal savings bank. Thus, when misfortune struck, it struck far and wide. Willie was overextended in every direction. Suddenly, for the first time in his life, he discovered he was not immune to the troubles of the common world.

He had begun the year without a care, reveling in his racing in Europe and returning again to cross the Alps in August, but all the while failing to take hold of his affairs. Now, it was too late; Willie was overwhelmed by the crushing weight of bank and market failures.

Unlike his cousin Neily who had walked away from a fortune for love, then built up a sizeable fortune through his own invention and business acumen,[1] Willie K. had undermined his marriage and squandered his assets on a dozen divergent ideas. In the face of so much trouble, he turned back to the railroad — the family he could always count on.

Willie had the hubris one might have expected from a fourth generation Vanderbilt; he relied upon the moneyed past as a key to his future, particularly his father's fortune and power. Had his father been more present and supportive, he might have provided a better road for the son to follow. Instead, he cast a shadow over Willie, just as his father had done to him and his grandfather to his father.

Willie had always desired to be taken seriously for his efforts, and yet he did not want to be taken *too* seriously; he still needed time to escape, play, and be frivolous. By 1905, being a financial man offered better prospects than a railroad man, something of which both his uncle Frederick William Vanderbilt[2] and his cousin Neily seemed well aware. Despite Willie's flaws, he had learned some valuable lessons in running his own businesses. He knew how to make his own money, and the taste of reaping his own dollars whetted his appetite. He had developed into a businessman, although he was still internally tormented by conflicting desires. On the one hand, he recognized the importance of focusing his attention on fundamentals, all the more valuable in order to bounce back from the slumping economy and get his financial affairs in order. Willie K. could not have been oblivious to his cousin Neily's rise to glory, as his cousin pursued his business efforts obsessively, building a reputation for himself even in the court of the Czar of Russia.[3] Nonetheless, Willie wanted to enjoy his life and, like his father, he knew keenly that money alone did not bring happiness. He needed passion, something money, in and of itself, could not offer.

This internal conflict was Willie's only constant. He was plagued by a restless appetite for change, his desire for fame and glory in the tradition of Vanderbilts, his pursuit of pleasure, and his hope of leaving his individual stamp on the world.

On October 30, 1907, his third child, this time a son, William Kissam III was born.[4] The nursery that housed the young infant son, brother to three-year-old Muriel and two-year-old Consuelo, was made of pure white marble, a fitting home for the next branch of the Vanderbilt family tree.

A constant stream of telegrams and gifts bombarded the delighted parents. Willie had an heir. And the pressure on his strained marriage was momentarily lifted.[5]

Despite the apparent reconciliation, Virginia had stayed true to her vow that she would never get into an automobile with Willie again. They now traveled separately, even when they were heading to the same destination. Virginia traveled by limousine to Aix-les-Bains from Lucerne, while Willie followed the next morning in his racecar.[6]

But the marital truce was short-lived. By the end of the year, Willie's financial troubles were adding dry tinder to the mounting flame of marital discord. The agricultural land of Deepdale was rented to Albert Hanlon of Little Neck,[7] and although Willie denied the rumor, Deepdale would soon be on the market. Deepdale straddled the county line and was assessed at a higher rate in one than the other. Unfortunately, the tax burden nullified the rental income Willie was hoping to achieve.[8] Willie's prized chickens had already been sold, as was the rest of the livestock. A polo player and fellow yachtsman, Paul Rainey, rented the rambling estate, but made the transaction conditional on the return of the prize pullets to Deepdale.[9]

Despite the birth of a son, the rift between Willie and his wife did not heal; for Virginia, too much had gone wrong. While she had adored her husband's enthusiastic spirit during their betrothal, she was now loath to see her family fortune squandered or used to pay Willie's expenses. Five months after William III arrived, Virginia no longer entertained any charades of familial peace. She entertained royal guests, including the Earl and Countess of Granard, Lady Cunard, and the Vicomte de Perigny, all without Willie, all despite her husband's obvious financial distress.[10]

Birdie took up residence at the Oelrich mansion where she had spent her early debutante years, enjoying the company of her sister Tessie once more.[11] Tessie, who had written an extensive letter to the press in the aftermath of the earthquake in San Francisco, in which she expressed her heartfelt sympathies to the city for their loss and her love of her hometown,[12] undoubtedly must have been enraged by Willie's clandestine attempt to sell Virginia's property there.

By the spring of 1908, the split was obvious. Fresh from one of his motor tours in Europe, Willie returned to New York on April 14, just as Virginia conveniently left for San Francisco. Willie would only say that he was returning from his annual trip abroad, declining comment on his motor tours, or the noted fact that Virginia failed to accompany him.[13]

Within the same week, Willie was arrested again for speeding.[14] He made quite the stir when he appeared in old Town Hall, full of spectators eager to catch a glimpse of another celebrity trial. Magistrate Connolly required Willie to post a hundred dollar bail on behalf of his chauffeur. But instead of reaching into his pocket and offering Clerk McGee one of a roll of one hundred dollar bills, Willie surprised the court by offering Deepdale as security.

"Is it worth $100?" McGee asked.

"Well I would like to buy another like it for $200," Willie replied.[15]

Later, on August 24, 1909, the *Times* reported on yet another speeding arrest, only this time Willie was quick to come up with the fifty dollars required by the magistrate.[16]

The very next day the *Times* again reported on an incident during which, "The policeman had a hot chase after the car, reaching at one time a speed of sixty-five miles an hour."[17] When Willie was confronted with the charge he quietly said, "I plead guilty, your Honor. I didn't think I was going thirty-five miles an hour."[18] He paid his fine without comment.

With failed businesses behind him and a marriage that teetered on the verge of collapse, Willie chose to escape on a cruise in the Caribbean aboard his motor yacht *Tarantula*. Months later, when he finally returned, he took up residence in the Brook Club not far from his 5th Avenue house.[19] All during this period in Manhattan, Willie kept a low profile and, before the press could badger him, he left once more for France on his annual voyage. Returning months later, on June 15, 1910, with his mother, Alva, he took up residence in Newport at her residence, the lavish Marble House.

When Alva and her son returned to New York, she had high hopes for reconciliation. Virginia, however, promptly departed, taking Muriel and Willie K. III with her on the North German Lloyd ship *Kronprinzessin Cecille*. Willie chose not to bid farewell at the dock. From then on, the two were never again seen together as husband and wife.

Willie's father reacted with surprising frustration. Soon after Willie arrived in New York, he sailed from Cherbourg back home on the same ship, *Kron-*

prinzessin Cecille, when it became public knowledge that articles of separation had been prepared. According to an *Evening Journal* report, allegedly William Kissam commented that "there had been too many divorces in the family and he intended to see that there were no more."[20] His abrupt return brought focus on the events at hand. His views of the family predilection towards marital failure were given no shortage of import. If he could achieve reconciliation, he would. The *Journal* reporters tried to squeeze a comment out of Alva. When asked, she said, "That is something which I cannot talk about and should not be asked about."[21] Despite her own theatrics, the troubles of her children were a matter of Vanderbilt pride, and there was no triumph in marital rift.

Yet Willie did not stop pursuing his passions; instead, he took up new ones. That same year, Willie K. took to his wings with the purchase of "the swiftest airship ever constructed."[22] The custom monoplane, built in France especially for Vanderbilt, was expected, he said, to "eclipse all records when we get started."[23] Willie intended to compete as a pilot and, if the rumors were true, he could expect to reach two miles per minute, about twice the speed of the fastest train. The idea surfaced that his motor parkway would be used as an airstrip for launching races. Pilots generally liked the concept, but as with so many of Willie's ideas, it never came to fruition.[24]

Virginia seemed to be of like mind. She, too, was soon piloting a plane. Of course, soaring about the skies was hardly lady-like. So she concealed her identity, appearing at the airfield garbed in a heavy dark veil tightly bound around her face. Her friends formed a defensive wedge to protect her from prying eyes. No sooner had Virginia settled in the cockpit than she placed a heavy foot on the accelerator, causing the airplane to lurch forward — anything but the smooth initial run characteristic of the takeoff. Harmon, the pilot, grabbed her foot. She took the reproof in style, replying, "All right, I'll be good."[25]

Of course, there had to be a reason for the irreconcilable differences between the pair, and the press had a field day speculating over the rift. Some alluded to their religious differences, while other publications cited Willie's attempt to sell Virginia's jewelry, silver, and real estate to finance his whims. The *Journal* ventured a few even more sordid ideas, including, "The name of a famous opera singer was connected with that of the young millionaire."[26] In April of 1910, the *New York American*,[27] swiftly followed by the *New York Times*,[28] would break the story of a French actress Mademoiselle Polaire, "the strange looking idol of the French theatre-going public, [who] will go to America in June for a four weeks' engagement on a New York roof garden."[29]

Emilie-Marie Bouchard, better known as Mademoiselle Polaire, was a thirty-six-year-old performer known as a tight lacer, with a corseted waist reported at an incredible circumference of fourteen inches, a figure made all the more extraordinary by a thirty-eight inch bust packaged in a petite body measuring only five feet and three inches in height. Always fashionably attired in lavish furs and jewelry, Mademoiselle Polaire possessed extraordinary gifts as a comedic actress, taking Paris, and later stage and film in the States, by storm. If Willie was hoping to maintain a clandestine relationship with such an odd and prominent figure, he made a poor choice. That June, he apparently helped the rising star acquire a lucrative theatre engagement in New York. Public curiosity was rampant to see the alleged mistress of another fallen Vanderbilt.

Willie would have been fortunate to escape with a cheap exposé. However, the mademoiselle would have none of that. She was a rising star with a story worthy of print and she had the press's ear. When asked why she had come to New York, she responded:

> What induced me to accept the offer? Well there is a big salary and that counts, of course, but especially I want to see what America is like and what the American man is in his native haunts. Americans are so strange, I had a very dear friend from New York but I couldn't understand him and now we are friends no more.[30]

The *Times* explained that "the little incident that broke the friendship between the whimsical actress and the New Yorker, who is W.K. Vanderbilt, Jr., was amusing enough and makes quite clear why they are 'friends no more.'"[31] In June of 1909 Willie had apparently invited the mademoiselle to dine with him at the Pavillion Henri Quatre. Coming home in the moonlight, Mlle. Polaire took a fancy to some flowers in a wayside garden, "Oh, Willie, get me those."[32]

> Mr. Vanderbilt sent his chauffeur to get them, but Mlle. Polaire had expected a greater gallantry from her escort, and she showed it very plainly, so he, too, got out of the motor and set about filching flowers for the spoiled actress.
> "And then," said Mlle. Polaire, "the whim struck me to see whether I could drive that big car all by myself. I could and I spun clear away into Paris."
> It was very late and young Mr. Vanderbilt and his chauffeur had to trudge along a dark road to Nanterre before they could get an early morning train to Paris.
> "He has no sense of humor," said Mlle. Polaire, plaintively. "He didn't see the joke. I sent back his motor car, but he never sent me the flowers. Are all Americans like that? Perhaps they are nicer when they are at home. Anyway, I'm going to see."[33]

The public scandal surrounding Willie's choice of consort had immediate repercussions. Virginia grew openly enraged. Immediately, she pursued a formal separation by September of 1910. Willie would have preferred a divorce, but he was trumped by Virginia's Catholic prohibition of the sin. The compromise was a separation allowing for Virginia to care for the children, and she would consider divorce only once Muriel and Consuelo were married. At this point, she was of considerable personal wealth and did not require funds from her relatively poor husband Willie. There was no public display of emotion, at least none that reached press coverage. They simply parted ways.

Virginia's sister shared the throne of New York Society with Mrs. Stuyve-

sant Fish; hence, the likelihood of her suffering social ostracism was minimal. The *Post* summed her up, "Mrs. Willie K. Vanderbilt, Jr., has rather delighted in being a moving spirit in playing the games of the smart set and has allowed others to quarrel over the actual leadership. She is universally popular."

Virginia leased the estate of the late Charles T. Barney, at Wheatley Hills in Westbury, Long Island, after their separation. Her new home was ensconced among wealthy neighbors that included the likes of Harry Payne Whitney, E.D. Morgan, Clarence Mackay, Stanley Mortimer, and Neily, Willie's cousin, who had just leased the home of Foxhall Keene.[34] Meanwhile, Willie kept to his club in Manhattan. Still, he was a devoted father and would make the effort and time to be with his children, even if he had lost the right for parental authority.

Upon arrival from Europe on the *Lusitania*, reporters surrounded Virginia, badgering her with nosy questions. Her response was pleasant and firm, "I cannot say anything at this time. I have been so much in the public eye that I do not wish to make any statement. Please do not attempt to interview me."[35]

Not everyone shared affection for Virginia. Willie preserved a humorous, if not slightly acerbic, note about his estranged wife in one of his scrapbooks:

> Mrs. Virginia Vanderbilt, recently staying at Karlsbad, has been using an electrical bed warmer, which the other night went wrong and set fire to the mattress. We respectfully suggest to the lady that there are other bed warmers equally efficacious and less likely on the whole to cause spontaneous combustion.

Despite the attention she drew, Virginia did not shy away from an active social life. Two weeks after her return, Virginia made her first public appearance at the Belmont race track.[36]

Willie sought refuge that autumn in Paris, but ill winds even pursued him there. He left just as flood waters consumed the city. As he arrived at Liverpool aboard the *Mauretania*, he described the flooded city as "a most distressing sight."[37] The sight of dead animals strewn across the Seine riverbanks was enough to send anyone packing.

On one of Virginia's trips to San Francisco, a reporter inquired, "Have you come West with the intention of going to Reno?"[38] At the time, the Nevada destination hosted a lucrative divorce colony, as the desert state was a haven for the many seeking marriage dissolution. Given the "rumors of domestic trouble,"[39] the supposition implied she was headed there to establish residency in Reno for purposes of filing quick divorce papers. Virginia denied it, saying, "Why no; I wish you would say that I have come here for no such purpose.

Opposite: A debate raged as the world decided whether the tight-laced actress Emilie-Marie Bouchard, known to the trade as Mademoiselle Polaire, was the world's ugliest with a 14-inch waist, a comparatively remarkable 38-inch bust, and standing at 5' 3". Apparently, Willie liked her enough to be caught in an affair with the steamy actress. Virginia, already strained by Willie's ways, would have none of it and filed for separation.

Beyond that I would rather not discuss the matter."[40] But the press continued to pursue her every step.

Virginia complained of insomnia[41] and sought a return to San Francisco and her children for rest. Instead, she found herself caught up in a whirlwind of social engagements, and since this was her first visit since the 1906 earthquake, apparently rest was in short supply.

By the end of the month, reports proliferated again on growing evidence that Virginia was, in fact, to join the Reno divorce colony, renting a cottage owned by John Werrin of Virginia City.[42] Reporters pushed for more details, but everyone involved remained silent, refusing to comment.[43]

Local counsel, indeed, had been engaged. Sardis Summerfield, of the law firm of Summerfield and Curler, alleged attorneys for Mrs. Vanderbilt, said: "I will not deny nor confirm it. I cannot talk upon the subject."[44]

Work in Reno was rushed in anticipation of an April arrival.[45] However, for some unexplained reason, Virginia returned to New York.[46] When Virginia came back to the city, occupying a house of H.B. Duryea,[47] Willie K. set out to Paris. They pursued their separate interests amicably, but would never remain in the same city as long as it was possible. Soon after his father's return from Europe, the *Times* mentioned in their society column that the younger Vanderbilt had purchased "a large country estate on Long Island near where, it is said, he will build during the present summer."[48] The home would be built by the famous architects Warren and Whetmore, designers of the Grand Central Terminal, at Little Neck on Huntington Harbor for $125,000.[49] While Virginia continued her ecstatic social schedule, Willie grew more reclusive.

CHAPTER 15

Harbor Me

Willie set out to build a refuge for himself now that he was once again a bachelor. He looked to the north shore of Long Island: Little Neck, now known as Centerport. It stood surrounded by navigable water on three sides, and lay well beyond the annoyances of Gold Coast colony millionaires. Here, Willie K. built a decidedly private residence consisting at first of a bungalow of seven rooms, offering a private view of beautiful Northport harbor. It was the perfect spot for a man who loved sailing and was far enough away from the bustling commuters of New York City. As his estate lay on a narrow stretch of land jutting out into the bay, Willie could literally pull his boat right up to his front yard. Unlike Deepdale, which had been celebrated as the consummate millionaire manse, his new home resembled an "English bungalow."[1] It was a comfortable residence, a retreat rather than an imposing mansion — perhaps even a place to *live*, unlike traditional Vanderbilt residences. Begun in 1910, the first house was completed the following summer. The first floor held three rooms and a connecting hallway. Four bedrooms, a bath, and quarters for servants sat on the second floor. Complementing his connection with the land and sea, a wide porch of heavy oak provided an expansive view of Northport Harbor.

When he first came onto the property, Willie saw an eagle flying out of its nest, which led him to give it the name Eagle's Nest. Two of the eagles that once embellished the old Grand Central Terminal were placed, like sentinels, at the entrance to his hideaway estate. A long wharf lit by gas lamps offered a breathtaking stroll down to the harbor. Climbing roses and vines covered the entrance of the bungalow, while the front garden blossomed with large profusions of rhododendrons. Eagle's Nest, unlike Deepdale, was not a stately residence but rather a delightfully charming and inviting *home*.

He acquired a bed that purportedly once belonged to French emperor Napoleon Bonaparte. Its headboard bore the insignia "N." But contrary to this one piece of regalia, Eagle's Nest was a comfortable and inviting home, with furniture and designs that reflected Willie K.'s own personal tastes and travels. It was from this safe haven that Willie would embark upon numerous sailing adventures, away from the societal pressures and familial strife that faced him

The original bungalow at Eagle's Nest, ca. 1910. Smarting from his separation and seeking refuge by the sea, Willie purchased a tract of land in Centerport, Long Island, considerably past the normal reaches of Long Island's "Gold Coast." Beyond society's eye and within reach of his strained pocketbook, Willie began small, adding only as needed. He had a good port and privacy (courtesy Suffolk County Vanderbilt Museum).

in Newport and New York City. Eagle's Nest became his solace and comfort; his own private harbor where he would develop his new pursuits and follow a lifestyle remarkably simpler and less ostentatious than the one he had known. In 1913, Willie K. would add a quaint Medieval-styled four-story boathouse. As Willie's interests changed and he put more of his time and effort into his sailing expeditions, Eagle's Nest became the repository of his marine collections that he accumulated from his trips around the world. Later, in 1925, he would maintain a residence in Florida on Fisher's Island, which served as a launching point for romance — the equatorial adventures of a succession of yachts.

It did not take Virginia long to announce her own real estate conquest, and in October, the *Times* reported that she had acquired 125 acres on old Glen Cove road, near the Jericho turnpike, where she would reportedly "build a fine mansion."[2] The *Washington Post* alluded to a real estate rivalry between the two.[3]

Willie needed to escape from the difficult baggage of his past as Deepdale rankled as a painful reminder of his own arrogance. Neither of the Vanderbilts had occupied the place in two years. Soon after he acquired Eagle's Nest, he put the property of Deepdale, the one he had struggled so intensely to own and control, up for sale.[4]

Slowly, he removed himself from his old property and the life he had known previously in Newport and at Deepdale, putting his energy into developing his simpler Eagle's Nest. Now he sought the comfortable, the quiet, and the solace of privacy.

Eagle's Nest was a retreat for a man who had grown, in the pattern of his father, increasingly fond of his solitude as he matured. At Eagle's Nest, instead of entertainment, he created a refuge that he could enjoy in near silence. Proximity to the sea was the first priority. Still, Willie's home reflected an adventurous personality and his love of the foreign, unknown, and exotic. Rather than an extension of life in New York, this was more a harbor from which to launch himself into more distant worlds.

In time, Eagle's Nest evolved to reflect the later, life-altering events in Willie's universe. For the first decade, as Willie separated himself from Virginia and Newport, his new estate expanded modestly as he added a garage, a boathouse, and a superintendent's cottage. But as his confidence returned and Willie grew more adventurous again, he added a swimming pool, a bathhouse, and the Vanderbilt Marine Museum, also known as the "Hall of Fishes." His father's death in 1920 left him a substantial inheritance, enough to turn Eagle's Nest into a sort of private world all its own.

A second phase of expansion arrived after he met Rosamund Warburton, who would later become his wife. This period of construction was by far the most extensive and ambitious, reflecting the change that was occurring for Willie internally as well, as he shifted from being a bachelor to a suitor and husband. Above all, Eagle's Nest reflected Willie's personal fantasies and eclectic tastes. His home was an anomaly of design styles. Warren and Whetmore created a simple residence in the Spanish style that was more popular in warmer climates of California and Florida. Yet the open rooms, wood floors, and terra cotta perfectly suited Willie's idiosyncratic ways. From 1924 to 1930, Willie embarked upon an expansion of the main house to include a central courtyard, as well as the addition of an elaborate polychromed entrance tower[5] and a second floor to the museum. The gardens underwent a dramatic transformation, becoming filled with tantalizing smells of fragrant blossoms and fruit.

The final phase began in 1933. With the death of his son, Willie again added to the complex, building a memorial wing in the young man's honor, as well as a library and Moroccan court and minor alterations suggested by the architect Ronald H. Pearce.

CHAPTER 16

A Fatal Accident of Sorts

When E.H. Harriman suddenly and unexpectedly died, new leaders rose immediately to challenge the existing status quo.[1] In the first eight months of 1909, Harriman had pursued a powerful policy of buying stock in the New York Central, and as chairman of the Union Pacific, he was poised to achieve his own transcontinental railroad composed of legally independent and yet unified railroads.[2] Harriman was known for his excellence in organization and the discipline that he had brought to the Union Pacific, transforming the railroad line into a highly efficient and competitive business.

While Harriman did not possess a seat on the board of the New York Central, he nonetheless controlled $14,200,000 in stock.[3] He had tried to buy out William Kissam Vanderbilt but the senior Vanderbilt would not budge, declaring his position secure and unwilling to part with his stock as long as he lived.[4] Rumors had circulated that Harriman would replace Chauncey Depew as chairman of the board. His death, however, dispelled all expectations. Instead, attention fell once more upon the Vanderbilts. How would William Kissam respond?

Within one week of Harriman's passing, William Kissam Vanderbilt was back in his New York office, reasserting his authority in a symbolic gesture that in many ways represented a return to the old order. Dividend earnings had shot up from 6 percent in 1906 to almost 8 percent.[5]

Despite public speculation that the senior Vanderbilt's decisions were the direct consequence of Harriman's death, William Kissam tactfully stated that he recognized the importance of providing a directing authority to the New York Central and that the views of Harriman regarding management would be adopted.[6] The execution would lie with President W.C. Brown, and his assistant, Willie K.

After completing almost a decade of apprenticeship, Willie K., at the age of thirty-two, finally achieved a seat on the board of the New York Central Railroad in July of 1910. Willie's ascendance was viewed as the natural progression from his great-grandfather to him, fourth in line in the succession of Vanderbilt men. He not only sat as a director, but as "Assistant to President Brown."[7] By extension, he automatically became the assistant to the president of every railroad line included in the New York Central system.

The younger Vanderbilt received the stamp of approval and accompanying authority through his new position and an office adjacent to the president. The decision also came with a stream of accolades, including a glowing view of the young railroad magnate's work ethic. His vote on thirty-two boards had continued the practice of interlocking directorships his father used to control the burgeoning empire. They were considered deliberate moves that did not go unnoticed or unappreciated by the board. The elder Vanderbilt continued to keep in touch with Central operations by daily wires from its offices in New York and visits from his son, while he remained in Paris. Willie's ascent was certain.

Occupying a four-square room in a new office building downtown, Willie's office resembled that of a well-traveled gentleman, with walls lined with bookcases, large photographs of horses and boats, a comfortable red couch facing large windows on Lexington Avenue, a large flat-topped desk, and numerous chairs.[8]

With Willie on the board of directors, the Central was once again viewed as a "Vanderbilt Road." Few doubted that Willie K. would soon take the helm of the family dynasty. He would never be anything less than a railroad man. Professing a lack of time to think about his future, being too busy learning about the railroad, Willie still offered impressive insight:

> I do believe, though, that the American railroad has about reached its limit of physical development. Its roadbed cannot very well be improved; maintenance of way men have seen pretty nearly all their dreams come true, I should say. Steel coaches lighted by electricity and fitted as they are already don't leave much to ask for. Motive power is the one thing left for us to work on.
> Electricity will unquestionably be the motive power of tomorrow. It's a good deal of an old story even now, but it is only a question of time, and not a long time, either before all eastern roads, at any rate, will use it wholly. They will for passenger service, anyhow. It may be that steam will never be supplanted for moving freight or for handling it in yards.[9]

Despite his lack of leadership experience, Willie was heralded as the heir apparent, lauding his "kindly disposition,"[10] "democratic"[11] tendencies, "keen appreciation of merit and worth wherever found,"[12] and "praiseworthy ambition to maintain the prestige of his noted family in connection with railroad affairs."[13] The press described his hard work for the past two years and his willingness to solve long-standing problems:

> Wall Street now forecasts that eventually William K. Vanderbilt Jr. will be President of the New York Central and that his determination to qualify himself to run the road cannot but appeal to investors. He is in his early thirties and his colleagues say he has abundant capacity for work coupled with the same sort of business ability which brought success and millions to his forbears.[14]

Yet, at this moment, the role was a demanding one to fulfill. Willie responded with complete honesty when asked whether railroad work came easy to him:

No, I don't think that's true. It has been easy for me, but that has been because I was interested in it, not because it was "born in me." I'm pretty sure of it. I took it up in the first place because I had a very real need for something to do. Every man of his generation, I think, realizes that need.[15]

His idealism was also readily apparent; Willie was taking on a job and the legacy of being a Vanderbilt,[16] but he also recognized his own powerful need to achieve something of personal importance, something fully his own:

I had to have something to do; something to occupy my mind. I don't mean that as we speak about the "something to do" that kills time. I mean something constructive, something creative, and something that has a living connection with the affairs of the world. I quite understand the feeling that makes a man keep in touch with his business by wireless when he's in mid-ocean; that makes him keep in touch with it by cable when he's on the other side of the world. I like that throbbing sense of having a part in things that are moving; having a part in planning and building and improving on them after they are built.[17]

Willie's fortune appeared on the rise. His father's, however, was in decline. By the following spring in March of 1911, the dividend rate on Central stock fell from 6 to 5 percent.[18] The 6 percent dividend was a sacred tradition at the Central. With freight rates frozen by the I.C.C., net revenues dropped on increased gross revenues, the result of steadily increasing expenses. The faltering dividend came as a shock to the market, a harbinger of troubles.

Change was brewing in every aspect of the business as workers, no longer content to accept wages determined by railroad executives, joined labor unions. The 1898 Erdmann Act had made it illegal for employers to forbid railroad workers from joining a union. In 1911, an additional charge of $3.6 million was levied on behalf of the railroad's workers. Additional service requirements, newly requisite in New York and Massachusetts, exacerbated the situation. Burgeoning annual expenses skyrocketed to almost twenty million dollars. Of course, ten million dollars for the construction of Grand Central Terminal only added to the line's woes.

Earnings were down across the board, subsidiary properties faring no better than the Central. The Lake Shore paid out a 6 percent dividend but recorded a decrease in net earnings of some $2.5 million. The Michigan Central's gross earnings increased by $2.3 million, while the net earnings decreased by $850,029. The Big Four gross increased by $2.2 million and its net decreased by 0.85 percent. Net earnings on the Pennsylvania Railroad alone fell off $6,660,332 from its tally the previous year.[19]

James McCrea, president of the Pennsylvania Railroad, pointed out to the stockholders that increased wages had a great deal to do with the relatively poor showing in net earnings, but that taxes and other expenses had also increased. Railroads were capitalizing at an amazing rate. Little of the new capital, however, found its way into improving infrastructure. Instead, it lined the pockets of shareholders. The dividend was now king, but it was bleeding the business to death.

In the spring of 1912, the board of directors appointed Willie K. vice-president of the New York Central Railroad and the Lake Shore lines.[20] His oversight of the roads during President Brown's vacation abroad left a generally positive impression of his ability and dedication.[21] Inexplicably, that same year, the unsinkable Willie K. suddenly slipped into a troubling depression, a condition he seldom acknowledged, though he knew it hounded his father. Alcohol, cigarettes, and Coca-Cola, which still contained cocaine as an ingredient, were his antidotes against this case of "the melancholies."[22]

In 1913, an aggressively progressive congress passed the Valuation Act. The Interstate Commerce Commission was charged with the responsibility of determining the "true value"[23] of a railroad property. In principle, the railroads were then guaranteed "reasonable rates"[24] that would provide a return of 6 percent on real investment. This concept had been broached in the Sherman Anti-Trust Act of 1890, but was dismissed then, as it was believed that the invested capital and the railroad value would be substantially watered down.[25]

Within weeks of the Valuation Act, railroads applied for 5 percent rate increases, which were granted on the basis that the income of the roads was less than was required for the public benefit. This "5 percent"[26] decision was a landmark as it linked a change in philosophy of government and industrial relations. The railroads were guaranteed a "living wage."[27] Later, the Transportation Act of 1920 would provide for a 6 percent return on capitalization.[28]

The *New York Evening Journal* vehemently opposed any legislation that would either "rob the public through extortionate rates or dishonest capitalization"[29] or rob the railroads through "unreasonable legislation or the imposition of unreasonable, unnecessary conditions." They recognized that the hard reality of increases in labor wages and cuts in freight rates would completely wipe out the railroads.

Unfortunately, Willie, too, suffered another kind of disaster; ironically, the direct product of a failure to maintain infrastructure on the railroads.

After a night out with some friends, the Laimbeers and Pells, Willie was about to drive away when suddenly Mrs. Pell jumped into the passenger seat beside him. Startled, Willie dropped his keys and fumbled a few minutes in the dark before he recovered them. His friends, Mr. and Mrs. William Laimbeer, had rushed off in S. Osgood Pell's motor car, with Charles J. Granveau, the chauffeur, driving with Mr. Pell seated beside him. With Mrs. Pell, Willie did his best to close in on the Pell Limousine.

Having sprinted past their friends, Willie K. and Mrs. Pell had just crossed the track when he heard a cry, then a horrendous crash. They looked back to see a train in silhouette strike the Pell car broadside.

The Pell auto was built on a heavy limousine body and, when the train hit, the car rose in the air and dropped, then was lifted again, turned over and over as it was swept ahead for hundreds of feet before the motorman brought the train to a stop.[30] It collapsed heavily on its side, crumpling and splintering.

Mrs. Pell watched painfully before fainting. Willie leaped from his car and ran along the train to the nearest wreckage. By the light of the train, he saw William Laimbeer's body stripped neatly of its clothes, but could not recognize the mangled face. Somebody cried in the darkness some fifty feet further up the tracks that there was a second body. Willie ran to the plaintive sound and recognized his friend, S. Osgood Pell, only by his cravat and the name embroidered in his hat. The head and body were crushed.[31] The train started to move with Willie running alongside it, but it quickly stopped when someone shouted that there was a third body under the train. Mrs. Laimbeer had survived, but suffered fractured limbs and terrible lacerations and bruises all over her body.[32] The chauffeur Granveau had perished.

The accident occurred at an unprotected Long Island Railroad crossing: there was no gate, bell, or flagman.[33] Autos formed a long single line of traffic leading to and from the crossing. The hurtling train sounded no alarm, but the crossing on the road from Long Beach to Hempstead was in clear sight for a quarter of a mile, allowing for an unencumbered view of oncoming trains. Unfortunately, however, there was not enough light. The train was powered by a heavy electrical engine and had thirteen cars crowded with passengers on their way from Manhattan to Long Beach. No one in the train was even aware that the accident had taken place.

There was no shortage of press coverage as the Public Service Commission inquired into the "Pell Tragedy." Willie K. was on the stand as the chief witness. The heir to the Vanderbilt throne, vice president of the New York Central, now became a key voice against the Pennsylvania Railroad's malfeasance.

The tragedy cast a pall over Long Beach and the Long Island community. The Long Island Railroad was quick to provide a storm of defending statistics. Charles B. Addison, assistant to Ralph Peters, president of the Long Island Railroad Company, appeared on behalf of the railroad. He outlined the costs associated with adding gates and flagmen to every crossing and, consequently, the increase in cost of commutation tickets of at least two dollars. He also added that earnings in the past years had been spent for improvements, halting payments of dividends to stockholders for fifteen years.[34]

As Charles Edward Russell, a writer for *Pearson's*, stated, "Our railroads have more fatal accidents than any railroads in the world."[35] Willie K. suffered dearly, learning the consequences of railroad policies adopted by the likes of his father that had left his close friend Pell a casualty.

Later that same year, Grand Central Terminal was finally completed. It was a bold American Renaissance design, offering a fitting crown to one of its most revered economic engines. The New York Central now had a terminus appropriate to one of the great American railroads. The reaction of the media was positive and abundant. It was a grand moment to be a Vanderbilt, as brief as that moment would be. Yet, in subtle but abundant irony, the stars on the rotunda ceiling had been painted backwards. The artist had laid the design on the floor and transferred the design as if one were standing on top of the building looking downward on the sky. Had fate provided an indelible portent of the future?

In an effort to put the Pell tragedy behind him, Willie returned again to sailing. He traveled aboard his new steel yacht, the formidable *Tarantula II*. Adapted for cruising deep waters, the ship measured one hundred and twenty feet in length with a beam of a slim ten feet. It was built at Lawley's yards in Neponset on the east side of Boston and plunged into the waters in January of 1913.[36] The vessel was built entirely of steel with teak wood decks, watertight steel bulkheads, and two motor-driven launches and two gigs.

Throughout the year, Willie took his beloved new friend from port to port. Traveling aboard the *Tarantula II* was exceedingly, perhaps excessively, comfortable. Outfitted with numerous modern devices for convenience as well as a gorgeous stateroom in rosewood, mahogany, and satinwood, the *Tarantula* could easily accommodate several passengers. The *Tarantula II* was no ordinary pleasure boat. Apart from the stateroom, saloon, two-berth guest stateroom with associated bath and lavatory areas, the vessel also had full sleeping quarters for the ten-man crew, a bridge deck with a charthouse forward for controlling and guiding the craft, a dining room, deckhouse, and a small connecting elevator. Powered by two speedway gasoline motors of two hundred and sixty-five horsepower, it could maintain a comfortable cruising speed of thirteen knots per hour.

For the first eight months of the year, Willie kept his powerful boat in New York and Newport harbors. Caricatures in newspapers depicted him as a popular hero and sailing veteran:

> William K. Vanderbilt, Junior
> *Tarantula*'s master on cruise
> Takes trips on the boundless old ocean
> To meet with Society's views.
>
> Just like him to take to the water
> According to social demand
> For this youth, who is popular sailing,
> Is even more so on land.[37]

Years later, Willie donated the *Tarantula II* to the American war effort. It was well suited for the job of patrol and pursuit, already the cut of an English torpedo boat. The *Tarantula* was painted a neutral gray.[38]

In 1914, when World War I broke out in Europe, Wall Street was in the midst of another depression. Railroad traffic had declined by 6 percent. With no rate increase relief on the horizon, revenues on the Central plummeted by eighteen million dollars.[39] What began as gradual erosion soon became a cascade. Despite Draconian cuts, the elimination of improvements, and a reduction in work force, the line was still left with an operating loss of two and a half million dollars.[40] Something drastic had to be done, but it was not up to

Willie always returned to the sea. In January 1913, he launched the steel yacht *Tarantula II*. Built at Lawley's yards on the east side of Boston, she had a length of 128 feet. Fast and comfortable, she was donated to the war effort (in 1917) and converted into a sleek patrol boat, serving the vicinity of New York Harbor. Here she is seen in military gray. At first, Willie commanded his own vessel, but was then recalled for railroad work. Just in time, or a little too soon, as she was sunk while on duty (in 1918) (courtesy Suffolk County Vanderbilt Museum).

Willie K. to decide how to proceed: the final decision still remained in the hands of his father.

In the pre-war years the economy prospered, and although the railroads did not keep pace with the increases in other sectors, they enjoyed the trend. The rise in earnings, however, was not viewed as an opportunity to put money back into the railroad for improvements and better equipment; instead, it was almost exclusively a source of shareholder income. Meanwhile, between 1900 and 1915, the general level of prices in the country increased 35 percent, railroad wages by 50 percent, and the taxes paid by the railroads by 200 percent. During this time period, the I.C.C. granted only one freight rate increase — 3 percent in 1913.[41]

In 1910, 66 percent of American railroads paid four hundred million dollars in stock dividends, offering about an 8 percent return. Three quarters of that was paid from current income, and the other quarter from a surplus. In stark contrast, the railroads stated they only used fifty-seven million of income for capital improvements — and very little was done to actually improve the physical condition of the roads.[42] Moreover, in the Central's case, money continued to pour into Grand Central Terminal, diverting even more revenue from other needed improvements.

The Central's debt consistently deepened. From 1902 to 1913, capitalization had increased, and since the Central owned one-fifth of the system outright, the rest was leased or converted into collateral trust bonds. Hence, management had to pay out fixed charges first before dividends. Despite these restrictions, the surplus remained high, yet the revenue only ensured that dividends were paid regularly, so the road itself went neglected. The railroad barons had gone from building and expanding a railroad empire to pillaging their own coffers, intent on squeezing out every profitable dollar. As the owners raided, they wailed against the progressive government climate. Despite their complaints, the rail industry paid the greatest dividends in history.[43] Shareholders ignored management, and the rape of the railroads continued unfettered. The fight between the railroads and government regulators became a continuous downward spiral.

Regulatory neglect and inadequate legislative action allowed business owners to strip assets. Government had guaranteed a fixed return against investment without assuming the responsibility for regulating it or assuring that a sufficient balance was retained to maintain the essential utility at task. In essence, the continuous demise was steeped in a combination of shareholder greed, complicated by regulatory failure to understand the problem. The railroads did not receive the improvements needed, operating on old equipment and lines in poor condition. The pitiful condition of the railroads became most evident when pressured by the traffic demands stimulated by World War I. While physical plants disintegrated, the I.C.C. refused to raise rates. It was only in 1914, after substantial damage had already occurred and numerous wrecks had forced public attention, that the capital structure was reorganized.[44]

Where was William Kissam in all of the unfolding drama? Semi-retired, the senior Vanderbilt was content to remain in France with his beloved wife, Anne, raising his horses, yet still holding the reins from across the ocean. All the while he insisted that the Central cling to its dividend. He had to in order to keep the investors happy — and he needed their money to finish the terminal. The elder Vanderbilt was caught in the same noose as the rest, unable to raise rates, ignoring his infrastructure, and paying out returns to ever-hungry investors. His son, Willie K., could only stand by watching. The New York Central was adrift.

Over time, through family ownership, the Central had allied with other railroads, such as the Lake Shore and Michigan Southern Railway; Geneva, Corning and Southern Railroad; Detroit, Monroe and Toledo Railroad, etc; and — through leases— the Big Four and Michigan Central. Each railroad maintained a certain independence, but was held together through the Vanderbilts' scheme of interlocking directorships. By vote and influence, the family laid claim to their far-flung empire.

By the end of the twentieth century's first decade, many railroad lines however, stood on the verge of collapse. William Kissam Vanderbilt understood the need for the constituent railroads to consolidate into one entity, allowing for a favorable capital reconstruction, centralization of management, and retrenching of family holdings. Yet, while the parent railroad had centralized control, Vanderbilt influence would decrease on the newly enlarged board, while other interests, especially those of Morgan and Rockefeller, stood to gain ascension. Still, the Central's survival depended on consolidation.

It took William Kissam two years of hard sell. He, along with Central president Chauncey Depew, and Alfred H. Smith, negotiated doggedly. On December 28, 1914, the shareholders of the Lake Shore, the last holdout road, ratified the merger. The newly restructured New York Central Railroad appeared on January 2, 1915. The elder Vanderbilt believed he had secured the line once more. By consolidating different entities, he increased his holding in the final corporate entity, the reconstituted New York Central Railroad. Thus, the great road would remain in Vanderbilt hands for years to come. In the wings, Willie K. stood in waiting, ready to soon take charge.

The railroad, at least for now, was saved from the onslaught of the changing times. William Kissam, most certainly exhausted by the events of the past fifteen years, was ready to retire to his loving Anne and their horses. But history would not relent. Europe was tearing itself apart in all-out conflict, and the United States was inching, day by day, toward entering the war. By late 1916, involvement seemed inevitable.

Willie, like many, had no intention of being denied his opportunity to serve. Approaching forty, Willie was no longer the young recruit, but he took his participation in naval affairs, even at the lowly level of junior grade lieutenant, quite seriously. At the first hint of United States involvement in the war, he donated his yacht, the *Tarantula II*. It was armed as a patrol boat and made part of the mosquito fleet patrolling New York harbor.

Still, Willie could not leave his responsibilities on shore altogether. During one routine assignment, he wanted to return home on his shore leave to check on the status of business at the Central. Captain Ballinger brushed his request aside, telling him to follow his protocol:

> The junior lieutenant saluted, turned away as if to leave, and then hesitated. "Please excuse my pertinacity, Captain, but this day's shore leave means a lot to me. Of course when I took up this naval work I meant to stick to it, and if you say so, why, of course I shall at once withdraw my request. The only thing is that I worked seventeen years to get this job I had, and I want particularly bad to tidy things up before putting to sea for good. After working so long to land the job, you see, I'd like to have it waiting for me when I come back. It's a good job and I'd hate to lose it."
>
> "As I said," returned the Captain. "Your application will be acted upon in due course of time. That is all."
>
> The Lieutenant again saluted and turned away. As if by an afterthought, Captain Ballinger halted him.
>
> "By the way," he said, "what is that job you're so anxious about?"
>
> "Why, vice president of the New York Central Railroad Company, Captain," replied the junior lieutenant, touching his cap and again turning away.[45]

The Vanderbilt family grew intensely involved in the war effort in different capacities. William Kissam and Anne donated millions for the war effort in France. Anne, a significant philanthropist in her own right, spent myriad dollars of her own. But she was even better known for her hands-on approach at the front. Indeed, she inspired William Kissam to reach beyond his own typically private boundaries. He founded, funded, and served as president of Official Government Pictures, Inc., which, with the approval of the British Government, went to the front to bring the war home in graphic footage.[46] Moreover, on October 11, 1918, the *Wall Street Journal* reported that William Kissam Vanderbilt I was presented the Legion of Honor as honorary president of the Lafayette Esquadrille, the intrepid battlefield ambulance service which he aided in founding.[47] For a man who had shown little passion for money, he certainly had found passion for life.

In 1914, Willie's uncle, George Vanderbilt, the builder of the grand Biltmore Estate in North Carolina, passed away. He left behind a large Fifth Avenue mansion that passed on to Neily, much to the delight of his wife, Grace.[48] Neily took the position of brigadier general in the New York National Guard, training divisions and fighting on the Mexican border. He also immediately gave up his ship, *North Star*, for use as a hospital for the British.[49]

Cousin Alfred, who had ignored service and instead cultivated a rather scurrilous reputation in England, made history aboard the ill-fated liner *Lusitania* in May 1915. So the story goes, when a German U-boat torpedoed the mighty ship, Alfred offered his own life jacket to a distraught woman, then ran back and forth across the sinking ship, rescuing children, scooping them in his arms with his valet, Ronald Denyer, as they vainly tried to save the poor infants. Though many survived, Alfred was not one of them. In the subsequent storm of international outrage over the attack on a civilian ship, Alfred had died a noble hero.

Willie's cousin Gladys (Alfred and Neily's sister, the Countess Szechenyi) housed three hundred children of soldiers who had died fighting in Budapest. His uncle, Frederick William, donated substantially to the Red Cross efforts and gave up his ship to the navy.

As the war effort lurched into full gear, and President Wilson organized the railroads under martial authority, the Central's president, Alfred H. Smith, was sent to supervise American railroads in the east. In turn, Willie was named president of the New York Central System. Willie K. Vanderbilt II at last had a titled position that appeared fitting of his diligent efforts and, more importantly, his family status.

CHAPTER 17

Railroad Man

Despite his eagerness, Willie's new role could not have come at a less opportune time. The very roadbeds upon which the railroads had been constructed were in disrepair and crumbling beneath his feet. Bankers and management had little interest in the function of a railroad as a transportation system; they were motivated solely by short-term profit. Inevitably, efficiencies between systems that did little to improve the bottom line were given little credence. In stark contrast, the progressives charged that the profit motive was undermining the roads and the national interest. The demand for war goods and an efficient transportation system only exacerbated opinions in Washington that the troublesome roads should be nationalized as common carriers.

In the two years preceding Willie's appointment, the United States became more and more embroiled in the Great War. Heavy traffic overloaded the railroads, which could not handle the increase in demand. European demand for American goods and munitions grew and the railroads, unable to handle peak traffic loads in the spring and summer of normal years, strained under the new burdens. Railroad management was reluctant to make infrastructure investments demanded by the increased traffic flows in the face of escalating costs and unwieldy and unpredictable legislation. Government borrowing and the new capital needs of war had skyrocketed debt while swallowing up dividends.

In 1915 President Woodrow Wilson had labeled the recalcitrant railroads "the transportation problem"[1] and recommended a general inquiry. Within several months a joint committee began investigations that continued until 1917. The New York Central, faltering from years of neglect, continued to disintegrate. According to Walter D. Hines, director general of the railroads, "The general opinion was that the railroad companies had not spent on improvements nearly as much as they needed to spend to keep up with the growth of the traffic."[2] In his analysis, the roads could ill handle the traffic swell brought on by the harvest of 1915 and 1916. They would fare even worse when faced with a full-scale war effort.

The year 1916 also brought other changes among the roads. The Adamson

Act finally won something railroad managers had fought against for years: an eight-hour workday. As the cost of labor rose, so did operating expenses. A steady stream of new laws requiring the installation of safety measures and equipment were passed. The railroads, despite their extensive network, were burdened by heavy capitalization costs. At the same time, the government approved and encouraged the growth of the automobile industry, with a colossal network of new roads and highways.[3] Suddenly, an entirely new rival, the trucking system, had come into being, garnering millions in supportive, state-by-state subsidies.

At the end of 1916 the Interstate Commerce Commission reported that the railroads could not handle peacetime peaks in traffic and could not be expected to handle emergency demands. The report concluded that peak seasons were approaching a year-round phenomenon as transporting grain in the autumn and coal in the winter was growing more and more bottlenecked. It was not just a shortage of cars, but limitations on other railroad facilities that were showing strain. Car and engine repair facilities were in short supply as were the personnel to manage them.

Railroad management refused to cooperate in the return of empty railcars to points west despite the pressing need to bring war goods to eastern ports. There was no profit to be had in hauling an empty car. By early January 1917, mills were being shut down and perishables destroyed because the ports were too backed up to carry goods to their destinations. Prices for commodities began to skyrocket. The escalation in prices made the cost of money even dearer and further discouraged bold refinancing. The situation was spiraling out of control.

When war commitment finally came, the rising tide of change grew to a deluge. Disparate corporate entities would have to set their own motives aside to respond to military demands. Clearly, the railroads would have to cooperate with one another. The proper functioning of the railroads as an effective transportation system required unification as well as government regulation. The initial approach of government was to allow the railroads to resolve the problem themselves.

Unfortunately, years of regulation and court precedent made "cooperation" impossible. A string of anti-trust legislation thoroughly prevented intercorporate collaboration. At the same time, without fixing the profit of each of the corporate entities and molding them into one cooperative unit, the traffic problems would not meet the needs of the war machine. It was unrealistic to expect corporate officers, responsible to shareholders for profits and dividends, to surrender profitable traffic to another railroad for the overall good; especially when the act of creating such a national system of cooperating railroads was monopolistic. Thus, even if the roads could have found their own solution, they would be legally restricted from acting in the common good.

As the war progressed, labor shortages were inevitable. It also followed that as labor became less available, the workers would be able to make increasing demands. Experienced labor would be drawn away to other efforts; the locomotives would not receive service as needed and the system would be further ground down. To make matters worse, as the system slowed to a crawl, fuel became more expensive.

Government subsidies and the pleas of the newly formed Railroad War Board, the railroads' effort to reach their own compromise, had been without effect. Meanwhile, new powers granted to the Interstate Commerce Commission could not clear the bottleneck in New York and New Jersey. In particular, the Central and the Pennsylvania were backlogged with empties while loaded trains could not access ports. The system was at a breaking point. The I.C.C. report to Congress in December 1917 left little doubt that railroad management could not achieve the unification required to facilitate the traffic demands of a nation at war. The Railroad War Board laid its dilemma at the hands of President Wilson "for protection, and for disposition as he may determine is necessary in the public interest."[4] It was his war, and it appeared as if the railroads would become his as well. It became management by necessity for the Oval Office.

At the end of December 1917, President Woodrow Wilson "took possession and control of the railroad systems of the country, for war purposes."[5] William McAdoo, who served as Secretary of Treasury, was anointed the Director General of Railroads. The governing body under his charge was dubbed the United States Railroad Administration. Federal control would last until the war was over.

On January 19, 1918, A.H. Smith, the president of the New York Central Railroad was designated to manage the railroads in the east, where the greatest congestion existed. His task was to merge the trunk lines into one cooperating unit. Numerous other managers were selected for leadership positions in the now nationalized system. Altogether, seven geographical regions were created, and the leadership of each was drawn from the constituent railroads. In early April, it was ordered that all members of the United States Railroad Administration were required to terminate their relationship with their parent railroads. With the departure of Smith, Willie K. took his place as president of the New York Central.

Willie inherited the mantle of leadership on June 1, 1918. Unfortunately, the timing could not have been more ironic. While, he had toiled for years to move up in the ranks of the railroad industry, Willie K. now found that his legacy was no longer regulated by government; instead, it had fallen under Washington's complete control. With the track crumbling, creditors at the door, and the entire New York Central an inefficient, rambling Cyclops lost in bureaucratic red tape, Willie's hands were tied. The newly appointed leader of the Vanderbilt roads had nothing left to lead.

The day after Willie K. took his new post, the *New York Times* published an article entitled "The End of a Railway Dynasty."

The election of William K. Vanderbilt, Jr., as President of the New York Central railroad is at once the end of a railway dynasty and the beginning of a new railway era. There have been three "Williams" in the Vanderbilt line, and it is no disparagement of any of them to say that none were the equal of the old Commodore, Cornelius, who founded both the family and the railway. His times and conditions called for initiative, enterprise, boldness, adventure, which some condemn as speculation. He fought through troubled times, and went his way leaving a work which grew after him.

The New York Central Railroad is a greater institution than in his times, although his line are not greater than he, but never again is it likely that the 125 companies now affiliated with the system will grow faster than the country. The cure of enterprise by the regulation of rates and profits, and prosecution has been so complete that we shall be fortunate indeed if hereafter the railways grow up to the country, instead of leading the growth of the country.[6]

Within less than a year, Alfred H. Smith returned to the Central, and Willie K. resigned his post. The unprecedented course of events had usurped all possibility of decision-making power and associated glory from the young Vanderbilt. A Vanderbilt would no longer be the power behind the chairman, nor would he unilaterally select railroad leadership.

For Willie, who had waited so long for his turn to come, the future was simply ripped from his hands. He was left only to rub his eyes in disbelief as his long-held dreams evaporated into the ether.

CHAPTER **18**

A Different Wind Blows

After more than a decade working his way up through his family's railroad, Willie now found himself a man without a purpose. Within days of leaving the offices of the Central, he made his way back to the sea.

In an odd but important sense, the ill winds of the railroad debacle, like the passing of a hurricane, had finally subsided. So much that had occupied his time and energy for years was stripped away. Now, a new wind was blowing in Willie's life. He had finally sold his Deepdale home and stepped down from his business duties. The relationship with Birdie that had grown cold by 1909 remained threaded only by the children; both Willie and Virginia led entirely separate lives. And still the winds continued.

With the wounds of his failed railroad career still stinging, Willie received news that his father, William Kissam I, suffered a heart attack and died of complications on July 22, 1920, at the age of seventy-one.[1]

With his father's death, Willie was, in a way, fully freed of the railroad business. William Kissam had left behind an estate valued at approximately fifty-four and a half million dollars.[2] His father's provisions had left Willie with a large fortune. The son was now assured of financial independence.[3] There had never been a better time — or opportunity — for a new beginning.

Perhaps now Willie would discover what truly brought him happiness.

It might have been the example set by his father that influenced him the most. William Kissam had always said that money did not imply happiness. Instead, he found his contentment with his wife, Anne. In their chateau in Normandy they discovered a quieter life away from the press and the social circles of Newport and New York.

Willie K. had always found solace in travel, in wondering at the horizon, seeking that next destination. Leaving the demands of others behind gave Vanderbilt the chance to revive his own spirits. But more than mere escape, discovery in the physical world often gave way to reflection in his own internal explorations.

Increasingly, Willie put more effort into describing his motorcar adventures in Europe. In his travel log *A Trip Through Italy, Sicily, Tunisia, Algeria, and Southern France*, he shared impressions that caught his eye for their beauty, historical significance, distinct culture, and numerous surprising challenges. Traveling with his friend Harry Payne Whitney,[4] Willie's love of the open road was contagious. Harry was not used to taking risks or undergoing hardships that Willie so easily and cheerfully accepted. Vanderbilt was a natural wanderer who adapted quickly to his surroundings.[5] Despite passing through delightfully charming villages and towns such as Capri, in Italy, where Harry might have enjoyed a brief respite, Willie pushed on relentlessly. Every day was an adventurous campaign to reach their destination of Algeria.

From the cobble-stoned streets of French-inspired Tunis[6] to the desert towns of El Djem and Sfax, where Harry and Willie encountered snake charmers[7] and a town full of people willing to mutilate their bodies for money, life on the road was strange, compelling, and at times, precarious. Willie marveled at the sights of the caravans and camels and even took to traveling by camel for a short while.[8] Passing through the desert, Willie was amazed by the golden hues of the sun setting as he stared at tall Bedouin tents and local men and women dressed in flowing robes and scarves, gathering water and preparing for their night's rest. By the time they reached Boyie, Willie and Harry had traveled four thousand eight hundred and twelve miles with their only misfortune amounting to nine punctured tires.[9]

After his father's death, however, Willie left his auto idle and turned back even further, seeking out his first true passion: sailing. Having earned a nautical master certificate in 1918, Willie was ready to sail in rougher, more challenging conditions. His travels could now extend beyond his visits to the Caribbean; Willie was ready to tackle the high seas of the Atlantic and Pacific.

Soon, Willie found a new love that could help him share the sea. In the shipyard of Camper

Until his father's passing in 1920, Willie traveled frequently between the continents. The senior Vanderbilt never relinquished a true leadership role in the railroad to his eldest son, always preferring to manage with the long reach of an investment banker or through professional railroad men. In this 1920 photograph, Willie has returned on the S. S. *Homeric* from a tour of Europe, lasting some three months (courtesy Suffolk County Vanderbilt Museum).

In 1921 Willie inherited 21 million dollars as his share of his father's estate. He purchased and re-outfitted the *Ara* as a luxury yacht. She was his new love and would
serve him well for nearly a decade. He began refurbishing her in early 1922. There
was an open fireplace in the living room and a special card table designed to hold
steady no matter how rough the ocean. Luxurious almost to a fault, she boasted a
Steinway grand piano, six staterooms with private baths and the most powerful radio
equipment ever seen on a private vessel (courtesy Suffolk County Vanderbilt Museum).

& Nicholson in Southampton, he found the diesel-powered *Ara*, a boat previously used by the French navy for only the last three months of the war, purchased by a Captain Heriot, and lying in the small harbor awaiting repairs.
Despite the fact that "partially the hull and engines would be all that would be
saved, even auxiliary machinery would have to be discarded," Willie insisted
at the time that her sad state "did not dampen my ardor." He purchased the *Ara*
and, by the beginning of 1922, began the process of refurbishing the vessel.

The *Ara* had a dining room, saloon, and a private bathroom for Willie, as
well as a full facility for storing food supplies for up to fifty people for an entire
year. There was an open fireplace in the living room and a special card table in
the dining room designed to hold steady no matter how rough the ocean. Additional embellishments included a gym, a large library, an Aeolian Duo-Art
Steinway grand piano, a Brunswick Panatrope, and a ventilating system
designed specifically to change the air completely every four minutes. To round
out the accommodations, the ship held six staterooms with private baths and
a dining salon designed to accommodate fourteen passengers.

Rigorously outfitted with state-of-the-art wireless technologies—so that Willie could keep up with the stock market while cruising the world—the *Ara* had some of the most costly and powerful radio equipment ever found on a pleasure vessel, rivaling those often mounted on big ocean liners and "almost identical with that on the S.S. *Majestic*, which is reputed to have the finest marine radio set in existence." However, the equipment, like almost everything that was purportedly "useful" aboard the *Ara*, also had the purpose of amusing his guests in some form or another. Willie and his guests imported news from the mainland and issued a newspaper: *The Ara Daily News*. Willie had indeed created the vessel of his dreams.

Willie began to spend nearly all his time aboard the new yacht, testing its engines in the harbor near Eagle's Nest, and contemplating his next destination. It would soon come into sight.

After hearing the tale of a frightening "devil fish" that inhabited southern waters, Willie K.'s interest was piqued. The story was one frequently told in sailing circles: a young man by the name of Fred Bishpam had encountered a terrifying fish that attacked him while he was out in a tiny wooden motorboat in Biscayne Bay. Fearful and trembling after the event, Fred was never able to fully recover, dying of fright within a year.[10]

Real or not, the story whetted Willie's appetite. Muriel and Consuelo, Willie's two winsome daughters, were equally inspired; a guest, Frederic Cameron Church of Boston, was also game. Church came from a Lowell, Massachusetts, family of moderate means, but prominent position. He had distinguished himself as a star student athlete at Harvard, and was an officer in the war. Consuelo had displayed an artistic bent, enjoying drawing and sculpture,[11] hobbies her father encouraged. At twenty-three, Muriel was a strong and independent young woman. Her debut in society three years earlier had brought her tremendous attention.[12] Athletic and outgoing by nature, Muriel, however, preferred the back of a "good-spirited horse,"[13] or a night of dancing at a society dinner. Muriel and Frederick had known each other since childhood. The two had been fast, albeit platonic, friends.[14] Yet all four of them — Muriel, Consuelo, Frederic and Willie — were swept up by the prospect of true adventure. They wanted to follow the course of Fred Bishpam, armed to the teeth in pursuit of the "turrible sea devil"[15] that had reduced him to wreckage.

There was, however, a striking difference between poor Bishpam's adventure and the Vanderbilt expedition. The former was that of a solitary man with a graying face in a waterlogged little motorboat while the latter boasted a steel hull and a crew of some fifty odd passengers in the two hundred-and-twelve-foot luxury yacht *Ara*.

The foursome and crew set out in April of 1925 to the West Indies where the giant sea monsters were thought to breed. To maintain a certain authenticity in their adventure, the group decided that they, too, had to engage the monsters in a smaller boat like Bishpam. When Captain Charlie Thompson spied the first devil fish, a dark shadow ghosting below the surface, the *Ara* dispatched its launch with a crew of four accompanying Church, Vanderbilt, Muriel, and Consuelo.

They had given considerable thought to how the beasts with "jaws capable of swallowing a man with ease"[16] would be conquered. The plan was simple: they would follow the monsters in the launch, and when the moment offered itself, a harpoon was to be thrust for the kill. If the harpoon failed to immediately dispatch the animal, a barrel attached by rope would provide the hunting party with the opportunity to follow closely and make a second attempt. Further armaments, including elephant guns, were also prepared if needed.

Soon after setting the launch at sea, they caught up with the first sighting. A huge black body, with wings measuring eighteen feet to the tips, lifted up into the air, breached, and returned to the sea in a splash of white foam and spray. Willie rushed to the bow with the harpoon and launched it, as the giant breached once again, not fifty feet away. The harpoon struck and the sailor charged with the barrel let out the line and threw the barrel over the side. Then a "merry chase,"[17] similar to the deadly "sleigh rides"[18] of old whaling days, ensued; the launch was jerked forward, and all went still.

A half hour later, a second and larger sea devil appeared and a second harpoon was forced home. It, too, fled and was not seen again.

Ten minutes later a smaller sea devil surfaced. This time Fred Church seized the bow holding a harpoon. He hurled it with all his young strength as the devil fish flew into the air, its massive wings flapping in a horrifying spectacle. The harpoon sank home and yet the monster did not run. "Instead it swirled in rage, and then, as a wounded swordfish attacks the fisherman's dory, reared savagely beneath the boat and almost upset it."[19] Water poured over the gunwales. Fred Church hung tightly to the bow to keep from being swept overboard. The thrill of fear sent Muriel clinging closely to him. For a moment, the monster swam darkly away, but then, as the boat rocked precariously, the ominous shadow reappeared, charging directly at the tender. Church saw it closing on them just as did Muriel. She screamed for the sailors to grab the rifles. A volley fired out, and bullets found home, but did nothing to slow the beast. As it hit the tender, it gave just a glancing blow, allowing the sailors to empty their rifles at point-blank range. Again the sea devil turned and attacked, its mouth gaping large enough to swallow Muriel whole. The boat was upset again. Additional rifle loads struck once more, and again their chambers emptied. Finally, the monster collapsed, rolling in a glorious cloud of its own blood.

The relationship between Frederic Church and Muriel Vanderbilt was never to be the same, their lives now entwined unforgettably by their "Sea-Devil romance."[20] It would not take long before the pair would walk down the wedding aisle.[21]

Willie sailed across the Atlantic five times in the next three years. He took

On the *Ara* in January 1924. Consuelo (left) and Muriel (right) Vanderbilt and Ellen Sturgis (center) (courtesy Suffolk County Vanderbilt Museum).

his *Ara* to Miami, the Bahamas, and Cuba. One clear day, off the coast of Florida, Willie felt the bite of a monster on the end of his fishing line. He tugged, arm muscles tight, feet planted firmly. The line was taut and the rod toyed with breaking, but Willie persisted; he would not lose. His interlaced fingers blanched as he gripped the reel until at last he brought to the *Ara*'s decks the largest devil fish previously recorded. With a tired triumphant smile, he

With *Ara* poised for adventure, Willie could not remain anchored off Eagle's Nest for long. There was the tale of one Fred Bishpam, who had encountered a fierce "devil fish" while out on Biscayne Bay, Florida. The poor man was frightened to death, dying within the year. Frederic Cameron Church (pictured here, center, with unknown crewmen, in 1925) and Willie's daughters Muriel and Consuelo headed south for the hunt. Armed with elephant guns, the result was inevitable and the devil fish, with "jaws large enough to swallow a man," fell victim. Actually, devilfish are filter feeders incapable of harming the most feeble of fishermen. Muriel was impressed by the feat of courage displayed by Harvard athlete Church. They were soon to marry, the product of a "Sea Devil Romance" (courtesy Suffolk County Vanderbilt Museum).

pulled the heavy fish on to the deck and paused, breathing hard. His passions, he found, were not limited to a business that moved him to radio from his yacht, but rather, it seemed that his business truly was on the yacht. Watching the stingray's flailing slowly cease, Willie came to a better understanding of his own true mettle.

CHAPTER 19

The Enchanted Isles

Willie had found a new calling—far from the morbid air of Manhattan. He was now a man of the sea, pursuer of passion in the ocean depths, a collector of natural history. Beautifully preserved trophies of mounted fish, stretched over blocks of wood and painted to mimic life, accrued in abundance. Like his father's mounts that had adorned Idle Hour, he slowly amassed a collection of trophies that surpassed a sportsman's private hobby. Shortly after traveling aboard the *Ara* on a thirty-eight-day cruise in the Caribbean, he had acquired enough fascinating marine life examples that he decided to create his own Marine Museum at Eagle's Nest in 1924.[1] Willie transformed the *Ara* from a pleasure cruise ship to one devoted to the more serious purposes of scientific expeditions to explore the vast unknown of the sea, an area "almost as little understood by man as the heavenly blue of the sky or the star-crowded expanse of the Milky Way."[2]

Willie decided to build a "unique museum of the sea."[3] Styled after a church he had seen in Guatemala, Willie K. built the marine museum at the top of the hill that made up his private golf course. In time it would showcase some four hundred rare sea specimens. He could now share his treasures with his friends, giving him the legitimacy he sought in every new effort he pursued. Willie now had a claim to membership in the scientific world. Or was it a rich man's ruse to fill a life searching for meaning?

Ever since Charles Darwin ventured to the Galapagos Islands to write his great scientific work, *The Origin of Species*, the islands held a special allure for those intrigued by the idea of evolution. Walter Rothschild, an heir to the international banking fortune, presented Willie with a role model. Considered both brilliant and troubled, Rothschild's fascination with the islands led him to amass the largest private collection of animal specimens in the world: over two million stuffed birds, mounted butterflies and live, giant tortoises. Other enthusiasts included William Beebe, the impassioned naturalist writer, and Allen G. Hancock, whose magnificent boat *Valero* was a "marvel of yacht-building perfection"[4] and would inspire Willie to outfit his own ship in similar fashion. William Beebe was a gifted storyteller, enticing the public with his well-written

149

essays exploring new worlds such as the Sargasso Sea, known as the dead spot of the ocean, an area that had grown "countless legends."[5] Beebe had a talent for appealing to both the scientist and the layman with his tales of the "sea of little grapes"[6] because of the "myriad tiny floaters, miniature gas balloons that look like the fruit of this wandering herbage."[7] Beebe also had validation: his efforts were under the auspices of the New York Zoological Society and his stories were sent by wireless for immediate publication in the *New York Times* magazine section from his ship, the *Archturus*.[8] Willie was no doubt familiar with the frequently published stories of Beebe's scientific discoveries of the "fabled Sargasso"[9] and other elusive sea creatures, but it was just as likely his inspiration to visit the Galapagos came from a less scientific source.

Zane Grey, better known for his tales of the Wild West than for his acumen as a man of science, outfitted a one-hundred-and-ninety-foot, three-masted schooner named *Fisherman* with the purported aim of conducting a scientific excursion in the South Pacific in 1923. Unfortunately, when a doctor and scientist he had hired were unable to travel, Grey was forced to go himself.[10] Quite oddly, instead of procuring suitable replacements, Grey instead managed to retain the services of other more interesting passengers, such as an artist, a motion-picture camera operator, and, as he writes, "Jess R. Smith, cowboy and horse-wrangler, straight from the Arizona desert."[11]

Fortunately, Grey turned his novelist's eye to at least a handful of scientific observations, as when he describes the harpooning of a giant ray and a subsequent battle lasting "for hours."[12] He admitted disapproving of such sport, despite the excitement and the strenuous nature of the battle, yet conceded, "On an expedition like ours, however, there is the justification of collecting specimens and data in relation to the strange creatures of the deep; and it is not possible to record very much about them without capture."[13] Unlike Willie, however, who was aware of Darwin but not particularly well versed on his theories or studies, Grey well understood the scientist's depth, deeming the famed book, *Voyage of the* Beagle, as fascinating as fiction. Grey also credited Darwin with being the inspiration for the voyage of the *Fisherman* and the source of his knowledge about the archipelago.

Undoubtedly a sportsman cut from Zane Grey's cloth, Willie K. appreciated that aspect of becoming an explorer. But he wanted something more. He truly yearned for the *validation* afforded by scientific discovery. After all, this was the Vanderbilt whose mother condemned an idle life: "It is a mistake to believe that any woman, no matter what her financial condition of life, can lead an idle existence. It is merely a question of the worthiness of her activities."[14]

Willie's true role model was Albert, Prince of Monaco. Albert was a man of science, a man who was seemingly unfettered by all extraneous trappings, yet retained at his core the adventurer's masculinity, determination, and will. Willie found royalty attractive yet detested a life spent without accomplishment. The idea that a prince had managed to receive acclaim on the basis of his *accomplishments* rather than his family's name impressed Willie, who felt a kinship born of birthright. If it was hard to transcend the name Vanderbilt, how much more difficult it would be to escape the constraints of royalty.

When the prince spoke at the Lotos Club in New York in 1913, he was introduced as "a man of achievement, a man of good red blood, a hunter, an aeronaut, and an explorer of the deep blue sea." In his own right, he brought his tiny homeland acclaim in the scientific community. He had been involved in the study of the sea science since his teens and had equipped four of his personal yachts for deep sea dredging. The prince had specially outfitted a personal yacht that he had sent all over the world to make oceanographic charts.[15] The Marquis de Folin, who had led one of the French expeditions for the prince, had described delightfully the many glowing creatures they had found in the deep waters and brought ashore; whose brightness lit up newspapers some six yards away, with magical flashes of light emanating from corals changing from "violet to purple, from red to orange, from bluish to different tones of green"[16] to create a "marvelous spectacle."[17]

According to newspaper accounts, experiments by the prince were instrumental in charting the drift of German mines in the North Sea. In 1910 he established a museum of oceanography in Monaco. He was also personal friends with Buffalo Bill and had conversely abandoned his close relations with the kaiser during the war. The prince was warmly welcomed for his contributions with great exuberance in the United States, eliciting strong admiration from the likes of Otto Kahn and other members of New York's wealthy elite, and asked to recount stories of his travels and expeditions. His contribution to science was unquestionable. He was a man who had put his efforts and substantial amounts of his own wealth to good use for the benefit of public knowledge. Willie, undoubtedly, was drawn to and inspired by the prince's efforts.

When Willie finally embarked on his own voyage, he must have been well pleased to find himself and the prince in the same clipping:

> In choosing the ocean as the field for his exploration and scientific study Mr. Vanderbilt is following in the footsteps of the late Prince of Monaco. The ocean and the myriad creatures that live therein were the Prince's particular hobby. For years he devoted a large part of the millions to Monte Carlo gambling hell poured into his pockets to scientific expeditions that penetrated all the furthest reaches of the Seven Seas.[18]

Beebe, Grey, Albert: here were men still caught up in the sweep of manifest destiny, the last of the nineteenth century's march to conquer the last grand frontiers. Their blood still boiled with a thirst for exploration. And, for them, the sea remained a vast unknown. It lay before them, a labyrinth, a mystery, and a source of greatness. Willie K. Vanderbilt was now one of them.

For the adventurer-turned-naturalist, Willie had an impressive résumé. He had already crossed the Atlantic nearly a hundred times. His travels included exploring the Caribbean, Labrador, Greenland,[19] and the far north,[20] and traveling through the Mediterranean on a six-month-long trip for oceanographic purposes.[21] On nearly all his trips, he brought back impressive trophies, including numerous rare marine specimens to add to his growing collection.[22] Willie's personal style, too, had evolved. He wore the classic navy blazers of a captain while sailing, and pinstripe suits while he entertained guests or waited to leave from the harbor off Miami Beach.[23] In many ways, he had been training for this role for years: the memory of Alva forcing her children to document all of their excursions, making every yachting vacation into a learning experience, would always remain with Willie. It was not enough for him to simply enjoy the ocean for leisure activities or even as a collector. Instead, he needed to find a higher purpose. Willie desperately wanted to go beneath the surface in search of greater meaning.

A Vanderbilt took to yachting as a seagull to the sea. There was, however, a difference between simply yachting and true exploration. The tried and true pleasures of foreign ports held an allure for Willie, but so did the unknown. It called to him like a siren. Willie needed to experience and believe in the unknown; its magic and allure remained forever a fascination.

Though more an amateur naturalist than a scientist, Willie's desire to experience the islands was vastly different from other travelers among his set who were largely trophy hunters and collectors at best. Willie fancied himself worthy of Darwinian achievements, and when it became fashionable for members of high society to take tropical vacations in the name of science, Willie, who yearned for the validation afforded by scientific discovery, prepared his yacht, the *Ara*, to embark on such an adventure. The American Museum of Natural History was in great need of donations, but, alas, was overflowing with trophies.[24] William K. Vanderbilt, Jr., recently inaugurated as a trustee, was eager to take on the challenge of providing the museum with new and better specimens and garnering the public's attention for a noble cause. He was not, however, inclined to financially contribute to the institution.

Assuming the title Commodore, Willie took the helm. With his inheritance in his possession, his railroad and marital misfortunes now behind him, and his children grown, the *Ara* was the beginning of a new phase of his life.

With six hundred miles of ocean separating them from the Ecuadorian mainland, the Galapagos Islands are a lonely and seemingly bleak place. Although relatively close to the equator, the Humboldt Current, sweeping its way up from Antarctica, keeps the remote island chain relatively cool and dry, allowing for a climate that goes part and parcel with its diverse and enigmatic animal life and flora. Though the highest points are often swathed in an eerie fog, called the *garua*, the islands themselves are each quite distinct from one another, numbering between thirteen and seventeen (depending upon what cartographers consider an island and what might be deemed no more than a large protruding rock). Their individual, unique characteristics were the very reason they provided Darwin his clues to the theory of natural selection.

Isolated and distinct, wildlife of common ancestry took different directions suited to the particularities of each island, including species that had never been seen or described. In essence, the singular isolation and multiple evolutions provided what turned out to be the world's largest living laboratory.

Off the west coast of South America, close to the equator, the Galapagos Islands had acquired mounting attention for the growing extinction of its famous tortoises. Charles Darwin had written extensively about the animal in 1834, native to the volcanic islands. Tortoises had provided meat for local soup and for whaling ships for several centuries, but by the early twentieth century had dwindled so severely in numbers on the Galapagos Islands that they were virtually extinct on ten of the twelve islands. Wild hogs and feral cats, born from years of strays left behind by passing ships, ferreted out eggs buried in the soil, dooming the tortoise. Alarmed scientists such as Charles Townsend, the director of the Galapagos Expedition, put together excursions to rescue the endangered species and bring them to the New York Zoological Society for sanctuary.[25] His endeavor was widely reported and hailed as a new kind of triumph of man over nature — this time in its service.

Having made earlier trips on the *Ara* with an assemblage of people all roughly his own age, Willie gathered together an entirely different group for his first excursion to the Galapagos. Invited for purposes of science were William E. Belanske, the brilliantly talented painter of fishes[26] and curator of Willie's own Marine Museum, and Capt. Charles Thompson, who was considered the most accomplished fisherman in all of Florida. Thompson had achieved certain fame for having captured a "monster of the deep,"[27] which had toured the country and been a source of both scientific speculation and controversy.

Dr. George Dixon, who had been at President William McKinley's deathbed after he was shot, was there to tend to illnesses that might descend during the trip. Dixon had also treated Willie's father, and perhaps this is the main reason he was invited. A wealthy man with houses in New York and Southampton, Dixon not only watched the rich die but also dined with the rich still living. At nearly seventy, he was the oldest member of the party. Just two years after this Galapagos excursion, he would marry his twenty-six-year-old French tutor.

Also on this second voyage was J. Gordon Douglas, an accomplished tennis and polo player whose father had won the America's Cup. He became close friends with Willie, and the two would socialize regularly for the rest of their lives.

Ostensibly to provide a female attraction, Josephine "Fifi" Widener was included. Her family was well grounded economically and in society, with founding ties to United States Steel, the American Tobacco Company, and the White Star Line of *Titanic* fame. Fifi was a rather notorious young lady who, at seventeen, had garnered national attention when she eloped with her young lover to Tennessee, much to the consternation of her family and the delight of the society press. Unhappily married, Fifi was eager to join the *Ara* without her husband, Carter. Rumors had long circulated about her interest in Douglas, and this trip would only add to the flames.

Mr. and Mrs. Barclay Warburton were the final guests aboard for *Ara*'s sophomore voyage. Barclay, known to all as "Buzzy," and his wife, Rosamund Lancaster Warburton, had been married just five years. He was the grandson of John Wanamaker of the famed department store in Philadelphia. The pair had reasonable wealth, but plenty of social ambition for higher circles. While Buzzy failed in his attempts to make a living as a journalist and the family fortune (which might have seemed large by Worcester standards but did not so impress in New York), Rosamund soon became a darling of the society papers. Described as a "sweet and lovely"[28] young woman, Rosamund was determined to be successful in society. A petite blonde with gray eyes and a "camellia-like complexion,"[29] Rosamund was considered beautiful, refined, mannerly quick-witted, and determined. Reinventing herself before traveling aboard the *Ara*, she removed her Worcester origins, instead titling herself Rosamund Lancaster from Boston.

Rosamund and Willie were acquaintances prior to the journey. In fact, Alva may have been instrumental in facilitating their introduction since she no longer had favor with Virginia after her separation from Willie. Having outgrown her husband's charms and fortune, Rosamund was ready for larger horizons. Buzzy, who signed Willie's guest book "cameraman de luxe," had all but acknowledged that he and Rosamund were not really going aboard as a couple.

The party was varied enough to never suffer boredom. The two very attractive women provided delightful companionship while Belanske and Captain Thompson, by the very nature of their professions, were bound to be interesting. Buzz and Gordy Douglas were sportsmen and ever game for physical activities like climbing and fishing.

The trip was scheduled to depart on January 20, 1926, when Mrs. Warburton's grandfather died suddenly and family duties called her away. It would have been easy to proceed without her, or to find another young couple to take their place, but Willie kept *Ara* in the harbor, bobbing at anchor, awaiting Rosamund's return. In February, the crew finally departed as Willie's patience was rewarded with Rosamund's eventual arrival.

As the tone of the trip itself gradually evolved, so too came an obvious change in the feel of Willie's journals. His previous travelogues had typically carried a sense of the simple guidebook, lacking any sense of fun or enjoyment. They were just like the lesson book journals his mother had forced him and Consuelo to keep on their childhood excursions.

While still neither eloquent nor particularly exciting, this travel journal, *To the Galapagos on the Ara*, had an undercurrent of emotion in nearly every passage, full of ebullient images and vivid sensations. The paragraphs flowed one into another with remarkable ease and eloquence. For example, when he and his guests found that the Hotel Tivoli could not appease their palates, a simple enough traveler's conundrum, he described their reaction as high drama, noting, "Howls of despair poured forth."[30]

The small island of Cocos, filled with nesting birds and small caves, left Willie gasping, "What a diversity of beauty here!"[31] Luxurious vegetation and swaying coconut trees on precipitous cliffs towered six to seven hundred feet above the beach. The silvery lace of spirited waterfalls ended in a bleach white foam as they exploded on the rocks below. Willie had never seen "such magnificence of color and grace of movement."[32]

All opportunities for complaint become opportunities to glory in life itself, "In the terrific heat we suffered no discomfort."[33] Instead, he recounts his ingenious solution, "The boatswain flooded the decks three times a day with the hose."[34] He speaks of his newly slimmed physique — a change that has come about with no apparent effort — and of how his skin has taken on a tone "such as even a chieftain of darkest Africa might be proud of."[35]

For the first time his guests became more than mere sources for name-dropping and instead emerged as living and breathing characters. The exploits of Thompson, in particular, excited Willie greatly, and he never ceased to delight in describing the various accomplishments of the famed fisherman. He was amazed at Charlie's boldness in chasing down strange beasts: "Large lizards, iguanas of the marine species, bold enough to watch us, were soon hanging by the tail from Charlie's hand."[36] Referring to Charlie as "a madman,"[37] Willie relates how he worked "like a beaver"[38] to capture, record, and occasionally even skin the various specimens he was charged to discover. Each capture led either to the dinner table, where the turtles were transformed into soup later to be rhapsodized about, or they became passengers. An on-board menagerie evolved: "Squawking sounds next attracted us—emitted by a group of penguins, indignant at our approach. At first we could not believe our eyes."[39] Willie was playing Noah and the *Ara* speedily transformed into a luxurious ark.

Willie took great joy in an attempt to capture sea lions who, when corralled by Charlie and the crew via a lasso,[40] emitted "roars such as might be expected to issue from a lion's den."[41] Once captured, the seals did not give up the fight and the mother "very much active with her fins and a fine set of teeth, kept the entire ship's company at a safe distance."[42] The ferocity of the mother seal and her youngsters astonished Willie. It seemed that new discoveries waited at every turn. The trip was fast becoming a marked success.

The *New York Times*, in an article so treasured by Willie it became a section of his book, reported on one of Thompson's many exploits and referred to Willie by his adopted title, the Commodore. Willie and Thompson came upon an enormous breeding area in the Panama Bay, where tiger sharks fed on red snappers that ate red shrimp, which in turn, were feeding on minute insects, also consuming seaweed. In between, large gulls hovering nearby would snatch and eat shrimp that the snappers failed to reach: "It turned out to be five

Willie and Rose spent considerable time fishing on one side of the island. Barclay Warburton and Fifi Widener spent considerable time on the other side of the island. Willie is pictured here with a 100 pound tuna. Galapagos, 1926 (courtesy Suffolk County Vanderbilt Museum).

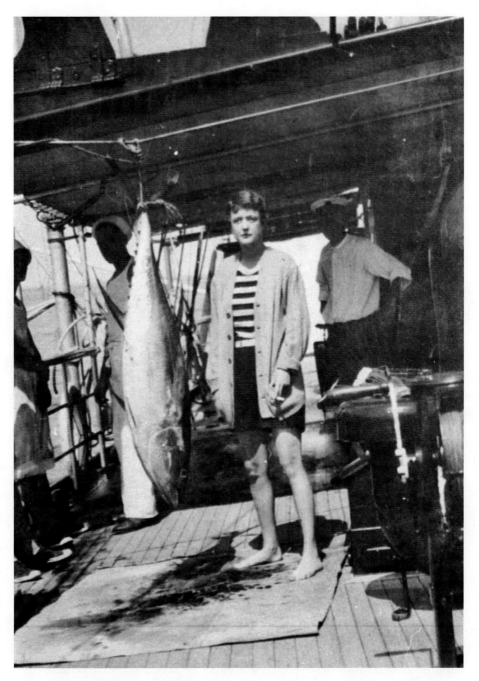

Mrs. Warburton becomes Rose, and she in turn becomes a tuna fisherman. Galapagos, 1926 (courtesy Suffolk County Vanderbilt Museum).

Carving the graffiti on Tower Island, Darwin Bay, Galapagos, 1926 (courtesy Suffolk County Vanderbilt Museum).

varieties of life, four of the sea and one of the air, gorging and, in three instances, being gorged."[43]

One day they hooked tuna almost by the bundle. Willie and his guests competed for the record of the largest fish, and Buzzy managed to snag the title with a catch weighing in at one hundred and forty-eight pounds, followed by Fifi with another giant at one hundred and eight pounds. Willie described both the women as "fine fisherwomen."[44]

Those fishes, which were not destined for the dinner table, met a different, though hardly happier, fate: struggling for their last breath beneath the skillful hands of Belanske. He made plaster casts of the fish and painted them, while still very much alive, so that "Mr. Rowland, our taxidermist in New York, will thus be able to reproduce the fish faithfully, just as we landed him."[45] The race against death's growing shadow was made all the more difficult when multiple specimens were caught at the same time. Painting five or six specimens would require rapid mixing and application of color. Belanske was challenged by the necessity of multi-tasking; first etching in the larger shapes and forms on all the victims and then returning to memorialize the important details. "They faded out palpably from the moment they left the water, so that color sketching had to be done very, very fast. One of the fish that fades out most rapidly is the dolphin. It comes out as brilliant and bright as a jewel, but its beautiful glow and cerulean blue spots and golden color fade to a muddy dirty brown that has no resemblance whatever to the original."[46]

The transitory nature of natural beauty and the concerted effort to retain some replica of it brought to light Willie's nearly obsessive efforts to capture a single moment. In a sense, the middle-aged Vanderbilt seemed to attempt, quite literally, to seize the day. His interest in stopping time rose with every degree of difficulty: "To keep smaller specimens alive, we set up on the after deck an aquarium with salt water running in through a hose. Sketches were made of these smaller forms as soon as possible, rough color sketches first, then accurate drawings of details."[47]

Although Willie's first entry into an entirely new body of water, the Pacific Ocean, on the first of March at 3:15 P.M. seemed to have held a certain symbolic meaning for him, one sensed that other things were also exciting him as the benchmark swiftly falls into the distance. As the *Ara* drew closer and closer to the Galapagos, his writing also took a more vivid turn. Willie's distance from the reader evident in his previous journals had all but disappeared. He now had become completely immersed in the physical world around him. His sentences overflowed with descriptions, odd details bubbling to the surface like so many fish crashing upon the deck, as he valiantly tried to describe all the rich detail of every day's events.

The pulse in his writing also quickened, equal to his growing excitement. Every detail, from the tiniest or largest of fish, the reptiles basking, seals at play, even to the steady grayness of rocky outcroppings and the dramatic brilliance of sunset, acquired some special significance to the awestruck Willie. Some were frantic scribblings; many were rambling descriptions, while yet others had a poetic and dreamy sensibility. Of Tagus he writes, "In the valley beyond was a vista — one volcano after another —fall on fall of ash — some grey, some red, some yellow — just a tumble of rock — ash heaps— haze — very desolate. But awesome as a spectacle.... After dinner all hands gathered on the bridge to look at the alluring distant mountains and their covering of purple-tinted foliage reminiscent of the heather-covered hills of Scotland."[48]

For Willie, there was the sense of riches beyond measure; riches that had nothing to do with his bequest or his last name. He was positively rejuvenated by his experiences in nature. He turned a new eye toward detail and minutiae —

the subtle things that might have eluded him in his youth. Willie began to cultivate an appreciation for every moment — the abundance of which would become a running theme of the enchanted journey. He was in paradise. Willie had finally found something he could call unequivocally his own.

But there was another noteworthy change in Willie's writing, one quite strange considering it occurred on the threshold of reaching his destination. With each day, his written accounts turned less and less scientific, devolving instead into the human. No detail was lost; rather his focus simply shifted — with particular concentration on certain of his companions. Mrs. Barclay Warburton had evolved into a different species entirely; he started referring to her as "Rose."[49]

The yacht, large as it was at two hundred and thirteen feet, must have felt extraordinarily cramped with Willie and Rose's budding romance. Such secrets are always difficult to keep, but on board a ship where so much was shared openly, it must have been outright excruciating. Willie was keenly aware of how his mother had been happier in her second marriage and he knew that the seeds of that union had sprouted while her first husband, the father to her children, had been close at hand. In fact she, too, had been on a yachting trip with her husband while she fell in love with Oliver Belmont. But it was not just his mother's example he was following; Willie had also noticed the tremendous increase in his father's quality of life after he married his second wife, Anne Rutherford. What was it his mother had once said? She advised that one should marry twice, first for money and then for love. It seemed to be exactly the option now before Willie. A very exciting one indeed.

Aboard *Ara*, the rules of secret pursuit made the hunt that much more exciting. Few thrills could surpass the danger of detection, and on board the sea-locked ship, with its cast of intelligent and alert characters moving to and fro from cabin to cabin, deck to deck, ever anxious for the juiciest morsel, such detection was a constant threat.

Inevitably, every movement, every look, every word spoke the unique language of secret lovers. Their energy was almost impossible to contain. Pregnant pauses, hands brushed almost inadvertently as a saltcellar passed across the dinner table, or lingering afterwards to enjoy a sunset together, all drew attention, no matter how surreptitiously cloaked in propriety. For Willie, the pain of not sharing his newfound enthusiasm for life's subtle pleasures was agonizing. After almost twenty years of being alone, his thirst for Rosamund's company was palpable. He followed her every movement tirelessly, drinking in her beauty; engaging all of his senses. He was eager to make Rose his own.

The Galapagos Islands, often known as the Enchanted Isles, actually held charms often too subtle to merit such a romantic name. Inhospitable and harsh, colored with the grays and blacks of volcanic rock, these lands were the outward thrusts of gigantic volcanoes, mountains of strength and hidden power that extended far beneath the surface of the water. Their so-called "enchantment" required a willingness to look closely and deeply. Ferdinanda, the largest of these, loomed another mile high, the dark cone veiled in transient mists. The rocks and crags emerged briefly, almost as apparitions, before drifting sheets of white, only to be shrouded once again in mystery. For the most part, the harsh Galapagos yielded little to those who could not see beyond the seemingly barren and uninviting.

Yet, at every turn, the islands taunted in a symphony of endless variety, spectacle, and wonder. Each niche was filled with some life form, there as if destiny meant it to have this singular special place.

Willie encountered the marine iguana, Beebe's "black lizards of the surf," everywhere on the islands. These seemingly living fossils, primitive in appearance, had survived millennia amidst the most inhospitable conditions. Black when wet and dull gray blotched by brown when dry, they were hardly beautiful in a conventional sense. Their beauty lay in their remarkable skill in survival. Willie studied mating contests, as the male opponents puffed themselves up and bobbed their heads back and forth to intimidate one another. When one or the other refused to retreat, the skirmishes escalated into head-butts and pushes until finally the loser melted back into the crowd and all memory of the unpleasantness disappeared. In such moments, Willie understood the commonality of all animals, including humanity. No doubt, as he wondered at these contests, he compared himself to Barclay.

Another creature that caught Willie's attention was a strange bird called the *booby*. Originating from the Spanish word "bobo" for clown, the booby was a bird frequently sighted by British sailors who considered them stupid for their trusting natures. Sailors would easily approach and capture the beautiful birds. Yet the locals called the bird *piquero,* which meant "lancer," appreciative of their long, pointed beaks and their habit of making sharp, vertical dives in the pursuit of fish well below the surface.[50]

A flock of red- and blue-footed boobies engaged in a coordinated plunge sounded like the staccato of many rifles firing an immense, syncopated barrage. So forceful was their strike into the water, one would have expected the impact to render any creature unconscious. But, inevitably, thanks to its skill and strength, the bird re-emerged, typically laden with fish. When noting this contrast, Belanske described the blue-faced booby thus: "The bird is rather clumsy and stupid on the ground, but once in flight it appears to be one of the most proud and powerful birds, darting down from a great height, at a rapid rate of speed, and disappearing under the surface to the accompaniment of a great spray of water."[51]

Simultaneously evoking the sentiments of clown and lancer seems an absurdity only apt in such a strange land. Yet how clearly such traits can also coincide in humans. Somehow these birds arrived in the Galapagos. Somehow they adapted. Somehow they became something almost entirely new. The same was true of Willie. Here in this extraordinarily brutish yet beautiful world, where life and death played out its eternal pageant, Willie was acutely aware of himself as a man. And — at the same time — he keenly understood the sweetness of his newfound companionship after drifting for fifteen years alone and unfulfilled.

When they had passed through the Cocos Islands, Willie noted the inscriptions in rocks and trees carved by other visitors commemorating their presence. But the party had chosen not to mark their voyage. By the time they reached Tagus Cove on the Galapagoan island of Albemarle, however, they were finally ready to do something to render their visit timeless.

As they approached the harbor, Willie was struck by "thousands of silvery bodies"[52] passing beneath the boat, and he marveled at their beauty as they dove and reappeared. Then, suddenly, he was overcome with empathy, seeing a scene "fraught with tragedy for the mullets as they attempted to flee for their lives."[53] This from the man who, during his speed craze, had run over thirty dogs and bragged about it; who had blithely, without a second thought, tossed money at the people whose lives his motoring sport had disrupted and maimed. Suddenly Willie could even feel for, of all things, these silvery little fishes.

As he observed the languid flamingoes at James Bay, he again seemed to see the nature of what was inside himself — this time an appreciation for beauty that seems almost as apt a description for Rose as for the birds who stood within "brackish water ... producing an indescribably charming effect with their long, slender legs, very long necks, their rhythmic movements, and reddish color."[54]

Nearby, on a tree, a hardly legible inscription in Spanish hung from a wire, the remnant of a previous visitor's sign of passage. Seeing it as an invitation and thus emboldened, the crew set about leaving their own carving to mark their trip to the island. Belanske set to work chiseling "ARA 1926" into a prominent rock wall for time immemorial. Finished with their rock carving, the expedition ascended the beach to a tidal pool where the sea lions of the prior evening were enjoying their freedom.

Ara's last stop in the archipelago was Tower Island, the island of birds.[55] Although it appeared low slung, less than one hundred feet above sea level, the island rose steeply from the ocean floor — a young volcano attempting to make its existence known. Conveniently for sailors, it opened on one side into a C shape, with the center forming Darwin Bay. Again, the group set off to make another marker. This time, Willie enthusiastically recorded the event:

At seven we were on the beach with cameras, dynamite, and carving implements to record on the rock *Ara*'s presence in these waters. Naturally, Belanske was assigned to the task of carving the stone. Chisel in hand, he sought the most conspicuous rock. And he cut deeply our good ship's name, so that for hundreds of years to come passing ships would know of our presence here just as we knew, by their records, of the presence of those who had visited Cocos Island before us. Belanske's was no easy job. The rock was hard — it took three hours to cut the name. Then he painted it black and white, with house flag underneath.[56]

For a few hours they occupied themselves with photographing the friendly birds that dotted the island. "How charmingly tame they were!" Willie wrote of the occasion.[57] It was hard to ignore a nesting male frigate bird with its bright red reproductive colors. His throat pouch inflated, he gave the appearance of a vibrant red balloon approaching the point of bursting. There were few behavioral demonstrations in nature to rival the display of the frigate bird. Willie noted, "If anatomical tricks are a criterion of perfection, the male frigate bird is far from being a failure."[58]

After witnessing a volcanic eruption in Tagus Cove, Vanderbilt sent a radiogram to William Beebe the naturalist, describing how the trip lived up to "expectations as you described them in your book."[59]

It was time for the visitors to turn homeward and return to the modern world. With the trip winding down, Willie's journaling grew pensive and reflective. The author took note of his last moments among the Enchanted Islands in uncharacteristically somber tones:

> As Tower Island slowly sank below the horizon, our little party looked over the tafrail wistfully, feeling that our time in this region had been much, much too short. At Tower Island one could spend many enjoyable days.... We carried away pleasant impressions and trust that any other yachting enthusiasts will be as fortunate if by chance they should voyage to this particular spot.[60]

The trip home was a heady blend of self-congratulatory dinners and clandestine glances, as everyone reflected on the momentous journey and Willie and Rose looked forward to what might lay ahead for the two of them. When they reached the Panama Canal they made gifts of two sea lion pups to the pilot. In fact, the entire menagerie that had so dominated the decks now was rapidly given away.[61] They trawled, dove, and fished. The expedition had developed a decidedly tourist-like air. They stopped, fished, bartered, bought, and visited as they and their host pleased. Their course was leisurely and with no rush to reach any homeward port. They capped off their Caribbean meanderings with a visit to Cuba.

With the trip winding into its last days, Willie finally made a scientific coup. Just after 8 A.M. on Wednesday, March 31, Willie and his crew "procured two new specimens of small shark, adults, eight inches in length; also several other specimens unknown to us."[62] Later, scientists that Willie engaged would determine these tiny sharks to be a new species of the band-tailed cat shark, otherwise known in scientific circles as *Apristurus arae*. For Willie this was a moment of immortality. A new vertebrate was, after all, a considerable contribution to science. Deserving of auspicious accolades, the new find was named for the *Ara*. It was a wonderful way to celebrate the end of the voyage.

Under the subhead "Got Many Rare Fish," the *Times* enthusiastically reported, as if Darwin or Beebe were the central character: "Besides the specimens not yet identified, the party dredged up many rare fish, including a strange eel. Off Miami, sending the net down 250 fathoms, several six-inch sharks, so rare they have no common name, being known only as '*Apristurus melastomus*,' were taken."[63] Dressed in a bathing suit, slippers, and hat, Willie K. directed the unloading of rescued tortoises, penguins, boobies, cormorants, blue and yellow macaws, bugle birds, and iguanas from his yacht.[64] The cormorants had bright "sapphire-colored"[65] eyes, small wings that helped them swim, and were tall, graceful, flightless birds. Many of the animals had grown accustomed to people by the end of the trip (including the six rare tortoises that he brought to Miami by March 16 that year, his second trip to his beloved Galapagos).[66]

After a successful two-month-long trip during which he had traveled off the Atlantic and Pacific coasts of Central and South America to the Galapagos Islands,[67] Canal Zone ports, Cocos Island, Tagus Cove, and Old Providence Island, Willie returned home[68] with rare specimens of fish, including the strange eel, six-inch sharks,[69] a penguin, myriad birds, iguanas, and an assorted menagerie of other creatures. The entire trip had covered seven thousand miles and Belanske had faithfully drawn and painted all the subjects with great care.

Spring was in the air and, released from the confines of the *Ara*, the lovers—Willie and Rose—were free to pursue their affair. Despite the fanfare marking the end of the *Ara*'s journey, the saga of Willie and Rose was only beginning.

CHAPTER 20

Fifteen Thousand
Miles Away

On the twenty-fifth of July, 1925, the press up and down the eastern seaboard gave top coverage to a new generation of Vanderbilts.

> This is the site selected for the most brilliant social event of a decade — the wedding today of Miss Muriel Vanderbilt and Frederic Cameron Church, of Boston. Although called a "cottage" by the wealthy, Beachmound to the average person would appear a palace, in size, beauty and furnishing. It is a fitting place for the nuptials of one of American's most beautiful and wealthy heiresses to a scion of one of Boston's oldest and most distinguished families.[1]

For Willie, Beachmound was, in essence, the finish line to a fiercely long and rocky stage race. Virginia had conditioned their own divorce on the marriage of both Muriel and Consuelo, and Willie had pressed the engagement of his eldest daughter for two years. With one married off, perhaps the next would soon follow suit.

The lovely and demure Miss Muriel Vanderbilt had met her future husband in the South, where the two privileged children of northern society wintered each year. From there, Frederic Cameron Church, the famous Harvard athlete, and Muriel found themselves one afternoon aboard the *Ara* chasing down the infamous devils of the sea. It would not take long after such an exciting adventure for the two to become rapturously engaged. Preparations were made ready for a grand Catholic Vanderbilt wedding under Virginia's pious, though quiet, approval. The only factor that lay in opposition was the groom's insistence on an Episcopal service. Miss Muriel, described as "the prettiest, best behaved, and most popular of all the Vanderbilt heiresses,"[2] held firm, but gave in at the last minute. Her capitulation caused a rift within the Vanderbilt family that rippled across an excited press.

Virginia, who apparently had kept her feelings to herself throughout the turbulent proceedings leading up to her daughter's marriage, had finally had enough. She would not be present for the ceremony, leaving Willie to give his daughter away. Unfortunately, Muriel's sister, Consuelo, and Willie III were also conspicuously absent. Consuelo had bowed out at the last minute, citing an unexplained illness, while her little brother had firmly declined.

When Willie and Birdie had married, Willie had agreed to his bride's wishes that they be wed in the Catholic tradition and raise the children accordingly. Virginia's feelings were well rooted in her history and she would give no ground. When Virginia threatened Muriel with disinheritance, however, her father was quick to tell her "not to worry."[3] Virginia refused comment, promising members of the press that she would provide full details at an appropriate time. The press noticed: "Never before has so little been said about a Vanderbilt wedding before the ceremony — and so much AFTER the wedding."[4]

Although Consuelo had not joined Muriel and Freddy in the search for sea devils, she had apparently caught a bit of the fever herself. The bells were soon ready to chime once again. The date was set for January 7, 1926. Consuelo surprised the public when she opted to drop the Vanderbilt name and become Mrs. Smith, the Smith in this case being Earl E.T. Smith, a Yale student.[5] At last, after more than ten years of separation, Willie was finally ready to cut the marital cord — and just in time to tie it again, this time to his new-found Rose.

Rosamund had already traveled to Paris in July of 1926, not for a leisurely yacht vacation this time, but to obtain a clean divorce from Barclay. Her task was completed within a few weeks. Now it was Willie's turn.

Unfortunately, Vanderbilt's effort was not to be so simple. The bitter seeds sewn by Alva in marrying her daughter off to the Duke of Marlborough had sprouted long ago and were now reaping their ill harvest. Just as Willie undertook clandestine tactics to steal away to France for his own annulment, his sister, Consuelo, beat him to the punch. Consuelo had suffered through a sad and lonely marriage. The Duke of Marlborough had been unfaithful, but so had Consuelo, and he had been far more discreet than she. Negotiations proceeded with great difficulty; the one term of separation on which the Duke would not relent was the right to flagellate his wayward wife. Strong hands, including those of Winston Churchill, intervened to achieve an amicable settlement that preserved the reputations of either foe. The Duke kept his cash flow offered by William Kissam as a settlement prior to the union and retained the children for six months of the year. By early 1907 the agreement had been consummated and the arranged, loveless marriage was legally, if not religiously, terminated.

However, in 1926, the Duke moved onward with another woman. For the better part of the year, the annulment filled the press in both New York and Europe. In order to prove the marriage annulment justified, the unhappy couple had to verify that there had been no real union in the first place. To do so, Consuelo revealed that her mother had threatened to kill poor Winty, Consuelo's lover in her youth, if her daughter went through with the planned elopement at the age of seventeen. The sentence of the Roman Catholic Holy Tribunal of Rota was made public on November 22, 1926:

On one occasion, the sentence says, the then Mrs. Vanderbilt [Alva] threatened that if Consuelo eloped with Rutherford she would kill him on the first occasion and would be imprisoned and hanged for the crime, her daughter being thus responsible for the tragedy. At another time Consuelo's mother declared that she would die if her daughter did not marry Marlborough.[6]

Alva's reputation was forever stained. She was cast as a social climbing, overbearing mother who had sold her daughter for a royal title. That she had dedicated much of her later life to the women's suffrage movement could do little to stem the near tsunami of press on both sides of the Atlantic. The truth was that much of her suffrage career had been rooted in championing radical and often violent measures, making the flood of verbose publicity appear fitting to those who knew well her methods. She had not been shy about using her fortune to leverage her demands, which often created jealousies and resentment among her colleagues. Alva would be remembered as a cruel parent, as it certainly did not mesh for a person advocating women's rights to sell her daughter for a title.[7]

Consuelo had gotten her wish, but the annulment was soundly criticized throughout the church and set off a ripple effect that would make Willie's efforts an uphill battle from the start.

It appeared to be a propitious time to get out of town and take his own scandal far from the reach of enquiring eyes. Best to dash from the stage and avoid further press comments such as "The Vanderbilt-Warburton romance has been the subject of animated gossip in European society for several months."[8]

Surprisingly, what he could not buy with money, he acquired with patience. As the holidays came and went, 1927 dawned clear and bright for the anxious Willie. Finally, seven months after Rose made good on her end of the bargain, Willie left for Paris on the ocean liner, *France*, to work out the details of his divorce from Virginia. Not surprisingly, it was a very different trip from his last voyage, his triumphant Galapagos expedition. Willie K. left New York for Marseilles on Sunday, January 30, with no one waving goodbye. He kept up entries to *Ara*'s log as if, indeed, he had taken his beloved yacht east across the Atlantic and not the liner. But in fact, *Ara* went on ahead and would await him in the Mediterranean, where he had scheduled a rendezvous with a few friends, and, of course, Rose. Not surprisingly, he recorded the semi-truthful trip with droll indifference. Once again, he was back to his motor logs of old. Gone were the rosy depictions of rugged rock outcroppings and brilliantly colored birds. Absent were the awe, the excitement, and the feverish enthusiasm. His ennui can be summed up in a single line from the log: "It was a delightful crossing for this time of the year, delightful but uneventful."[9] Uneventful indeed, for Willie had not even been aboard his yacht. Yet, inexplicably, he preferred the ruse, as if he still needed to maintain some kind of lie.

In February of 1927, upon his arrival in Paris, the *New York Times* recounted how Willie "emphatically denied that he had come to Paris to obtain a divorce."[10] It was a statement that would come back to haunt him later that year.

He went from Paris to Villefranche where he anxiously awaited his guests aboard the *Ara*. A week later, Willie reported, "Our party today was augmented by the arrival of Mr. and Mrs. Winfield Scott Hoyt [friends and traveling companions of his parents], Mrs. Lancaster Warburton, and Doctor George A. Dixon, and the ship's company now being complete we set out upon a trip to certain of the Mediterranean ports."[11] Thus would begin a new journey for Willie and Rose, the former still married to Virginia and the latter now divorced from Barclay.

As for Virginia, her interests had turned to horses over the years since her separation from Willie in 1909. She had built and managed her own racing stable.[12] Her two-year-old gelding Sarazen was her pride and joy, winning numerous accolades,[13] including a fifteen thousand dollar match race of six furlongs for all two year olds in 1923.[14]

The arrival of "Mrs. Lancaster Warburton" was certainly pressing business and Willie took the unprecedented measure of appointing Mrs. Hoyt to continue chronicling the journey. She had a smoother and more descriptive writing style than Willie. She also enjoyed a turn as gossip columnist. Upon arrival at Monaco, for instance, she played at intrigues: "It might be put on record that at least two members of the party resisted the lure of the Casino and were prosaic enough to turn in while the rest of us set out for the shore with an idea of breaking the bank — at least to a certain extent."[15]

In another passage she again alluded to Willie and Rose in her furtive way, "The first glimpse of Rome is thrilling. One pities the blasé who have forgotten or pretend to have forgotten sensation — what is life without an occasional thrill? I would say quite a little about that were we not speaking of Rome."[16]

Meanwhile, the press was having its way with Willie: "Mrs. Vanderbilt arrived in Paris last Friday and it was currently believed that she would immediately take the steps necessary to obtain a divorce."[17] The reporter pressed the intrigue on, insinuating: "Further changes of mind in this kaleidoscopic domestic picture are not, of course, either impossible or unlikely, but today's situation is providing a subject of piquant gossip in the American colony here."[18] The gossip heated up even more five days later when it was announced for the first time that Willie had "started action for divorce in the Seine tribunal from the former Virginia Fair, to whom he was married April 4, 1899."[19]

It was not until two months later, on June 3, that Willie finally got his divorce. From the headline to the coda, the press painted Willie as a liar: "When Mr. Vanderbilt went to Paris last February, accompanied by his attorney, he denied that the trip had any connection with divorce proceedings"[20] while Virginia was deemed the wounded wife and triumphant heroine.

Virginia would retain sole custody of their son, Willie III. It was Virginia who had fought against the divorce "because of her religion, it was said; she flatly refused for many years to entertain thoughts of a divorce."[21] A millionaire in her own right, Virginia asked for no alimony. Reports of his infidelity with Madame Polaire would later emerge: "The judgment says that Mr. Vanderbilt drove his wife from their conjugal domicile and showed himself excessively cold toward her."[22] By August, reports of the "Secret Arrangements in Paris"[23] for the Vanderbilt-Warburton marriage began leaking, and soon Willie's second life was ready to begin.

Without fanfare, pomp, or circumstance, September 5, 1927 dawned clear and sun-filled in Paris. The *New York American* dutifully reported: "In a large stately room at the City Hall of the Sixteen Arrondissement, amid furnishings of red plush chairs and faded red curtains, William Kissam Vanderbilt, Second, and Mrs. Rose Lancaster Warburton were married this morning at 11:30 o'clock."[24]

The couple was quietly married by the city mayor with only a handful of others present. Photographed immediately after the ceremony on the steps of the Paris registry office, the happy couple remained demure for the camera, with Willie's hands behind his back and Rose wearing a large beige cloche hat with an emerald pin and holding rose orchids close to her waist. The shadow it cast masked her face in the photo. Willie, as usual, wore his impish grin. After a wedding breakfast at the Plaza Athenee Hotel, the pair left for Southern France to board the *Ara*. At long last, the happy couple was homeward bound.

Willie kept a journal of his travels, and titled it *15,000 Miles Cruise with Ara*. While Willie's voyage was by no means a single 15,000-mile journey but rather the compilation of a series of shorter trips with *Ara*, it was most assuredly a long one. What had started two years earlier, after myriad hurdles and much personal cost and public embarrassment, had at last come to an end. Perhaps the 15,000 miles were symbolic. After all, in this most singular voyage he managed to conclude his divorce, ride out the vociferous press, and finally remarry. He left America with one wife, and returned with another. If Willie's inner journey were measurable, it would have covered far more than fifteen thousand miles.

Subsequent to their marriage, Willie and Rose returned to their beloved Galapagos Islands. Staying for four weeks, longer than they had the first time, the newlyweds fell in love with the Enchanted Isles all over again. The contrast of soft love against the sharp edges of volcanic rock must have been acute. They were exotics in a world famous for pushing life to its limits. In those environs surrounded by powerful currents, there is no escape; one either adapts or disappears. Willie and Rose found peace in their love and a sense of belonging on the Isles.

As a married couple, the pair returned to the inscriptions their group had made into the rocks on their last trip to the Isles. William Belanske had carved "ARA 1926." Now, as if to legitimize their marriage, Willie and Rose changed the numeral "6" to an "8," and added an inscription to a boulder at Cocos Island.[25]

After visiting Morocco, Spain, Cuba, and Florida, it was natural that the newlyweds would consider the architecture so popular in those environs for additions to Eagle's Nest. Certainly the exotic stucco façades with their intricate detail and flamboyant appeal rang true to Willie; the shapes and forms would be so different from the usual Gold Coast fairy tale construction that they would not compete, but rather serve in their own unique category.[26]

Along with the maritime collections came furnishings that were idiosyncratic, and therefore perfectly typical of the man. He needed his own style to house his new identity; Willie had always needed a form of expression that allowed him that. It remained a very personal fantasy, saying more about the personality of its owner than it did about any architectural or cultural precedents of the day.[27]

Willie's collection of maritime specimens took on a new level of commitment when the Marine Museum was completed in 1922. The bounty acquired in 1926, mainly represented by Rose and her two small children, required a building campaign of a different sort. The cottage would not suffice for his growing collection of specimens, both familial and marine.

The courtyard gained a wing to the east of the cottage, including an immense organ hidden behind a rug on the wall along the stairwell to the second floor. An arcade connected the original bachelor's cottage to a new nursery wing, so named because it was intended to be the quarters of Rosemary's young children, Rose and Barclay Warburton. The courtyard was then completed by a garden wall and service road on the fourth side, entered through a fanciful tower crowned by a guest bedroom and a sailing ship weather vane. The courtyard side of the tower was embellished by an electrically driven tower clock, linked to a collection of antique bells positioned in the tower belfry. "Vanderbilt's choice of several period styles, executed in ways which suggest various historical times in non-specific ways, reflects very clearly the fantasy-like way in which the owner sought to create a gracious and light-hearted environment for his seasonal retreat."[28]

Essentially, if he liked it, he did it; if he collected it, he displayed it; and if it represented a pleasurable memory, he surrounded himself with it. He steeped himself in the treasures of his journeys and relived his better days in a sort of museum of whimsical retelling.

The low-profile estate was quite satisfactory for Willie. His home gave preference to the back door exit — his route to the sea. The eagles at the gates had provided him with reasonable privacy and, with Rose, his life's strategy would be to envelope himself in the people and things that he loved. There was no need for a repeat of the opulence of Deepdale.

Across the road from the eagles, set in a similar arrangement, the superintendent's cottage was guarded by two stone lions saved from the Deepdale debacle. Passing the eagles on the eastern side of the road, Willie was greeted with a gorgeous view of Northport Harbor through a colonnade of six ancient columns reminiscent of the beaux arts so popular in his parents' day. He captured a memory from his own past, one from his father's and a hint of his mother's, all in a single architectural moment.

Stucco walls, recessed windows with intricate ironwork grills, roofs of red tile, romantic balconies and beautiful stone decorations enveloped the mansion. An elaborate balcony oversaw the entire courtyard. Nearby, a guest bedroom boasted views of harbor and golf course as breathless as all the other whimsies and adventures that Willie now lived.

Considered among the top twenty best-dressed women in the world by virtue of a poll of Paris fashion designers,[29] Mrs. William K. Vanderbilt, Jr., was now a New York social leader in her own right; a lady of high fashion and an equally high lifestyle. Her celebrity was quite a different sort than the demure Anne Rutherford, Mrs. William K. Vanderbilt, Sr., sought to share in public.

Other American women receiving the distinction made luscious company, such as Mrs. Cole Porter, Mrs. John Marriott, Mrs. Gilbert Miller, Ina Claire, Constance Bennett and Kay Francis.[30] The price tag for all this glamour was estimated to be between $10 and $40 thousand from Willie's coffers.[31] Still, while Rose drew appreciative glances for her style, she was even better known for the loving support she offered Willie as he embarked upon new adventures. To everyone who knew him, Vanderbilt had greater vitality than ever before.

We Know Who Put
the Bang in "Sabang"!

In April of 1929, Willie K. Vanderbilt achieved what few men have ever undertaken — he sailed around the entire globe. Over seven months aboard the *Ara*, he traveled twenty-eight thousand miles through the Atlantic, Pacific, and Indian Oceans, as well as the Mediterranean, Arabian, Chinese, and Red Seas.[1] In all, K. called on more than sixty ports.

The following year, Vanderbilt privately published the journal of his voyage, *Taking One's Own Ship Around the World*. In it, Willie declared: "For years I had waited and toiled for the moment when, as captain of my own ship, I would be able to undertake a voyage rarely accomplished — the circumnavigation of the globe."[2]

This travel log, lovingly dedicated to Rosamund Lancaster Vanderbilt, also contained a quote from Lord Byron's famous poem *The Sea*:

> And I have loved thee, Ocean! And my joy
> Of youthful sports was on thy breast to be
> Borne, like thy bubbles, onward: from a boy
> I wanton'd with thy breakers,
> And trusted to thy billows far and near,
> And laid my hand upon thy mane — as I do here.[3]

After suffering through a costly and difficult war, the time had returned for Americans to enjoy living again. They had earned their stripes, and now so much had changed. Victorian ideals were replaced by F. Scott Fitzgerald's *This Side of Paradise*. The fragility of life in war encouraged living in the moment. This message of *carpe diem* was taken by youth who smoked cigarettes all day, danced to jazz until exhaustion, drank in defiance of Prohibition, and drove fast cars. Advertising campaigns spoke to a hungry consumer of hundreds of new products promising modernity and a life of discretionary leisure time.

Willie had time, and was more than ready to enjoy a newfound spirit of camaraderie. It was his second chance, indeed his second life, and he intended to live it. History, with all its tragedy and troubles, couldn't follow Willie onto his floating island. Where else could one find a better place for the luxury of good living than on one's own yacht, loaded down with cigarettes, immune to Prohibition, with a scientific mission blessed by an admiral, and a lover at your side, all under the flapping of a commodore's flag? Willie reminisced not of the railroads, but rather the time he had spent in his youth gaining knowledge "in the handling of small boats."[4] Now it was his turn at the helm and he would take it.

His preparations for this trip were meticulous. Health and hygiene were primary concerns. All crew members and passengers "underwent a rigid physical examination"[5] before they could come on board. Willie also brought along a physician for this special global voyage. The *Ara* had limited capacity to carry ten thousand gallons of fresh water and, hence, part of Willie's route was, by necessity, guided through the various ports in which he could refuel and replenish water supplies. As a safeguard against malaria, "every part of the ship was screened."[6]

Willie and his passengers left New York harbor for warm southern waters in October. Immediately, troubles seemed to disappear: "Our whole attitude toward life seemed to change and the feeling of repose crept over us. New York now was only a bad, vague dream with its noise, dust, and gasoline fumes."[7] Hugging the eastern seaboard, the *Ara* steamed ahead and the mood of her passengers improved considerably with every passing mile. On Friday, October 26, 1928, his "friends found much amusement in designating me a half-century plant."[8] He could not have been happier.

The purpose of the trip, ostensibly, was to collect fish in the hopes of discovering a new species. The wildlife was abundant off of the coast of South America. "We sailed all day in a smooth sea, accompanied by many varieties of fish. Swordfish, marlin, sail fish, and tuna broke the water many times during the day."[9] Throughout the journey Willie took advantage of frequent opportunities to collect for the Northport museum, with Belanske busily preserving the colors of specimens on canvas.

The *Ara* cruised around the globe marking such highlights as the Philippines, Saigon, Cambodia, Singapore, Ceylon, India, Cairo, Spain, and Morocco before heading back to Miami and terra firma. They made purchases, talked with locals, and visited innumerable museums and temples. It was, to be sure, a passage of fits and starts, of new beginnings and strange endings. There was trouble with drivers, and the weather on the voyage home was a collusion of storms. Willie seemed to have found, if not validation, then at least ample opportunity for exploration.

Willie's journal entries revealed a man driven less now by science and more by raw emotion and a boundless fascination with life. At witnessing the effects of a hurricane in Florida, he muses philosophically, "The elements had exercised their powers over the labors of the human race."[10] The journal included both the poetic: "Havana is to me somewhat as the Riviera is to the

On the return leg of their 1929 voyage around the world, an appropriate stop was Cairo and the pyramids. Here they see the Great Sphinx at Gizah. The pyramids of Cheops are in the background. March 1929. Pictured here on the camels, left to right, are Rosamund, Willie K. and Pierre Merillon (courtesy Suffolk County Vanderbilt Museum).

European who during the winter months sojourns along the brilliant shores of the Mediterranean,"[11] as well as the perfunctory: "NOON, Lat. 18°36' N., Long. 129°09' W. Distance run 320 miles. Wind NE., force 3, long swell from NW. by N. Bad weather to the northward reported by wireless. Air 76°. Barometer 29.99."[12]

There were lows on outbound leg of the trip, as well as highs. Honolulu did not live up to its reputation, nor did the beach of Waikiki. Waves did not bear sun-kissed surfers, as Willie had been led to believe. While the guests enjoyed their stay at the Royal Hawaiian hotel, they were told to steer clear of flea-infested movie houses, and the consistently rainy weather did not always allow one to feel as if he were in paradise. As Willie dejectedly noted, "It does not rain, it pours, and this every few minutes of the day."[13]

While the *Ara* left the Hawaiian Islands in her wake in late December, a reporter for the *Oregon Daily Journal* interviewed Willie. Willie spoke candidly with the young man:

I was born on October 26, 1879, in New York City, so I have just passed my 50th birthday. I have always been very fond of the water. When I was a boy I loved to swim and sail boats. I served in the navy during the World war. I was a lieutenant, junior grade. My present rank is lieutenant commander. I started in the railroad business at the bottom. I wanted to learn every detail. When I was in my early 40's I became president of the New York Central lines. I had enough money to get along on, see something of the world, but to try to do something worthwhile in the way of scientific research. We have secured a large number of most interesting specimens of marine life, which I am sending to the museum I have at our home at Northport, on Long Island. When we secure duplicate specimens I present them to the American Museum of Natural History in New York. My wife and I are greatly enjoying this cruise.[14]

The reporter observed as well Willie's quintessential nature:

I studied him carefully. He is of medium height, has a forceful face, a kindly expression; his hair is slightly gray, his voice low and pleasant; he has charming manners and a certain magnetism that makes you like him. If I were going to pick someone to go camping with I wouldn't hesitate a moment to select him as my camping mate.[15]

Willie spoke, too, of his son, William Kissam III, in a private moment: "My son, W.K. Vanderbilt, Jr., is going to follow my example and start at the bottom of the ladder in the railroad business and learn the business from the ground up." He was fond of having a protégé. Though the younger Willie lacked the sea legs of his father, they had shared much. The boy kept a photo log much as his father retained journals, and times with his father were punctuated throughout. They sailed, hunted and fished together, the youngster referring to Willie as "Father" with an air of apparent pride, much as Willie K. thought of him.

By Thursday, December 27, at the Jaluit Atoll in the Marshall Islands, the passengers and crew aboard the *Ara* "made our first contact with Japan."[16] Waiting for them were customs officials and sixty tons of oil Willie had shipped from Yokohama in advance of the trip to offset their nearly six-thousand-mile cruise onward to Manila. They did not linger long, and by New Year's Day, they were already exploring the Caroline Islands. A few days later, at the Island of Ponape, another island under Japanese control, they were forced to endure a difficult anchorage. Everyone on board, though, welcomed the intense rain that ensued, since bathing water had been rationed to two quarts a day.

The *Ara* continued to hop from one island to the next on her way across the Pacific. Willie was fascinated by the still-active practice of head hunting on various isles. Warrior raiders in the Truk Atolls were said to "attack others within the atoll and to bring back headless corpses of those fallen in battle, which were to be roasted, so many say; while the heads, trophies of war, were to adorn the huts as ornaments highly prized."[17]

Traveling through foreign waters also meant enduring foreign rule. Willie did not understand the restrictions imposed as they sailed from one island controlled by the Japanese to the next. At Eten Road, Japanese authorities quickly came aboard and dutifully scrutinized their permits and papers. Permission to land was only granted for the limited scope of the trading wharf and forbidden on any of the islands making up the atoll. The inspecting authorities informed them that they "were dangerous ... this somewhat dampened our spirits, but orders are orders, and we gracefully acquiesced."[18]

Willie's hope to pay respects to the local governor was thwarted when he threw his right knee out of joint during the ascent to the governor's residence: "This knee, by the way, has been troubling me a lot on this trip."[19] The governor graciously came to call on the *Ara*, bringing his family and a cluster of lower lieutenants. A brother who came from the Catholic mission reminded the travelers of the fast-changing times, informing Willie "that Truk's native stock was dying off and that there was little chance for their survival."[20]

Off the coast by the San Bernandino strait, Willie was thankful to have missed typhoons before and after his stops, and appreciative of the rain that ensued.[21] By the end of January they were in Saigon, a French colony at the time and considered the "Little Paris of the East." However, Willie was notably disturbed by his surroundings there and repulsed by the motley crowds of sweat-soaked people that he described as looking "less like human beings than we could have imagined possible."[22] He wanted to leave as quickly as possible, feeling unsafe and ill at ease.

Amazed at the local Anamese who pulled the rickshaws "at a gait that is equal to that of a horse at a trot.... All were emaciated, and some so aged as to make us wonder how they could carry on so long."[23] Willie was astonished by even the slightest minutia, even their sitting posture. He wrote, "Were we to assume their position, that is, if it were possible, for five minutes, we certainly should never be the same again."[24]

In Southeast Asia, Willie's favorite destination was Angkor in Cambodia, whose ancient temples and scrollwork he knew and admired.[25] Willie, Rose, Belanske and Charlie arose at five A.M. to board auto cars chartered by the manager of the Continental Hotel, only to be informed by the owner of the two vehicles that the price was insufficient. Willie, with the assistance of the hotel manager, debated with the auto car owner until negotiations broke down. Their luggage was summarily ejected from the vehicles, and they were left on the road *sans* transportation. Frustrated, Willie reluctantly admitted defeat, finding it "necessary to abandon the trip, to our great disappointment."[26]

In Singapore, he found the traffic so daunting that the one-time master of speed proclaimed that "the motor cars went like the devil, and it was all we could do to get across the street. Had we lost our skill as New York pedestrians?"[27] However, this bout of forgetfulness did not last long once he put himself behind the wheel: "We soon found ourselves tearing down Singapore's streets with the rest."[28]

As they skirted the Indian coast during a placid day with smooth seas, a large whale broke water on the port side. There was a trampling of feet and exclamations of excitement to see what Willie called "His Nibs" as it broke the quiet shipboard.

> As a young boy I bicycled one day to Coney Island from Fifth Avenue and Fifty-Second Street (being arrested en route by a bicycle cop for speeding did not deter me!) Arriving on the beach, I found a tent bearing the sign, "25 cents to see the Prince of Wales." Childish curiosity had to be satisfied. Inside the tent a small decomposed whale was on view, but no one stayed long to examine His Nibs.[29]

The humpback whale played around the *Ara* and, although admittedly there was no proper way to handle the fifty- to sixty-foot catch, the sportsman in Willie was overcome:

> Charlie Thompson had already importuned me so many times to stop the boat for fishing that I did not have the heart to resist his plea now. A whale? Charlie Thompson was a great fisherman, but never had he had such an adversary, one that filled him with keener anticipation. A launchman and a sailor quickly manned a boat, with Charlie in the bow, while the crew lined the deck to watch the chase. The glistening harpoon in Charlie's hand was tremulously poised for action. The humpback whale, fifty to sixty feet in length, cavorted alongside and twice cruised around us. But when the launch was finally lowered, with the Ara following in its wake, the whir of the propeller incited the humpback to change his course, and he started for Bombay. Twice Charlie was close to the would-be victim, but the kittenish manners of the whale gave him no chance to throw the harpoon. When the recall signal was sounded, Charlie's pose was not that of the conqueror. The victor was on his way to Bombay. However, we still look upon Charlie as a great fisherman.
> As a good-by, a couple of bullets were sent after the whale from the elephant gun. Both went wide of the mark, but we were glad of it, for what could we have done with the poor thing had we managed to bag him or her?[30]

In mid–February of 1929, the *Ara* was docked in the harbor of Sabang on the island of Pulo Weh, off the northwestern extremity of Sumatra. Once again, it was a sketchy landing for the well-heeled Vanderbilt party:

> SABANG! And they did—we know who put the bang in Sabang! A hundred men, more or less, probably less, letting drive with their hammers this morning at the rust on the iron pier where we lay. Mon Dieu, how relentlessly they worked! Such an hour to start, too: six in the morning. The planks on the dock were torn up, the entire structure was to be repaired and painted, and we poor sufferers had arrived just in time to receive the full benefit of this Anvil Chorus.[31]

Back at home, the romance of an earlier adventure was taking a turn for the worse. Willie's daughter, Muriel, secured a divorce from her husband, Frederic Church, on grounds of non–support in February.[32] It was yet another Vanderbilt marriage following the fate of so many that had come before it.

Willie soon arrived in India and was surprised by the country's stark contrasts of beauty amidst abject poverty. While they enjoyed viewing impressive hotels and fine buildings in Bombay and the gorgeous marble mausoleum, the Taj Mahal, he also observed with distinctive sympathy, "The natives were a sad,

In Jaipur, India, 1929, Willie (holding the pith helmet) reported, "From now on I shall never again envy an elephant rider in the circus. What a movement! And ours had the bad luck of having a cold. His manners, consequently, were not at all what they should have been, for when he blew his trunk, we all thought it was raining, even though there was not a cloud in the sky." William K. Vanderbilt II, *Taking One's Own Ship Around the World*, 1929.

thin, and aged-looking lot, even those still young. They were pathetic, yet during our entire Indian trip we failed to notice a single glance that would indicate reproach on account of our superior estate."[33]

Willie took numerous photographs of the country, with its vast and magnificent ruins, citadels, tombs, and façades, and was mesmerized by the colors and intricate designs. However, he also expressed a cynical view when it came to the local population's fascination with self-proclaimed "holy men":

> The holy man of India is the man for business. The priesthood is a profession that can be taken up by anyone. India has over a million of them. In order to enter holy orders one need only stop work. Become eccentric, wear extraordinary clothes, get a stick, and look wise. The populace falls for this and immediately proclaims the novitiate holy, looks up to him with fear and admiration, and feeds him. What surprises me is that more have not taken up the profession.[34]

What is a trip to India without a ride on an elephant? Willie, of course, enjoyed the opportunity with his characteristic humor, explaining how his elephant had a bit of a cold: "His manners, consequently, were not at all what they should have been, for when he blew his trunk, we all thought it was raining, even though there was not a cloud in the sky."[35]

As the *Ara* negotiated the Arabian and Red Seas, the group stayed close together, marveling at the colorful costumes of locals and the steady pace of soft-footed camels through the desert. There was ample reason for concern along the Arabian coast, where foreigners were not welcome: "Off goes the head if the victim who is not lucky enough to have received a bullet before they got to him."[36]

The Red Sea was over a thousand miles long. Its shores on the Arabian side were lined with reefs forming an inner passage that allowed ships to pass. As in most other places, the English were at war with the locals. Yet Willie elevated himself above the fray — an ambassador to the world:

> Their planes drop bombs on the villages of these poor devils, blowing them to pieces ... but let us hope that some day we will be able to return and look things over. I would anticipate no trouble, for I have, in my day, been in a number of wild countries where, people said, I would be bound to have difficulty. I have never been molested, and I went without arms. I respected their customs and greeted all with a smile. A smile, I have found, will take one a long way in any part of the world.[37]

In the Sahara, they suffered through a powerful sandstorm that burned their eyes with dust. Willie fretted over his ship: "Will we ever get rid of it? Poor Ara looks as if she had not been varnished and cleaned in months, and only yesterday morning she looked so spic-and-span."[38]

At last, they were past the desert and reached the modern city of Cairo. Willie exclaimed delightedly, "Cairo! What a change!" Willie and company warmly accepted all that the "modern city" had to offer: "fine boulevards and splendid shops; tourists everywhere." It was their pleasure to join all of the other tourists visiting the sphinx and the pyramids, museums, and the Valley of the Kings (unfortunately, King Tutankhamen's tomb was off limits as it was Sunday). They imbibed in Turkish baths, lunched at the Shepheard Hotel and the Semiramis, "bordering the Nile and by far the best."[39]

Willie continually complained of pilots who knew not where to go, but only what to charge. He was clearly galled by the endless string of pilots who took them to the wrong berth through dangerous routes and those who came aboard after they were anchored and demanded a fee for no effort.

Enjoying the thrill of winning at virtually anything, Willie paid particular attention to bargains they purchased along route. In the Greek Isles there were amphorae brought to the surface in fisherman's nets; beautiful antiques that cost but a dollar apiece. In Aden, Arabia, one vender offered Willie a nice prayer rug for five pounds: "I suggested giving him two pounds and got it. Later in the day he offered me a similar one for four pounds. I started at one pound and finished there." "It's yours, he said. Stung again, said I."[40]

Morocco, by contrast, did not seem to enliven Willie's spirits. "The charm had gone," he observed.[41] Mosquitoes, foremost amongst other things, bothered him to distraction. But when a hotel proprietor explained to Willie the lack of mosquito netting, the response gave K. a good laugh, reminding him of Long Island: "We have no mosquitoes."[42]

He developed hay fever and it raged ruthlessly, weakening his already tired body. When the condition subsided, his right leg gave out. Willie wrote, "What is wrong I do not know, but it won't function properly, and our guide addressed me as if I were an old man, which helped to irritate me."[43]

Willie's assiduous nature when it came to hygiene was clearly evident in Malaga, Spain, when he refused change from a merchant on his yacht, saying, "Keep the change and the microbes with it."[44] He was also disturbed by the occasional air of local insolence. On the island of Sao Vicente, Willie took portage in Porto Grande, which he found desolate and unwelcoming. Furious at the arrogance of locals who refused to assist them with needed water and supplies, Willie complained repeatedly and eagerly set back to sea.[45]

At last, with a celebratory "Heigh ho!,"[46] on May 11, after a monotonous passage across the Atlantic, *Ara* entered the Caribbean. Wireless messages had been coming in from New York, and the feeling of approaching home boosted their morale once more.

Still, Willie was disturbed to see the aftermath of havoc wreaked upon the local towns such as Pointe-à-Pitre on the island of Guadeloupe, which had been demolished by a hurricane in the previous year. In that area alone, the storm killed over one thousand, five hundred people, while destroying the town.[47] Nearby Basse-Terre had also suffered devastation with buildings left roofless, but whose walls remained intact. For the first time in his life, Willie revealed religious wonderment:

> But, strange as it may seem, a large statue of Our Lord Jesus Christ, standing on top of a church and in full view of the sea, and a statue of the Virgin Mary in a niche nearby, had both weathered the gale. I had seen the same queer omen at Messina, Sicily, after the earthquake of December 28, 1908, when most of the buildings had been destroyed and 90,000 lives snuffed out. Yet the statue of the Virgin Mary had been spared in almost every case.[48]

The travelers were all ready to return home after a long voyage across the globe. As they passed the French cruiser *Aldebaran*, the *Ara* dipped her colors. According to Willie, "Her officers gazed with wonderment at our homeward-bound pennant, streaming gaily in the wind from the truck of our mainmast."[49] The pennant, all one hundred feet of it, was raised again for Willie's triumphant return at Miami.

Willie's own aging was reflected in his descriptions of the *Ara*. Over the years, he had come to call his ship's anchor the "old hook"[50] and the *Ara* his "old ship"[51] or just plain "old *Ara*."[52] In a storm she "yawed quite badly."[53]

At last, by Thursday, May 16, 1929, they were due to make landfall in Miami, a grand entrance that Willie eagerly anticipated:

> We ran slowly up the coast, arriving off the jetties at 3:30. Here a dozen or more ships, dressed for the occasion, met us. Accompanied by them and the blowing of

whistles, we proceeded to our dock, which has been named Ara Base, to which we tied up at just 4:00 P.M. after the doctor had passed us, and the customs, immigration, and prohibition agents had performed their various duties, the Reception Committee came on board and welcomed us back to the U.S.A. and Miami.[54]

Specimens had been collected, friendships forged, photographs taken, but now it was time to face their first night back in the States since beginning their episodic journey some seven months before. "A sad evening for us all!!" was how Willie put it, adding, "As we stepped over the side of the good old ship, there was a lump in my throat. It is something that comes to every yachtsman whose association with his ship has been close for so long a time."[55]

Like the meticulous yachtsman, Willie kept to his journal throughout the trip. Rose dutifully typed from Willie's "scrawled notes"[56] and prepared it for eventual publication. Typical of Willie's obsessive pursuit for detail, the journal consisted of a preface, an introduction, and two hundred and sixty-four pages describing their jaunt from Hawaii to the Far East, back through India, Egypt, Morocco, the Mediterranean, the "little known Caroline Islands,"[57] and finally back to Miami. At the end, he added no less than five appendices, including newspaper articles, "Totals and Averages: Nautical Miles, Revolutions of Engines, Diesel Oil, Lubricating Oil, Water Consumed," and a piece by Belanske describing some of the fish they had captured and documented in the name of science.[58] Likewise, Belanske again offered his artistic talents, with one hundred illustrations as well as twenty-one color plates.[59] Willie printed five hundred copies, giving out several to friends and family as gifts, donating a book to the Brooklyn Public Library[60] and offering a fraction of them for sale at one hundred dollars apiece.[61]

Welcomed home like a hero, Willie brought back *Ara* from her long voyage. His ship had traveled some 28,738 miles at an average of 13.05 miles per hour, and in his fiftieth year, Willie had at last made his long-awaited trek around the globe.[62]

A marvelous accomplishment indeed. Yet a sad and curious passage stands out from the rest of Willie's journal. It speaks volumes in its own right — not of the journey at sea, but of the journey inside Willie's own wandering heart. March 21, 1929, found the *Ara* dropping her old hook at the entrance to the harbor at the island Rhodes. "A great day! *Ara* had circumnavigated the globe, and I had been her commander all the way. It was one of those moments in a lifetime when vague emotions flood one's being. I felt I had accomplished something. But mixed with this delight there was also a restless urge that seemed to say, 'What's next?'"[63]

Willie had gone around the world, and, still, he could not find true satisfaction. What would it take for him to find the peace he so ardently pursued?

CHAPTER 22

The God of Palm Island

"Winter is turning to spring, and [Rose and I] are restlessly dreaming of distant places. We have decided to circumnavigate the earth once more, this time south of the equator."[1]

Since childhood, the urge to explore had been an insatiable force in Willie K.'s life. It drove his acquiring ways, ever prodding him to lust in consumption, to look for something better, faster, more powerful. And it served as the spark for his creativity, leading to his innumerable ideas, feats, and even his failures. Now, exploration would become an even more literal pursuit — the next horizon was, in fact, a faraway land, a point where the sea met the sky, the next destination, wherever it may be around this vast globe. Allowing himself to indulge the image of commodore and the naturalist, Willie added that of the global explorer. And leaving the rest of the world behind for months at a time may have been an act of delusion, but in K.'s dreamscape it was just as real — indeed, more real — than a daily trip to an office on Park Avenue. Rose provided his loving audience, cheering each tale. Willie, at this stage in life, could finally allow himself to be happy with what he truly was — a seeker, a man without destination.

In preparations for his second global voyage, Vanderbilt was again assiduous. Once acquiring full provisions and a crew of forty-eight men, all that remained was outfitting his ship. However, this time the *Ara* would not do. He was well aware of her limitations and, in many ways, he and his ambitions had outgrown the beloved French sloop. It was time for Willie to get a new ship, one that he could custom-design to suit his varied purposes. That ship would be *Alva*, named after his mother — the second so christened on her behalf. Perhaps in his newfound Rose, Willie K. was remembering the happier times of his childhood, when his mother loved his father and the family set sail in cheerful unity — when all was innocent, or so, at least, it seemed.

Far superior to any existing luxury yacht on the seas, the *Alva*, built by Krupp Germaniawerft in Kiel, Germany, was outfitted with the latest scientific gear, luxurious living quarters, and an elaborate laboratory for the pursuit of science. A magnificent ship, the *Alva* had a displacement of thirty-five hundred tons.[2]

Alva at Krupp Germaniawerft, still in the ways eight days before her launch, November 10, 1930. Willie inscribed in his book of her first global journey a quote from Byron: "She walks the waters like a thing of life, And seems to dare the elements of strife" (courtesy Suffolk County Vanderbilt Museum).

Willie proudly reported, "At fifteen knots *Alva* has a cruising radius of 15,000 nautical miles" (courtesy Suffolk County Vanderbilt Museum).

After accompanying his ailing mother, Alva, on a trip to the Nile River in Egypt[3] (a reminiscence of the excursion he had taken as a nine year old,[4] when Alva was still married to his father), Willie decided to purchase his new ship and name it after her. Launched November 18, 1930, from the German shipyard, *Alva* measured two hundred and sixty feet in length, forty-six feet in width, and traveled swiftly at a speed of sixteen knots.[5] Immediately, Willie hoisted the American flag as *Alva* was put to sea.[6]

No corner had been trimmed, no savings sought. Willie gushed about *Alva* like a proud father: "We did not want to have to say later, 'Too bad we didn't add ten more feet,' or 'Isn't it a shame we didn't raise that deckhouse?'"[7] He describes the *Alva* lovingly and radiantly, and for page after page, details every inch of her majesty, from her "water-tight doors" and "pneumatic gear" to her large stowage space, refrigeration and cold-storage capabilities, even a seaplane, calling her the "most powerfully constructed yacht in existence."[8]

Powered by two diesel engines, she had an auxiliary electric motor and resembled a cruiser with a slim body, high bow, and low stern.[9] The *Alva* featured eight large staterooms with accompanying baths for luxurious travel.[10]

Working for several months to ensure the comfort of all their passengers,

Rosamund and Willie pose on the bridge of their yacht *Alva* at Newport, just prior to setting sail for their 1931 voyage of the South Seas (courtesy Suffolk County Vanderbilt Museum).

Rose and Willie[11] made special arrangements to send part of the salaries of employees directly home, while offering regular postcards and communication by radio to ensure the peace of mind of their staff. He also promised each of the men an additional ten dollars per month for good behavior.[12]

Back on land, the Vanderbilt Cup still lived on, having a new purpose and location. But Willie was no longer directly involved, although the event and the trophy maintained his name. In January of 1930, the Vanderbilt Cup resurfaced as an annual prize for the fastest American driver of an American stock car at Daytona. The Cup was the only award, prestigious enough, without an additional cash award.[13]

Despite their frequent travels, Rosamund and Willie still dedicated significant efforts in revamping their home, Eagle's Nest, overseeing improvements costing two million dollars. Their travels at home included river excursions, including notable guests that included the celebrated Indian poet and philosopher Rabindranath Tagore.[14]

Willie also received a twenty-five-foot, rare white finback whale for his Marine Museum, donated by John Wanamaker, Jr., in Montauk Lake.[15] Wanamaker had taken a deep sea fishing trip when the celebrated hunter Captain Charles Thompson harpooned the six-thousand-pound animal. Though "swift and dangerous,"[16] circling precariously close to their boat, they finally subdued the whale after several hours of battle.

Despite the looming disasters in the nation following October 29, 1929, or Black Thursday, when the Great Depression began, Willie seemed entirely unfazed by the country's economic woes. The Roaring Twenties had come screeching to a painful halt and the era of flappers, fast driving, and Fitzgerald was all but forgotten in the daily worries that plagued the populace. The papers that once adored Willie's every action were too busy printing pictures of bread lines in Time Square and packed houses in soup kitchens. They did worse than decry the mediocre millionaire. They ignored him.

But the *Alva* was Willie's world now. He had built not just a new ship, but also a new empire — a floating island — over which he had complete dominion. He had his queen and now his kingdom: "I am in command, a responsibility and a pleasure. Rose is with me. Our dream is being realized."[17]

The man who had once held the land speed record, who brought racing to his home country, and who had experimented with seaplanes and now held one on his ship, had come to a new revelation that "speed is not the only thing in life."[18] *Alva* was built for relaxation and for slow, luxurious, and lazy days on the sea.

Just as they were about to set sail, Virginia, who was in Paris, announced the marriage of Muriel, Willie's eldest daughter, to Henry D. Phelps, the son of a "gentleman farmer."[19] Interestingly, Muriel consistently referred to her mother, Virginia, as "Mrs. Vanderbilt" despite the divorce of her own parents, revealing her own loyalty to her mother and rift from her father's second wife, Rosamund.

Alva left Northport in Long Island on July 7, 1931, on a world trip of thirty thousand miles to collect marine specimens.[20] Rose and Willie could prepare for the voyage with meticulous vigor, but they could not prepare for departure: "We had parted with relatives and friends, who stood on the dock, waving

Perhaps casualties of Rosamund and Willie's whirlwind romance and subsequent travels were the Warburton children (Barclay, left, and Rosemary) (courtesy Suffolk County Vanderbilt Museum).

farewell. Though we lay far out we could distinguish two small figures more active than the rest — Rose's children. We thought of our long absence, and our eyes filled with tears."[21]

They would have left the continental United States one day prior to their actual departure but they were not as well stocked as Willie preferred and he openly admitted his superstitions, saying "it was the thirteenth, when no good sailor sets out on a voyage."[22]

The next day, Tuesday July 14, "We let go the lines and broke our last ties with the United States. There was another brief moment of wistfulness, but soon we felt again the bliss of being alive."[23] Fifteen days later, Willie and his party of guests arrived in Cristobal in the Canal Zone.[24]

Willie's diplomatic and generous nature extended to the people he met along the way. Intent upon pleasing locals during one visit, he bought several dozen bracelets, necklaces, earrings, rings, mirrors, magnifying lenses, thermos bottles, and alarm clocks at a small store to take with him on his voyage to the South Sea Islands.[25]

A formal tone returned to his travel journal when Willie listed himself in the published List of Crew and Passengers as "William K. Vanderbilt, Lieutenant Commander, U.S.N.R.,"[26] the rank he had achieved prior to the outset of the Great War. He also shared how he had been rejected by the Army to serve during the Spanish-American War due to a "weak heart," when he was a freshman in 1898 at Harvard. But, he added with some obvious glee, "Apparently, at thirty-nine I had staged a comeback."

While formal, the overall mood of this travel journal was also upbeat, joking in the preface: "Cartons of cigarettes presented to all on three or four occasions found a ready welcome."

Yet some internal drive to prove his mettle and lend some purpose to his travels resurfaced once more in his journals. The table of contents for *West Made East* reads more like a childhood geography textbook than a pleasure cruise: The Galapagos Islands, Tahiti, Samoa, Australia, Sumbawa, Bali, Java, the Mediterranean Sea, France and Spain, the Cape Verde Islands. Along the way, Willie did as always: he took pictures. He requested that Belanske render drawings of strange and exotic creatures exactly to scale, filling every space of the *Alva* with memories, thoughts, reflections, and observations.

Willie had chosen again a quote from Lord Byron for a preface to his first nautical memoir, *Taking One's Own Ship Around the World*, and saw fit to do the same for the sequel, from Byron's poem *The Corsair*: "She walks the waters like a thing of life, and seems to dare the elements to strife." Willie was obviously in a state of ecstasy: "No day seems to pass without offering something of beauty. In one of the sunny spells we witnessed a thrilling thing when two sailfish, about ten feet long, jumped their full length out of the water and hurled themselves through the air at express speed. First one brilliant silvery body leaped clear of the sea, a shower of diamonds sparkled for an instant, and it was gone. Then the second sailfish embarked on a flight through the air and quickly vanished."[27]

Considered the queen of high fashion, Rosamund's yachting attire, carefully designed by Molyneux in Paris to accentuate her figure, was soft, flowing, and utterly feminine.[28] It was no wonder that she would top society's well-dressed list as "American swelldom."[29]

Willie could run away from the Great Depression in grand style, and bring his friends along with him. His weaknesses were many and his strengths equal in their fervor. While Willie had high esteem for those he came in contact with, such as his servants and deckhands to whom he offered generous bonuses, he still did not offer any sympathy for the masses of suffering Americans back home. His life had been strikingly devoid of charity.

Few writings included thoughts of home. In his journal of a voluminous three hundred and eighty pages, Willie remarked on the Great Depression only four times. Despite the fact that he received daily news updates from the New York Stock Exchange, had a newspaper, the *Alva Daily News*, that discussed domestic issues every day, and boasted a radio station the likes of which then reigning National Broadcast Company (NBC) might have envied, Willie showed little interest in the troubles at home. *Alva*, instead, was his new home.

Still, one passage reveals that Willie could not hide his eyes completely when he finally encounters reality. In Havana, "it was a still morning, sultry and sticky ... the harbor looked empty; hardly a ship was there. Never before had I seen it so. The depression is making itself felt. Everyone here is in the throes of despair, for the sugar market has gone to hell."[30]

But from sea, it was easy for Willie to remain the casual observer. Although he still owned some railroad stock, he had few concerns for the market: "By noon the weather had cleared and the sun shone. It was a perfect day until the *Alva Daily News* announced that New York Central was selling at 28."[31]

He described their travels in great detail from "Our visits to shops were cut short by a tremendous downpour,"[32] so "Rose and I worked in the gymnasium, for we are trying to keep thin."[33] He detailed every port of call, customs boarding, and squall line. He noted the tiniest details about specimens, fine ports and sherries, and the marvels of athleticism and mastery among his crew.

Peaceful and happy relations were his primary focus. Early in the preface, Willie commented, "I have tried to catch something of the significance of other peoples. In certain respects, people all around the globe have common adventures. To understand this makes for peace between nations."[34] He would boldly go in the company of Rose, Mr. and Mrs. Pierre C. Merillon, his daughter Consuelo and her husband, and a crew of fifty-one including William Belanske, curator of the Vanderbilt Museum. Willie chose his company wisely: "Without a happy ship's company, one might as well get in to port and stay there."[35] She would sail under the flag of the Naval Reserve yacht pennant, the first to do so in a global journey.

Off the coast of Miami, Rose and Willie had created a home and private naval base, which they had named Ara Base during *Ara*'s time in the sun. Although she remained moored there, *Ara* no longer ruled, and the name of this southern home was changed to Alva Base.

On board the *Alva*, Willie included a young cinematographer trained in Hollywood, whom he had hired to chronicle his adventures. Robert "Bob" Joseph Bronner, an eager and talented whippersnapper, enjoyed his work and deeply admired Willie, whom he, like the others, called the "Commodore." He described K. as a "fine gentleman; wonderful personality and not snobbish; very conservative in his manner."[36]

Upon reaching his "Enchanted Isles," Willie burst with anticipation: "Tomorrow we shall see the Galapagos Islands again. How well I remember poring over charts as a boy, wondering whether some day I should make a voyage to this weird place. And here I am on my third visit!"[37]

The self-proclaimed naturalist, Willie finally tipped his hat to those who preceded him as visitors and intellectuals: "I have scanned most of the books written on these islands, for I have wanted to know what people thought about them. I have read early navigators' stories, tales of pirate adventures, Darwin's account, William Beebe's *Galapagos: World's End*, and reports of other expeditions."[38] All the more reason Willie could not believe that a steamship company intended to land tourists on the island:

> I am surprised to put it mildly. I cannot imagine tourists willing to endure the discomfort that is inevitable here. In some places landing on the beach of a Galapagos island is like jumping from a moving elevator. Once ashore it is difficult to move

In 1925, Willie traded his yacht, the *Eagle*, for a piece of Fisher's Island, Florida. It was soon named *Ara Base* after his then-current yacht, a name that was superseded by the moniker *Alva Base* on the christening of his final luxury yacht, the *Alva* (courtesy Suffolk County Vanderbilt Museum).

about. Inland the rays of the sun beat down mercilessly. Because of sharks, bathing is dangerous except in a net put over the ship's side or on certain sheltered beaches where the water is shallow.[39]

At last they arrived at Tagus Cove, taking note of the records they had left during *Ara*'s 1926 and 1928 journeys. Under observation of a pair of sea lions, Mr. Belanske proceeded to carve a record of *Alva*'s visit "on the volcanic ledge, with chisel and paint."[40]

Willie sadly noticed that the friendly birds and wildlife were gone. They remained in seclusion, having learned to fear visitors: "Tagus Cove has lost much of the charm it had five years ago. Not many vessels had called here then.... The creatures of this once fearless animal world have had too much contact with human beings. It is a sad commentary on the havoc civilized man inflicts on a primitive world."[41] Despite this disappointment, Willie was the mayor of happiness: "Running a ship is like running a small town. Every detail must be watched. Days go by, and I wonder where they have gone to. I run up and down steps continuously from cabin to upper bridge. I have lost eighteen pounds; the life at sea has invigorated me. Yet I am greeted with, 'What! Aren't you going to the gymnasium today?'"[42]

Willie was also thrilled to get another visit from his old friend "Nibs":

Suddenly another whale blew on our port hand. He advanced rapidly, swimming on the surface, back and snoot out of water, malice in his eye. Something told me to pay attention. He looked like an ugly customer, and as he was coming head-on, we were in a bad position in case he should sound, for his tail might smash the boat. Nothing, it seemed, would stop him. He continued to come straight at us.

I saw him within twenty feet of the launch, close to the bow. Then I dropped the harpoon, picked up the elephant gun, and let him have a ball in the middle of the back. Hard over right rudder! I shouted. Full speed ahead! We turned about, and as fast as our motor could take us, we sped in the other direction. Probably the shot did no more than tickle him.[43]

Indeed, back in the Galapagos, his floating kingdom was more complete than ever. Willie's energy surged to new heights. He even adjusted his sleep pattern to his role as commodore and officer of the deck. He slept lightly and awoke to action on demand, "almost automatically if things are not right."[44]

Tahiti rose to Willie's expectations: "Superb country. Brilliant foliage, flamboyant blossoms, natives who beamed when addressed — all lent reality to our romantic dream of the South Sea Islands."[45] In a small French café, Willie met the first cat that took a liking to him, stealthily handing food to her as she hid beneath his chair.

Willie's sense for superstition was again confirmed on Thursday August 13, a day that "began with fine weather." Approaching Tahiti "the sky was lowering. The glass was dropping. I felt that we were in for a storm."[46] The weather became ferocious. The winds were of hurricane strength. "I feel tremendously proud of Alva. She far exceeds my anticipations. I have no cause to worry over how the ship is going to weather the storm.... We are approaching the dangerous barrier reef of Tahiti, which ought to be on our starboard hand during the early hours of the morning. Alva might pile up on it if an error occurred in my dead reckoning. The course I have set down should put the island with its dangers about twenty miles distant on our starboard hand."[47]

The next day, Willie reported: "As soon as the thirteenth was over, things began to look better. Again it was wonderful to see how Alva had behaved. She always does the right thing.... A mariner cannot sleep in such weather."[48]

The thirteenth of each month never seemed to fail him; it was always punctuated by a storm or some other reason for caution.

The voyage through the South Seas continued. Natives, now familiar with European culture, made their impression. The trinkets that Willie had purchased as gifts were not willingly accepted as points of barter; the locals had graduated towards more practical commodities. Cultural changes had taken place and human sacrifice had ceased a century ago. However, in the Caroline Group, "The people appeared to be unspoiled, un–Europeanized."[49] Willie carefully collected bones at a sacrificial altar to bring home to the museum.

Local festivities intrigued Willie, who recognized that the "dances were symbolical, suggesting a ritual or story by the sequence of their movements."[50] Playing anthropologist as well as naturalist, he watched their movements with interest, running "the gamut from the graceful to the studiedly awkward, from the languorous to the energetic, they exhibited far greater invention and fervor than do white men when they dance."[51]

Willie had developed a fear of germs on his previous trip and, on one occasion, he was caught up in a procession of natives gaily joining planned festivities in celebration of the *Alva*'s visit. As he walked among the natives, "A jolly toothless woman, eating away merrily and carrying on her shoulder a little flower-bedecked model of *Alva*, tried to kiss me. Earl and Pierre saved the day by catching hold of her and dancing on down the road. They made a picture I shall never forget."[52]

Back on board the *Alva* adventures continued as well. Two men deserted and trumped up a charge against the *Alva*, citing that Willie had treated them poorly and breached their contracts.[53] Willie appeared in court to defend himself and the charges were dismissed. The men were ordered to appear an hour prior to the *Alva*'s departure and to be boarded by police escort. Willie was ordered to present the men with their clothes and possessions in the morning and pay their wages through August 31. The sailors came by in the evening to apologize and Willie expressed that all was forgotten. The men returned ashore.

The next morning Samoan chiefs came by way of a twenty-eight-oared cutter and boarded *Alva* for a ritual kava ceremony. Willie and Rose had one hundred and twenty native guests. The chiefs bestowed honorary titles on their hosts. A memorable scene: Chiefs squatted cross-legged on one side of the deck, and girls, arranged in a row opposite, dancing their appreciations. Willie and Rose were at the forward end. A kava bowl was prepared for Willie and Rose to share a drink. Willie was horrified: "It would have been an exceedingly pleasant ceremony if, after the chief made a speech, the half-shell of a coconut filled with kava had not been presented to me."[54]

Willie knew enough about the making of kava to be aware that on some islands locals prepared the drink by chewing the kava and spitting the milky residue into a container. Here on primitive Samoa, it was unlikely that the Kava drink had been machine squeezed. His mysophobia roared up like a volcano, but he did his feeble best to remain diplomatic: "I took it, but drank as little as possible, praying that the germs I swallowed would come to an unexpected death before they should have time to play havoc with my physical condition."[55]

Straining to obtain a hunting permit in Australia, and rather than waste it, he made one more attempt and scored: "The chauffeur picked it up. 'My God,' he cried, 'you have shot a cuckoo. That's against the law.'" To which Willie replied, "That cuckoo should have stayed in his clock."[56]

Willie was persistent in everything he set out to accomplish. Desiring photographs of marine life, he employed an underwater moving camera manned by a helmeted diver. Movies of the voyage were kept on his own camera and included hundreds of feet of footage.

While in Australia, Willie had an unexplained and disturbing experience

Willie was something of a germophobe in his later years. In Samoa he took part in a Kava ceremony. Willie knew the drink was prepared by first chewing the kava and spitting it into a container. He wrote, "I took it, but drank as little as possible, praying that the germs I swallowed would come to an unexpected death before they should have time to play havoc with my physical condition" (courtesy Suffolk County Vanderbilt Museum).

after having taken a launch to Great Palm Island. Finding no appropriate place to beach, the crew had waded the last fifty yards to shore. They had become accustomed to the casual dress of tropical islands; the hot winds and piercing sun beckoned as little clothing as possible, and it was assumed that the natives did not require American formalities:

> Friendly, smiling black men greeted us. The expression on their faces, however, quickly changed to astonishment and excitement. This made us a bit ill at ease. We asked for Mr. Cornell, the superintendent, and they ... showed us the way. Mr. Cornell came over and greeted us courteously, but there was a slight anxiety in his manner as he glanced critically at Pierre. Then he told me that one of my guests was not properly dressed. Pierre had come ashore in flaming red trunks made of a material he had bought in Suva. Mr. Cornell said that Pierre must put on the coat, which he was carrying on his arm. This he did, but we were at a loss to understand the reason for the request.[57]

Mr. Cornell's request seemed wholly out of place to Willie. He found an explanation nine months later, after returning home. He fell upon "The Mad God of Palm Island," in the book *Crimes of the Year*.[58] The published account told of one Robert Curry, an Australian, who was sent by the Queensland Government in 1921 to serve as superintendent of Great Palm Island. Aborigines on the island had once been renowned for their habit of raiding neighboring villages on the mainland; they were deported to Great Palm Island in an effort to get them under control. His wife and two children, as well as a physician and his wife, Dr. and Mrs. Maitland Pattison, accompanied Mr. Curry. The foursome had made tremendous progress with other aborigines, and it was hoped that they could repeat their performance at Palm Island.

For ten years they worked with the notoriously difficult Bushmen of Great Palm Island. The group succeeded; advances in both social and economic spheres measured their progress. Curry's physical stature gave him god-like status among the aborigines; he could jump higher, swim faster and out-wrestle all contenders. "And he was so gentle and taught them so much wisdom that they thought he must be a god."[59]

Sadly, however, Curry's wife died in May of 1931. "With his support for all his new concepts of values gone, he went mad within a few days of her death."[60] Thinking that all around him were hostile, he donned the same fiery red trunks that he had worn when competing with the aborigines in the early days of their tenure. Using a hypodermic needle, he administered fatal doses of morphine to his two children and placed incendiary devices under their beds, the explosion of which set fire to the buildings. He shot Dr. Pattison in the thigh and killed Mrs. Pattison. Destroying one speedboat with dynamite, Curry and his abject aborigine worshipper "Mad Jack" fled in a second boat, shooting at everything in sight.

Still wearing the flaming red trunks, Curry returned in the morning, standing in the stern of the motor craft. With difficulty, Dr. Pattison explained to the aborigines that their god had gone mad and had to be killed. Fearing the danger that the wrath of a mad god could place them in, the aborigines reluctantly killed Curry. The natives experienced a combination of remorse and fear when they buried Curry — they had killed a god and feared reprisal.

Willie concluded, "I now believe that the Great Palm Islanders, when they saw Mr. Merillon in his red trunks, wondered if Curry, their god, had returned."[61]

For Willie, the story was symbolic of how instantaneously a man's life could change, and how he could one day have everything, and the next day have nothing. Change came suddenly and abruptly.

After the encounter, Willie's mood grew somber and his reflections turned back towards home. Suddenly, he was forced to contemplate the upheavals in his own world: "with economic conditions in the United States growing worse, we cannot stop everywhere." As the Depression raged onward, he was aware that any event beyond his control could consume him. He now wondered what fate had waiting for him on the other side of each hour. At twenty-one, he had been the accidental heir to the entire railroad kingdom. At forty-two, he had lost that kingdom to a government that was fighting a Great War. The Curry story reminded him just how much of his life had been an accident, and how little of it he had controlled.

Their travels home carried a sudden sense of foreboding. *Alva* carried them through shark-infested waters, islands once inhabited by cannibals, and waterways that were the denizen of pirates. In Ceylon he questioned his choice of residency: "Why do we continue to live in New York where there are elevated railroads, street cars, gasoline fumes, noise, and an Eighteenth Amendment to help make life unbearable?"[62]

Joined by his son, William Kissam Vanderbilt III, they proceeded to Marseille: "I am afraid he did not enjoy the trip, because we struck a bad mistral and a heavy sea from the westward."[63] A few days later, the younger Willie bade his farewells and returned to Paris, having spent precious little time with his father. Again, time seemed all too fleeting.

Willie K. in an informal pose, trawling from the launch off the coast of Viti Levu Island. September 1931 (courtesy Suffolk County Vanderbilt Museum).

Their voyage was over: "Rose and I are deeply moved as we take leave of *Alva*. We felt somewhat the same way when we left *Ara* after her last voyage. I have even stronger feeling about *Alva*, because I had a hand in her creation."[64]

In all, this third world voyage left Willie with feelings less triumphant and more sorely aware of the passage of time. A sense of mortality seemed to dog him at every turn. When Willie intersected with the International Date Line on the evening of Sunday September 6, he entered this journal entry:

It suddenly became the evening of September 7, and a whole day was completely erased from our calendar. Tomorrow morning will be Tuesday. Thus is West made East with the loss of a day! We shall keep on sailing westward and reach our starting point from the eastward. Inasmuch as this is my second voyage around the world to the westward, I have lost two days out of my life. To recover them I ought to make two circumnavigations to the eastward. But what would I do with them if I had them? If one could only gain two decades as easily![65]

Willie was worried about losing days, and yet could not find value in the ones he had. He was living life on his terms, living for the moment, and yet had no sense of how a few more days might be employed. It was the race he

had run all his life. The determining moment had arrived to tell if he had lived his life well or simply frittered it away.

Willie remembered Phineas Fogg, the hero of Jules Verne's novel *Around the World in Eighty Days*. Fogg wagered that he could travel around the world by balloon in eighty days. He headed east gaining a day and arrived to his reckoning five minutes late. Sequestered in his apartment, ensconced in a feeling of loss, he believed it to be Sunday. He sent his servant out on an errand, and it is he who discovered that they had gained a day and it was now Saturday. He had actually won his wager! At the realization of his accomplishment, he was overcome by a sense of loss. Where would he find meaning and how would he discover passion, when his entire journey was consumed by the passage of time?

Opposite, top: Rosamund and Willie among the natives of Great Palm Island, 1931 (courtesy Suffolk County Vanderbilt Museum). *Opposite, bottom:* Willie meets Palm Island native, Palm Island native meets Willie — "Each thinking how funny the other looked." Great Palm Island, 1931 (courtesy Suffolk County Vanderbilt Museum).

CHAPTER 23

Weep No More

Willie had spent much of his life trying to learn what it meant to be a Vanderbilt. Only upon the unfortunate deaths of close family members was the pressure alleviated, allowing him to finally see his own life in completely different terms.

His mother, Alva, considered "a martinet"[1] with an iron will, was always more lenient with him than with either of his siblings, Harold and Consuelo. She was partial to Willie K. stating, "He's the only Vanderbilt in captivity who ever got over his accident of birth."[2]

In May of 1932, a year after Willie had launched the *Alva*, his mother suffered a paralytic stroke, and by January 24, 1933, she was still in critical condition.[3] She died two days later.[4] Consuelo and her husband were there in Paris to comfort Alva, who died peacefully at eighty years of age. However, Harold and Willie K. were in New York, too far away and too late to rush to her side. While her life was celebrated broadly, her death was suffered personally by those closest to her.[5] Services were held in Paris, and when the body was transported to New York, they were echoed again. Tributes came from the National Women's party, which she had aggressively led and financially supported: "Mrs. Belmont's courage and encouragement in continuing the struggle for equal rights for men and women has been outstanding, not only in this country but throughout Europe.... There is not a woman living today who is not nearer the benefits and beauties of freedom because of Mrs. Belmont."[6]

Even in her death, Alva remained completely in control. She orchestrated her final rights, leaving strict instructions in her will for the funeral, which were carried out precisely. Limousines pulled up to the church and the ancient disembarked. Society's remaining greats arrived to celebrate the passing of the queen of the old 400. And she trumped them all by flying banners that read, "Failure Is Impossible."

The woman who had divorced first and best was, in death, a national symbol of woman's suffrage rights. The congregation rose during the processional as a choir sang the hymn "Weep, Ah, Weep No More," a "jubilant funeral hymn"[7] composed for the event by — of course — the deceased. In nothing less

Alva's death came among a triple spate of passings for Willie K., seen here leaving the funeral in early 1933. His son, Willie K. III, died in a car accident that year and his first wife, Virginia, never recovered from the tragedy, dying in 1935. Presumably, Rosamund is cloaked in black at left (courtesy of Suffolk County Vanderbilt Museum).

than a national tribute, Alva was laid to rest with her husband, Oliver Belmont, in Fairlawn Cemetery. No mausoleum on Staten Island would cherish her bones. The rights and freedom of women had replaced the Vanderbilts, their money, and all they stood for of the old Gilded Age. They could bemoan the misery of their money. It was past her now. She who had tumbled Mrs. Astor, built mansions that were havens of emptiness, and led the 400 as if it were a religious sect, now snubbed her nose for a higher cause.

Her last will and testament reflected the closeness achieved between Consuelo and Alva, who had paralleled in spirit, if not in method, their shared hopes for women's rights. To Consuelo went the honor of chief beneficiary, while Harold and Willie shared the responsibility of joint executorships. Marble House was destined to go to Harold, but never completed the journey as, after drawing the will, it was sold to Frederick H. Prince[8] for a fragment of its original cost at a mere one hundred thousand dollars.[9] To Willie she left a chapel in Woodlawn Cemetery and the premises at 9 Rue du General Lambert, Paris. Rosamund received rare recognition and was given "a long diamond chain and a single pear-shaped emerald pendant."[10]

Despite their mutual desire for women's suffrage, Alva and Consuelo shared little else in common. Alva had always been a domineering parent, controlling Consuelo's every action and forcing her into marriage against her will to a philandering and nearly penniless Duke of Marlborough. Consuelo finally divorced the Duke and became the wife of Jacques Balsan, enjoying a happier marriage and lifestyle. Alva's death also allowed Consuelo the freedom to renew her relationship with Harold and Willie.[11]

Willie's grief showed vividly as he departed his mother's service. He then embarked upon another cruise aboard the *Alva*, this time to Europe.[12] The passengers on this journey were few: his son, William Vanderbilt III, Mrs. Vanderbilt's children, Rosemary and Barclay Warburton, Pierre Merillon of Paris, and Robert Lancaster of Boston.[13] On November 8, after visiting Mediterranean and Caribbean points, they returned to Willie's new island estate on Fisher's Island off the coast of Florida.

Willie's son was not much of a sailor. Residing primarily in London and Paris, Willie K. III was anxious to return to New York to visit his own mother, Virginia. The two were close, as the twenty-six year old had spent much of his childhood with his mother.

After a few days, he left the group heading north, traveling with Erskine Gwynne, grandnephew of Alice Gwynne Vanderbilt. The chauffeur who would purportedly drive much of the distance from Florida was J.W. Guppy.

It was behind the wheel that Willie K. III would bear a striking and unfortunate similarity to his father. On November 14 at Bunnel, Florida, a bird flew through the windshield, sending glass flying and lacerating the young Vanderbilt's face.[14] Treated by a physician at Jacksonville, Florida, for minor injuries, and after the windshield was replaced, young William got behind the wheel again. The three men proceeded northward, a little less for wear.

The very next day, Mr. and Mrs. A.B. Stavely, New Jersey produce dealers, were driving their truck filled with Florida oranges and grapefruits when they suffered a flat tire along the long and straight road north of Ridgeland, South Carolina. Mr. Stavely jacked up the machine. Frustrated without a spare tire, he carried the flat for repairs into Ridgeland while his wife waited in the truck.

Sitting quietly in her passenger seat, Mrs. Stavely was unaware of the European limousine flying down the road. Willie K. III was behind the steering wheel. According to policeman Q.A. Nettles, first to investigate the crash scene, "Mr. Vanderbilt's car was probably going seventy-five miles an hour.... Mr. Vanderbilt thought the truck was moving and thus misjudged the distance necessary to turn the steering wheel and pass it."[15] It was one of those transfixed moments, with the rush of speed and wind, and that damn truck looming up ahead, altogether just too fast for even young reflexes to make appropriate adjustment.

The auto was wrecked from the steering column backwards, where it had glanced off the truck, shearing the right hindquarter. The younger Willie was jettisoned into the air, landing on his back on hard concrete. Erskine Gwynne was thrown farthest but landed best and suffered nothing more than scratches and bruises. J.W. Guppy had a broken leg and was pinned under the smoldering vehicle. Gwynne and Guppy were tossed from the vehicle as it tumbled over and crashed some one hundred and fifty yards away into the ditch. Remarkably, the truck suffered no appreciable damage and Mrs. Stavely was only mildly shaken. With the aid of four motorists, Gwynne rushed his relative to the hospital, but the last male descendant of the William Kissam Vanderbilt line died ten minutes later.

Gwynne took the young Vanderbilt's body to Savannah, where he awaited instructions from the family while the chauffeur went to the hospital for treatment.[16] A private car on an Atlantic Coast Line express train left at eleven o'clock carrying Gwynne and the body. In the company of his son-in-law, Earl T. Smith, Willie K. rushed to Washington to collect his son and bring him to New York where Virginia and his daughter, Consuelo Smith, were waiting.

Lying in a silver coffin under a "blanket of spring flowers,"[17] the body of William K. Vanderbilt III was brought to St. Thomas Protestant Episcopal Church where a few hundred witnessed the family's grief as a choir of seventy sang traditional hymns. Sitting next to the body of his only son, Willie was "motionless through the brief Episcopalian funeral."[18] After the ceremony, young friends bore him to an unadorned interment in the New Dorp Mausoleum.

Willie did not speak much about his loss. Instead, after the death of his only son, Willie handled his grief in traditional Vanderbilt fashion: he built an edifice. This third expansion on Eagle's Nest was profoundly personal and expressive. The death of his son precipitated construction of a memorial wing, closing the three-sided house with a fourth wing that enclosed the courtyard.

Willie K. chose one six-week expedition to represent the life of his son. He was deemed the Great White Hunter, and it became a trophy room of a single trip to the Sudan that Willie K. III had taken in 1931. A photograph of the victorious hunter and heavily armed native aids standing over an elephant unlucky enough to cross their path is converted into a mural-sized painting. The fantasy of a big-game hunter is made complete by an African diorama filled with a victims quarry and a room cluttered with trophies. It was a successful illusion: indeed he was "a big-game hunter." But he would never be a railroad man, as his father had hoped. Then again, neither would Willie. The imagery gave peace to the grieving father.

Ronald H. Pierce, a friend of Vanderbilt's and a Beaux Arts architect, assisted in the design work. The architectural details complemented the Spanish renovation of the house that Willie had commissioned a few years earlier during his second and most expensive expansion of the residence. Although fanciful, each room was functional and sized for its purpose. A narrow extension connected the new wing to the earlier house. The first floor of the memo-

In the fashion of an earlier time, reminiscent of his father and his grandfather, young Willie K. III traveled in 1931 to the Sudan, where, in one six-week span, he took so many trophies that even his proud father urged him to stop (courtesy Suffolk County Vanderbilt Museum).

rial wing expanded on housing the burgeoning museum collection, both ethnographic and marine.

It provided for a second floor breakfast nook equidistant between Willie's Napoleonic and marine-themed bedroom and Rosamund's newly created feminine, French-accented bedroom.[19] Rosamund gained a Hollywood-style dressing room, walk-in closet, and a bath of appropriate elegance.

The reasons for Rosamund suddenly requiring her own bedroom remain unclear. There were many theories. Some attributed the different rooms to their different schedules; Willie was reportedly an early riser and Rose enjoyed sleeping late. Some say that the two were copying European royalty who often slept in separate rooms, generally, because their marriages were arranged so they preferred sleeping apart. Of course, it could be as simple as the fact that Willie snored. But it was strange that suddenly, after nine years of marriage, Rose would need her own bedroom. Perhaps the death of Willie K. III affected Willie more than can be understood. He had lost his only son, the heir to his fortune and the final bearer of his name. Willie also grew severely ill around the time of his son's death. The heart condition that had prevented him from entering the Army during the Spanish American War had worsened until he required a nurse to live with him in residence. Rosamund was twenty-two years younger than her husband and perhaps a sick and grieving man was more than she could undertake. The creation of a distinctly masculine bedroom and a feminine counterpart also gave the two partners space for their distinct lives.

Through the eyes of a small boy, no greater image existed than his father as a great hunter. This photograph was found in William K. III's personal photo album. The boy accompanied his father to their Canadian hunting lodge, where this triumphant image was taken (courtesy Suffolk County Vanderbilt Museum).

Willie's relationship with Virginia was a deep connection to the past, a scarred wound, but perhaps with a lingering beauty as well. Certainly he had suffered his most difficult personal times with her. They had been separated for a quarter century, but at each family occasion there was warmth between them. They had parted as husband and wife, but had never broken the spirit of love that connected them.[20] Though in their divorce papers she had charged Willie with moral desertion and continued absence, and he had charged her with incompatibility and coolness, she kept the name Vanderbilt for the rest of her life.

Willie and Virginia had shared the most scarring event that two people can experience: the loss of a child. They both took the blow hard, but Virginia seemed to suffer physically from it in November of 1933, undergoing extensive medical care for severe shock.[21]

Indeed, the blow proved to be too much for her, and Virginia passed away on July 7, at the age of fifty-seven. While her death was merciful, considering the six weeks of torture her body had been subjected to, it was nonetheless unexpected and jarring.[22] Muriel and Consuelo were at her side when she died. A small memorial service was held and, while the children were present, Willie was not in attendance.[23] Nonetheless, when her will was read, her sentiment

Eagle's Nest mansion, ca. 1933. The Memorial Wing, the final addition to the mansion, was not yet constructed (courtesy Suffolk County Vanderbilt Museum).

was made clear. Willie K. was named executor, and he was referred to as "the father of my three children,"[24] but was not a beneficiary named in the will.

When she died, she was known as two things: "Mrs. Vanderbilt" and the "Silver Heiress."[25] Her glitter took form "as that of a sportswoman, art patron, and philanthropist by virtue of her father's silver fortune, her husband's social position, and her own vigorous personality."[26]

In experiencing the deaths of three family members in such chilling and rapid succession, Willie seemed struck with the idea of creating something immortal. His answer lay in the film that he had shot during his travels. The *Times* made note of a showing of *Over the Seven Seas*, "a travel film produced by Mr. and Mrs. W.K. Vanderbilt on a recent world cruise, will be presented today and tomorrow at the Lenox Little Theatre by the Finch Alumnae Association for the benefit of the Finch Day Nursery."[27] A month later it was shown at the Plaza Theatre[28] and reviewed by Mordaunt Hall as "an extremely interesting compilation of scenes, with a few sequences pictured by the multicolor process."[29] By September, *Seven Seas* was playing at Loew's Ziegfeld.[30]

At the same time, to find purpose and joy in his life, Willie K. turned inward. It was Alva who had stated that the secret to happiness was the pursuit of the day-to-day, to live in the world she was born to. For her son there was no solid footing in the world, no place to call his own. It was always a universe in transition. He was not to find himself in philanthropy or social causes that brought so much dignity to his mother, sister and other accomplished Vanderbilt women. Success in his first four decades was measured by meager business accomplishments, and later had literally washed out to sea. He may eventually have shed the prison cell of achievement but not without the help of a little delusion. For the seeker, it was always a universe in transition.

What was a rich man to do? Giving gifts would reduce taxes. Willie "gave to an unnamed recipient 2,000 shares of capital stock in the New York Central Railroad on June 26. The stock had a market value on that date of $34,000. Mr. Vanderbilt retained 40,085 shares of the road's stock."[31] In the ten days that followed the president's tax speech, Willie K. gave away five thousand shares of Western Union stock having a market value of $201,500.[32]

His cousin Neily shared a conversation he had with Willie:

"There is no point in dodging facts, Neil. In another ten years there won't be a single great fortune left in America. The country will come back — it always does; but we won't."

"What do you propose to do about? I asked.

"Do? What can we do? Everyone for himself ... I personally shall spend some of the remaining time in cruising aboard my yacht, seeing the world and trying to have a good time. If I were twenty years younger, then perhaps. Oh well, what's the use! I am not twenty years younger."[33]

CHAPTER 24

The Advancement of Science

In the last decade of his life, Willie received national recognition for the auto races he had commenced. In celebration of the thirtieth anniversary of the running of the races, the Smithsonian Institution added the Vanderbilt Cup to its collection. Before the Christmas of 1934, the cup was domiciled in the museum's division of engineering and placed on exhibit in its new glass case.[1] It was more than a silver trophy; it was a piece of Willie's life.

Legacy was also on Willie's mind when he decided to publicly display his marine collection, throwing open the doors of his museum to the public by invitation every Wednesday from the period of July 4 through November 4.[2] The *Times* greeted the news with the following splash: "The museum, which has been enlarged [a second floor was added to the marine museum] by the erection of an addition during the last year, is considered one of the finest private museums of its kind in the world and is filled with specimens taken by Mr. Vanderbilt on his several long cruises on the yacht Alva."[3]

William Belanske, the museum's curator,[4] had a cottage at Eagle's Nest, so he was always available to take people on tour. This kind of public exhibition was decidedly different for Willie K. Behind the rudder of his yacht he easily commanded and enjoyed attention as the commodore. However, public scrutiny of his museum was akin to an artist revealing his work in an exhibition.

Willie chose the now-comfortable role of the naturalist. For the first time the concept of systematic collection creeps into his lexicon. Choosing the often peculiar, he gave commentary on his collection for an appreciative audience. For instance, after a flying fish struck him "a glancing blow on the head," Willie, the author of thousands of pages of travel writing, decided to question, analyze, and explore this fish: "Does a flying fish really fly? We were struck by the beauty of the sight when, in one glistening shoal after another, flying fish, taking to the air, shot away from the sides of the ship as from a common enemy."

He wondered how these creatures that expanded "their pectoral fins into wing like gliders"[5] could "stay afloat for such great distances if they do not actually fly like birds."[6] Willie came up with his own reasons, deducing that these fish soared in the air like "motorless airplane gliders, making use of air pockets in the troughs of the waves and upward-deflected currents above the agitated surface of the sea."[7] He considered taking slow motion film to discover the pattern of flight.[8]

Willie employed scientific tools at his disposal, as in using native divers who could stay underwater for two or three minutes, while he collected his specimens, repeating the dives numerous times until he ensured that "a given area is covered systematically."[9] He also demonstrated his sensitivity to variations between habitat and the passing of the day: "Because the animals that appear on reefs in the daytime are not always the same as those that appear at night, arrangements were made with Tane to fish on Punaruu reef by the light of bamboo flares."[10]

Willie's descriptions now leaned towards the language of the scientist. Employing proper Latin names in describing species, Willie differentiated between genera and other higher orders of faunal organization, positing detailed analysis that showed both his newly acquired skills as well as his love of form and function. For example, in describing a burrowing clam *Tridacna elongata*, he wrote: "Its fleshy mantle, protectively colored an intermingled green, blue, orange, purple, brown, and yellow, to match the coral, makes it hard to see. It possesses a strong adductor muscle, and when a man gets his fingers caught in its grasp, the consequences may be serious."[11]

Willie's penchant for self-deprecating humor was also still evident:

> Sometimes the net comes up fairly full, but frequently it takes time to discover what is in it. Then the crew is amused. "The mountain is in labor and brings forth a mouse." I have often thought that something like this must flash through their heads: "Think of it! Here's a large ship, with a personnel of fifty men, put to scratching up the bottom.... All this time and labor for a fish we cannot even see. The Commodore must be crazy!" But I am satisfied if we can only get a few new specimens occasionally.[12]

Yet, he persevered without the need for aggrandizement. Something else was feverishly eating at him; Willie was restless and unhappy when he was unable to find specimens: "Our haul today contained no contribution to the advancement of science."[13] Feverishly, he continued to collect for the museum. It had become his new child — perhaps the only mark William Kissam Vanderbilt II would leave on this earth.

CHAPTER 25

Flying Lanes

Willie and Rosamund were spending more and more time in Miami, acquiring a new residence there and attending various balls and charity functions.[1] His daughter Muriel, after a short-lived marriage to Henry D. Phelps, had filed for divorce in Reno by the summer of 1936.[2]

Still restless, Willie sought out another voyage. This time, rather than the *Alva*, it was a seaplane that carried Rose and Willie to their next adventures. Perhaps as Willie got older he preferred the easier mode of travel, though he would never have admitted such a thing. With a private air yacht at his disposal it was time for a trip, something more than a jaunt to Rio. Willie was off on another of his adventures, this time a flight around South America and over the Andes, which "had been our dream."[3]

Though the trip would recall yachting journeys of the past, Willie was not to be commodore on this voyage — he did not have a pilot's license. He had to be content with the role of navigator, passenger, and occasional linguist. In the company of Robert and Edie Huntington, and piloted by Earl F. White and Henry Gerstung, they logged some fourteen thousand miles in about one hundred hours from January 18 to February 11, 1937. Their choice of transportation was a Sikorsky S-43 amphibian, similar to those operated by Pan-American Airlines in their normal routes. Of course, for Willie, it had to be outfitted to his specific taste for luxury: "This type of plane, the largest in the world equipped for both land and water.... The spacious fuselage will be treated in the style of a living room with settees and deep arm chairs about the sides and special murals will decorate the walls."[4] Modified to suit Willie and Rosamund, the craft enabled them to carry up to eighteen passengers, two pilots, and one thousand pounds of cargo, while cruising comfortably at one hundred miles per hour.[5]

The only other privately owned Sikorsky S-43 belonged to multimillionaire Howard Hughes, but even he could not have made the trip with the support of Pan Am the way that Willie did, as Hughes was busy attacking Pan Am's grip on international routes. Willie, on the other hand, had familiar ties to the Whitney clan, one of whom was the president of Pan Am. This connection made the trip a possibility, as Pan Am dominated the skies over Central and South America.

As usual, Willie had taken every precaution to map out routings and obtain the required permissions from the various nations along the route. Pan-American Airlines provided considerable assistance, including strategically placed fuel. Always resourceful, Willie planned well in advance of his trip. He also expressed appreciation for the spaciousness in their aircraft as well as its numerous gadgets.[6]

Travel to so many countries required special permits. As Willie joked: "Tell him you want to get permission to fly over Cuba, Haiti, Santa Domingo, Dutch, French, English West Indies, Venezuela, British, Dutch, French Guiana, Brazil, Uruguay, Argentina, Chile, Peru, Ecuador, Colombia, Panama, Costa Rica, Nicaragua, Honduras, Salvador, Guatemala British Honduras and Yucatan; and then have a drink ready as he starts to keel over."[7]

Willie had loved speed his whole life, and was utterly impressed by the velocity the plane was able to achieve: "What a shame they had come and gone before it was even possible to remark about their beauty! And still there a lot of us looking for faster planes. A speed of 250 miles is not too fast nowadays, said a friend of mine, and it won't be long before we reach the 300 mile per hour average. And he predicted the time is not far off when planes will be able to encircle the globe along the equatorial belt in seven days' time."[8]

The schedule was rigorous, with early morning wake-up calls and very little flexibility, even when Willie himself wanted to stay longer at a particular destination.

Dedicated to "Bob *and* Edie, *Our Flying Companions*,"[9] Willie titled his first flying travelogue *Flying Lanes*. Far from the dry recordings of the journals of his youth, this later work revealed a more sentimental side as well as an understanding that most of his readers would not know much about the places he was describing. Yet as in all of his writing, his recounting of historical and geographical details was inadequate, save for his vivid description of French Guiana.[10] The most interesting stories lay always in his personal encounters and experiences unique to his trip. In Trinidad, he convinced a man with three large boas in a box to show them to the ladies. The man wrapped himself in the snakes and moved over to the motorcar. "My! Such an exit from the car and what they said to me — well, I better not write it. In the confusion and noise that followed, the snakes got irritated; one bit its owner on the nose and another proceeded to put its fangs into the calf of his leg."[11] Traveling by boat on the Amazon River, he was amazed by the steady stream of "chattering monkeys and all manners of tropical birds of the most brilliant plumage imaginable."[12] He marveled at the enormity of Victoria Regis water lilies, measuring some twenty feet across in width.

Every location Willie visited reminded him of somewhere he had already been. Santo Domingo city was "typical Southern Spain."[13] As they passed over the island of Martinique, Willie reminisced about visiting the area in 1909 with his friend David Barnes. He was separating from Virginia at the time and the process was painful, staying a week at the hotel, "a nightmare even now, when I think of it."[14]

Willie also began to show signs of aging. He no longer was up at the crack of dawn, ready to break speed records.[15] He also fell asleep during picturesque moments of trips.[16] His old superstitions crept in as well with Willie certain that he would succeed only on his sixth attempt along any course; six being his lucky number.[17]

As they flew over Buenos Aires in Argentina, arriving at Mendoza airport and greeted by the press, he was struck by the similarities to home. He was impressed by the cleanliness of the city of Mendoza with its spacious tree-lined boulevards and excellent climate. Surrounded by attractive vineyards, Mendoza lay in the basin of an irrigated plain, "an enchanting little spot dropped here in the middle of the desert."[18]

From Mendoza, the group flew over an amazing vista that included glaciers and handsome peaks in Santiago, Chile. Upon arrival in Santiago, they experienced the heavy rumblings of an earthquake in the Andean city.[19] After being temporarily lost in the clouds, they arrived in Peru where they took a tour of the capital city of Lima and its outskirts. From there, they ventured out to the Guano Islands of Peru, an area that Willie found exceedingly dreary.[20] Yet he optimistically took notes for future trips on the *Alva,* paying attention to areas for mooring as well as collecting marine specimens in the future.

His beloved *Ara* was converted by the Ecuadorian government into a gunboat to patrol and protect the fishing banks of the Galapagos Islands.[21] At one point they flew over her as she, in military dress, was being made ready for sea. There were global rumblings of war on the horizon.

The trip could best be described as an aerial tour hopping from one region to the next, with ample share of spectacular panoramic views. There was no giant whale attack or collecting for the museum. Nothing was hauled home except memories of a good time. Mildly plagued by the press, who turned out to be more interested in the plane than them, Willie expressed delight in being "ordinary."[22]

Willie's stomach for pain also seemed diminished. Skipping prison colonies and avoiding lepers, he stated, "There is enough sorrow in this world and, in our two voyages around the globe Rose and I had seen plenty of it. So we decided to remain where we were."[23]

The more of the world that Willie saw, the more he grew fearful about what he ate for fear of sickness and disease. After flying over Central America into Colon, where they spent the day, Willie remarked that the town's name had "no anatomical significance but was chosen in commemoration of Christopher Columbus. Formerly a hell-hole of yellow fever, the campaign against the mosquito has made the place as sanitary as a roll of surgeon's gauze."[24]

The whole crew adhered to strict diets of "coffee, eggs, chicken, bananas, oranges, and potatoes,"[25] and soon found the lack of variety in their meals maddening. Mainly to quell his own internal fears, Willie concluded: "Again I say I believe the imagination is the cause of eighty percent of all illnesses."[26]

As they passed through Panama, Willie grew sarcastic again, remarking that the canal was the "route that William Nelson Cromwell and Theodore Roosevelt used as a big stick to force the Panama route upon a hesitating congress and a bewildered citizenry."[27] Every place evoked memories; some more recent with Rose, including visits by dignitaries such as President Hoover who stopped on the *Ara* during his goodwill tour of 1928 when Willie and Rose had anchored their ship off the Gulf of Fonseca.[28]

His descriptions of his own sensations during his trip revealed the same childlike appreciation that had won the affection of Virginia and then Rosamund: "For fun try dropping 20 feet over the water and then see how things rush by. It certainly gives one a sensation and a realization of how you are being hurled through space."[29]

Guatemala to Willie was a "magnificent country"[30] that he found "colorful"[31] for both its "scenic beauty"[32] and its population, "largely descendants of Mayans."[33] By February, after flying all over the western side of the Southern Hemisphere, Willie and his companions eagerly looked forward to returning home: "Think of it! Home! My, how good that sounded."[34]

Upon reaching Miami, now home to Willie and Rose, after an aerial tour that covered 12,439 miles in 101 hours and 40 minutes, Willie said to Mr. White: "Congratulations from all of us, a wonderful flight!"[35]

CHAPTER 26

Repose

World War II did not stop the sweet romancing and socializing of the Vanderbilts. They danced and dined in public. One of their favorite haunts was the night club El Morocco, famous for its card tables where much of New York's café society escaped their fears of war over games of gin rummy and where the press agent reported to Marcia Winn of the *Chicago Daily Tribune*, "You see few privates here." Said Winn, "That was only partly correct. The visitors saw none."[1] After scurrying away to greet someone of consequence the press agent of El Morocco returned, "Now over there are Mr. and Mrs. W.K. Vanderbilt. They're in here often, and always at table No. 2."[2]

While the club was considered exclusive, there were many socialites such as Oscar, the owner of the Waldorf-Astoria, who never went to the informal bar. On his first night there, however, attending a birthday celebration, Oscar stayed until the wee hours of the morning. When asked if he found the club quite different from his hotels, Oscar replied: "There's a great difference. At the Waldorf when W.K. Vanderbilt sees me, he bows from the waist and says: 'Good evening, Oscar.' But here, in a night club, he sees me, slaps my shoulder and says: 'Hello, Osk.' It's wonderful — pure Parisian."[3]

Now it was *Alva*'s turn to wear battle gray. After ten years of traveling that included three trips around the world, Willie gave his *Alva* to the Navy on Oct. 27, 1941.[4] He donated his beloved yacht for war service.[5] The Navy quickly renamed *Alva* the U.S.S. *Plymouth*.[6] She became part of the squadron escorting merchant vessels from New York to Key West as a patrol vessel.

In the preceding year, though America was not yet in the war, preparations were already underway. In January, Willie also donated his airplane, a Lockheed Zephyr airliner, for American maneuvers in Orlando, Florida.[7] The following month, Rosamund acted as honorary chairman to host a tributary dinner at the Waldorf-Astoria, the proceeds of which were donated for civilian relief in France.[8]

Now sixty-three years old, having witnessed the shakeup of the railroads, the demolition of trusts and monopolies, the rise of populism, and having lived through one World War as America braced herself for the next one, Willie was well aware that the world was changing under his feet. His lifestyle had already become a relic of the past.

His daughter Consuelo filed for divorce from her second husband, Henry G. Davis, to whom she had been married for only four years.[9] Two months later, in April, the Reno court granted her divorce on grounds of cruelty.[10] Interestingly, Consuelo asked the court to then allow her to use her maternal grandfather's last name, Fair, instead of reverting back to Vanderbilt. In January of 1941, she remarried again, for the third time, to William John Warburton, formerly the husband of her cousin Grace Wilson, daughter of Neily and Grace.[11]

Anne Harriman, the wife of William Kissam Vanderbilt, passed away that same month in New York. Anne was famous for her philanthropic efforts during World War I and was presented the Legion of Honor by France in 1919.[12] She was buried at St. Thomas Episcopal Church.[13] Willie K. did not attend the funeral of his stepmother, but instead stayed in Carmel with Rosamund and Muriel.[14] The Vanderbilts, apparently, were not even popular among their own.

More passings ensued. Willie was deeply saddened by the loss of Arthur E. Harding in January 1941, a former lieutenant commander who had served in World War I and then acted as ship captain for many of his world cruises.[15] The time of pleasure cruises and flights had come to a standstill. The world was embroiled in a war and, despite Willie's desire, he could not maintain his leisure pastimes the way he once had. His pilot, Bill Cleveland, was put in charge of ferrying British bombers to the new flight base located in Bermuda.[16] The "Willie K.'s"[17] as they were now known in social circles, grew more involved in fundraisers for the Red Cross,[18] contributing ten thousand dollars.[19]

In all matters automotive, Willie K. had established a reputation as a pioneer, garnering approval and perks such as an honorary lifetime membership of associations such as the Automobile Old Timers, who held him in high regard.[20] In October, when the nation's auto show opened in New York to display more than two hundred new car models for the next year, President Franklin D. Roosevelt sent a letter of congratulation, approving of the industry's substantial contribution to the nation's defense. Older models were also on display, as were such invited veteran race drivers as Henry Ford, Barney Oldfield, Guy W. Vaughan, Captain E.V. Rickenbacker, and, of course, William Kissam Vanderbilt II.[21] The Automobile Old-Timers Association presented Willie with an award for "distinguished service in the automobile field"[22] at their annual reunion at the Roosevelt Hotel. Willie K. had gone from being the young whippersnapper at the wheel to the trusty stalwart of the first automobiles.

After the war broke out, the Willie K.'s stayed briefly in Paris in a quiet hotel near the Bois du Boulogne. Their stay would be cut short, however, as food shortages hit the city and many members of the French noblesse dined on turnips and water.[23]

In August of 1943, the U.S.S. *Plymouth* was on routine escort of a convoy from New York to the south. Ninety miles east of Elizabeth City, North Carolina, she made sonar contact with an unknown target later determined to be the German submarine U-566. She swung to port and was lifted upward by a torpedo exploding just behind the bridge. The *Plymouth* rolled starboard from the force of the explosion. From the middle of the ship to her stern she was in flames. Quickly, she rolled to her port and began to list. In two minutes the *Plymouth* was gone. It was one more sad loss for Willie.

The sinking of the *Plymouth* was tragic, resulting in the death of more than half the crew, a total of one hundred and fifty-five members, in shark-infested waters. Five other ships, including a submarine and destroyer, were also sunk.[24] While he was extremely proud that the ship's captain was awarded a Navy Cross for his bravery, Willie nonetheless was heartbroken to learn of the demise of his *Alva*, his erstwhile pride and joy. Ironically, both the *Plymouth* and the torpedoes that sunk her were built in the same German shipyard, Krupp Germaniawerft in Kiel.

The *Plymouth* had barely settled to the murky bottom of the Atlantic Ocean when her creator's heart gave out. The year had just turned 1944, it was January 8, and Willie passed away of heart failure at 12:32 A.M. at his home at 651 Park Avenue. He was sixty-six.

The *New York Times* had this to say as a summary of his life:

> Although Mr. Vanderbilt maintained interest in the affairs of the New York Central Railroad with which his family has been identified, he was best known as a sportsman. A man of reticence, not particularly given to social activities, he moved in limited circle of friends and was happiest when "inching" a giant yacht into her berth.[25]

Throngs of people attended the funeral. The lucky thousand or so that could fit into St. Thomas Church were joined by a few thousand more lining Fifth Avenue. Atop Willie's flag-draped coffin was the cap and sword of a Naval Reserve officer, an honor bestowed in gratitude for the generous donation of his yachts to the war effort.[26] In the crowd were leaders of the railroad world, naval friends, and representatives of all remaining corners of the old society. The pallbearers carried his coffin to the sailors' hymn, "For Those in Peril on the Sea," one of Willie's favorites. Willie K., the commodore, was at peace.

Despite leaving behind a sizeable fortune of thirty-five million dollars, thanks to Roosevelt's death taxes, the federal government was able to claim $25,000,000, and the state claimed $5,000,000.[27] All that was left for Rosamund was a scant $5,000,000.[28]

Other Vanderbilt estates began to plummet in value as well, thinning out the possibilities that the younger generations could inherit like their parents had. "Thus the capital accumulated over many years by older men is being appropriated by *the government* rather than passed on to heirs. At the same time, tax rates now make it impossible for new large estates to be accumulated."[29]

By late 1946, only one Vanderbilt was among the top thirty shareholders in the New York Central Railroad. Of the 6,447,000 shares outstanding, Willie's brother, Harold Vanderbilt, held 45,100, less than one percent and valued at just over $1 million.[30] When it came to American royalty, the reign of the Vanderbilt family had reached its end.

Willie's final act of generosity was the donation of Eagle's Nest as a public museum.[31] Within three weeks, Robert Moses, president of the New York State Park Commission made it overtly clear that the State of New York had no interest in taking Willie's bequest under its jurisdiction, declaring the endowment too small.[32] Moses, the road builder, had much to hold against Willie who justifiably could claim to be a pioneer in an arena where Moses would seek to make his mark. The Motor Parkway had been a bone of contention between the two men, with Moses seeking to build public roads that made the rich man's highway irrelevant. It was Moses who had resisted the logic of making the Motor Parkway part of a publicly planned effort. Instead, he forced the issue until Vanderbilt gave up.

Robert Moses announced the state's preference before the state had an option. Rosamund was alive and residing in the estate, nullifying Federal-State-County-Town options until she surrendered the property. The will had not been admitted to probate and the grieving for Willie was still in process when Moses co-opted the state's choices for the future. At a later date the County of Suffolk reacted in what appears to be a less personal manner and accepted the gift for the benefit of its residents. By decision of the Suffolk County Board of Supervisors, the county took possession of the estate, museum and grounds on August 30, 1948.[33] The museum was opened as the first Suffolk County Park in July 1950.[34]

Rosamund, at the young age of fifty, passed away from breast cancer at Eagle's Nest three years after losing her beloved Willie.[35] She bequeathed her personal possessions to her children, Rosemary and Barclay, and created trusts of her residuary estate to be provided for them. Apparently her heirs were unhappy with the arrangements and protested to the courts the validity of the trusts. It was their intent to have the corpus distributed.[36] They were unsuccessful in overturning the will, but stripped Eagle's Nest of all her possessions and sold them at auction.

Willie's mother, Alva, who had dominated the social scene during her tenure at the helm of the Vanderbilt family, had said, "Happiness is seldom found through personal romance but through practical usefulness,"[37] believing that her daughter Consuelo could replace her own loneliness with a "stream of engrossing thought for others."[38]

Consuelo had responded by reiterating the belief held by her father that work gave true meaning: "But if we have striven to think and to do work based on thought, then we have at least the sense of having striven with such faculties as we have possessed ... and that is in itself a course of happiness, going beyond the possession of any definite gain."[39]

After divorcing the duke, Consuelo had found happiness in the arms of Jacques Balsan and in her philanthropic efforts while residing in France, although she remained known as the Duchess.

Willie had eased the demands of gilded society by an amalgam of Rose's love, a bit of fantasy, and a dusting of illusion. Rose was uniquely dedicated to him, even at the expense of her children. He was the commodore, captain of all-sized vessels on all seas and he served the American Museum of Natural History as contributor and collector.

But where did Willie truly stand? For what would he now be remembered? The great-grandson of Commodore Cornelius Vanderbilt, he was the last Vanderbilt to operate the family railroad business. He was a racecar driver, pilot, yachtsman, amateur scientist, and travel writer. His love of the sea led him to launch trips all over the world, create a marine museum, and collect rare and endangered specimens.

As a young man, Willie K. had gained a reputation for his motorcar racing feats and daredevil nature. Willie had pioneered the concept of a speedway, the sixty-mile Long Island Motor Parkway,[40] launched an automobile race that bore his name, and left behind thousands of travelogue pages filled with amusing anecdotes, detailed directions, photographs, and illustrations that would serve as the first travel guides for the American Automobile Association. His Vanderbilt Cup paved the way for the famous automobile races at Daytona Beach. His other racing-related venture, the Long Island Motor Parkway, was the forerunner to the first limited access highway.

And in many ways, Willie K. was, in fact, a visionary. He consistently looked to the future and pushed good ideas ahead of their time.

Willie K. Vanderbilt came of age just as America drew the curtain on the era of the "royally wealthy," and he found himself demoted from American royalty to "plain old rich." He was not in the same social position as his great-grandfather Cornelius Vanderbilt, who had created the family fortune and whose legacy was one of privilege and favoritism, passing along the bulk of his estate to his son William Henry. Subsequent generations did not possess the same genius for business as the founder, diluting the power of railroad domination wielded by the family.[41] Wealth, as the commodore proved, was the result of hard work, drive, intelligence, and vision and only the desire for success could sustain such an empire. Mere management alone, in the form of maintaining stocks, was insufficient.

The Vanderbilts, once one of the most powerful families in the country, had become more famous for their leisure activities such as racing, yachting, and contributing to the social 400 than for any business acumen. The Vanderbilts were also a family of individuals with each member following his own course and lacking the same devotion to tight-knit family affairs as members of wealthy dynasties such as the Rockefeller and Ford families.

It was a vanishing legacy; one that William Kissam Vanderbilt II was acutely aware of in his own lifetime. It vexed him deeply. By the time he arrived on the scene as a fourth-generation Vanderbilt, it was too little and too late. Neither Willie nor any of his cousins possessed the same purpose, vision, or prowess of the Commodore. The world that Willie K. inhabited was also no longer infatuated with the costume balls that had made his mother, Alva, famous.[42] He had seen the crash of the stock market, two world wars, a great depression, and a complete restructuring and pillaging of the railroads themselves. New taxation introduced by Roosevelt ate away at Vanderbilt fortunes, which no longer reaped the same dividends they had enjoyed earlier in the century. Expectation and compulsion to actually accomplish something during his lifetime, to live up to his inherited social status, haunted Willie K. throughout his life.

Willie was an enthusiastic and energetic man; the kind of person who could jump wholeheartedly into an endeavor without hesitation. Trustworthy and amiable, Willie always enjoyed the company of friends. His possessed a curious and imaginative nature, ready to engage quickly in new ideas as well as athletic pursuits with ease and good humor.

Willie had tried his hand at many things: running a business, racing cars and yachts, working in the railroad business, and serving in the navy. In the last two decades of his life, however, Willie no longer sought the approval of the public or his family for what he did. Instead, he turned to the sea and to his favorite pastime as a child, sailing. It was here that he found his greatest joy and solace. The mighty ship *Alva* that became his ultimate pride and joy was, in the end, a grand recreation of his first little sloop, *Osprey*, on which he had discovered his truest love.[43]

Here he found the joy and serenity of a life, developing an appreciation for the wild, natural, and untamed. Perhaps his greatest value would lie in his efforts in revealing the beauty and wonder of the world, with both its fascinating variety and the universal nature of people that stretches across mountains, oceans, and continents. Through this kind of understanding, Willie hoped, we all "might make peace for nations."[44] Or better still, it might lay in our appreciation for the simple happiness of a man whose life had been so rich, who experienced so much, and who had managed to discover in the latter half of his life, the company of his beloved Rose aboard his yacht, the *Alva*: "I am in command, a responsibility and pleasure. Rosie is with me. Our dream is being realized."[45]

Epilogue

Willie and his close friend Charles Tiffany were hard at work, generating a solid blue haze in the nearby smoking room, doing their wicked best to chase the girls out in search of fresher pastures. It did not work, however. Mrs. Tiffany was happily sated by dinner and all the more happily tipsy from a generous sampling of madeira. Thus emboldened, she was in no mood to be dismissed.

Nodding toward Willie, she prodded Rose, "I know he wants to show it to us. It would be darling." As Rose spied her husband, circled in the wreath of smoke wafting from his fat, imported cigar, her female companion gilded the lily a touch more. "I hear it's magical. Charles and I would feel absolutely remiss if we didn't see what all the fuss was about."

Rose thought to herself, "He *would* enjoy it. What harm could come of it?" No doubt the prospect of a night surrounded by towering beasts and drifting through exotic locales was far superior to one spent bathed in the glow — and stench — of her husband's favored cigars and lulled to sleep by talk of mergers and acquisitions. To Mrs. Tiffany, the hostess signaled both acquiescence and a warning: "*Darling*, you must be careful on those horrid steps! If you will promise to hug close to that man of yours, I'm sure it could be arranged."

Meanwhile, smoke in the parlor was reaching proportions that might soon require a visit from the Centerport Fire Department. Both men were putting robust "Cubans" to good use, as if some unforeseen ban was approaching and they were compelled to burn as many as possible before the witching hour. To circumvent an indoor bonfire, Rose called to Willie, "Darling, I know you were once captain of a fire department, but must we have all your old chums here for our quiet dinner party for four? Why don't you put those glowing embers to better use and take us to the Habitat?"

Willie put on a look of stern consternation at the prospect, but Rose knew better. Few things pleased the middle-aged magnate these days so much as meandering amidst the accumulation of his life's travels, and she suspected that half the fun was making a grand show of just the opposite.

As if saddled with a great burden, Willie arose dramatically, motioning to

Charles with a loud sigh that they should "suffer the interruption and humor the girls." The women winked at their conspiracy while the men busied themselves with refreshing their drinks and wiping ashes from their creased trousers. With Rose at his arm and cigar in hand, Willie led the party out of the comfortable dining room and into the grand hallway that served as the entrance to his modest manse. Relatives from glories past stared down from their portraits, scornful witnesses to the wobbling exodus of the four friends. The quartet teetered out the heavy doors and through the roofed walkway, pausing at the sudden fresh reprieve of evening air. Continuing on down the steep, dimly lit stone stairs, the couples snaked a meandering course into a small cluster of boxwood gardens where day lilies huddled, closed for the night. Were it a sunny midday, the boxwoods would have offered an enclosed effusion of splendid, carefully planned color to guide the way, but now they made for little more than an obstacle course along the passageway to sights much grander.

A handsome sundial stood timeless in the path as shadows, cast by an array of lanterns overhead, gave the sensation that it was any time one wished it to be — depending solely upon the mood.

The stairs farther on, leading to the grotto's lower level, were even more dimly lit. From the woods, a stone elf peered silently, observing the slow deliberate steps of the ever-so-slightly inebriated ensemble. Finally, out of the woods and on a landing as unsuspecting as it was unassuming, they found themselves before two massive wooden doors framed by an intricate wreath of stucco ornamentation. There was no lock, yet Willie hesitated at the entrance. While the guests may have sensed drama, the host was merely waiting for an attending servant to arrive with the requisite bottle of champagne. Glasses clinked, announcing their arrival in mysterious chimes and leveraging the moment with a sense of exotic expectation — equal parts a night at the opera and day in a foreign land.

Before them stood the "Habitat."

The doors swung majestically open and, as if passing from one dimension to another, all walked inside. Before them lay an underground memorial to one man's idiosyncratic, emotional formulation of his autobiography.

They hesitated only for a final moment at the threshold so that their eyes might adjust to the preternatural dawn. At this point, nothing was visible except a luminescent blue floor, eerie in its glow and surreal in its presence. There was no other dimension. This was exactly as it was meant to be: an entirely new world where floors glowed and monsters prowled. Visual dissection was less the goal than simple awe. As was true of Willie's other collections— his mansions, his cars, and his speedways— this place was part science, part technology, part entertainment, and mostly sheer delight.

Ever the patient host, Willie allowed his guests time to acclimate to the unexpected environs hidden at the bottom of a grotto. Even so, he had to force himself to recall that this was their first time, and that what to him was commonplace was to the Tiffanys a unique and somewhat unsettling experience. As if relishing the anticipation, Rose delicately slipped her hand under Willie's elbow, secretly pleased to take the journey once again — and with such fine company. It was always more enjoyable when the guests were new to the experience.

Willie smiled in the darkness, now the ringmaster to the awaiting circus of visual and visceral delights. Rosamund stood by his side with her right arm now entwined in his left, and her fingers reaching tantalizingly down the inside of his wrist. She clearly knew he was enjoying the moment and wanted to heighten his sensation in a way only a woman's touch could provide. Her fingernails lightly traced the tendons above his wrist, offering both a slight tickle as well as a mild seduction.

In the past year they had orchestrated visits such as this repeatedly; it was sweetness for Willie and she understood — and shared — it. Hosts and guests enjoyed the habitat tour alike, if separately. For the Vanderbilts this was a living photo album, each element reminiscent of past adventures, be they retreat or romance, adventure or amour.

With Willie purposefully on the left, the guests had no choice but to pass through the right door. Their eyes were fixed on the luminescent blue square; all else was a velvety darkness. Their natural reaction, like so many others before them, was to stop at the threshold, then inch forward and to the left, pivoting toward their host and hostess. Such specific posturing now allowed Willie to lead them at his will.

Moderate steps by Willie brought small steps by his guests, who made feeble progress toward their left. Each time they hesitated, Willie pressed on in seeming acceleration. But he led them away from the blue intensity, instead into a murky void. It was a deftly practiced and well-choreographed ballet for the tour guide. To seduce one by the allure of the magical room, first impressions were of the utmost importance, and therefore needed to be firmly controlled by the host.

To his practiced eye, Willie could make out familiar shapes and the reflection of brass foot rail, the signal to the end of their short detour. By design, his guests remained blinded by the void. Quietly, with implacable stealth, he reached forward with his right foot, his toe feeling, stretching for something. All was silent. Then he found it, and with a satisfied, invisible grin, his toe moved on, applying a most subtle, undetected pressure.

Suddenly, an expanse of light shot open before them, sending a gloomy radiance against blackness all around. Before them two shining black orbs, drawn together by a curving line made of row upon row of sharp white teeth, drew a gasp of terror from the Tiffanys. They stood face to face before certain death. The black eyes that stared back were so evil in their menacing glare that the couple was convinced they would be pounced upon in the next instant. Jaws agape, teeth gleaming, the great creature meant no less than to devour. It was only after the shark remained motionless for innumerable heartbeats that the guests understood. They slowly gathered a sense of the glass between them and their doom; they began to understand that what they saw before them was real, but bore no real threat. Calm and good sense gradually returned.

The great white hovered in magical suspension, seemingly occupied with other prey. Below lay some kind of shipwreck, accurate in detail down to the placement of barnacles and shattered beams. Beneath the shark and the ship's broken ribcage lay a bed of crisp white sand marking the waterless ocean's floor, dotted here and there with odd crustaceans of the deep-water variety, carefully showing their best sides. Nearby slunk another shark, this one in profile, his gills alight and his muscular, rippling skin awash in the shadowy glow that doubled for the ocean's briny depths. Grouper and other saltwater fish lingered in the wings, but the great white commanded center stage, its endlessly open mouth and immortalized rows of sharp, white teeth symbolizing into perpetuity his ability to inspire fear.

The surprise was over, and Willie had had his chance to steal years of good health from these guests. He asked them to make a careful about-face and retrace their steps around the blue light to the other side of the room. More delights awaited them — and not all of them visual. They were met with a selection of delicious canapés and more champagne, doled out on silver trays by liveried servants, their presence no less surreal than stuffed sharks or lungless grouper. Not surprisingly, in Willie's strange undersea world, the only thing to drink seemed to contain alcohol.

Meanwhile, the guests became happily consumed with the game of searching for the brass foot rail and whatever gave Willie the power to bring light over darkness in the room's murky depths. He again separated himself, this time behind them, and threw them all into a mild conniption when he struck a match and lit a cigar. But, for once, it was not part of the act. Willie was simply a dedicated lover of fine cigars. Thankfully, though, the intermittent glow of another Cuban was like a bell tied to the neck of a stealthy cat. The guests could follow Willie more easily as they spied the glow of what might well have been a giant firefly in the night.

Off he went with his guests in pursuit, Rose trailing behind, full of champagne and giggles. His foot finally found its mark, and a scene of startling color exploded in front of them. Given their recent harrowing brush with death, the layered rainbow of Caribbean coral reef was a welcome relief. Cheery striped sergeant majors, with bars of color vertically lining their sides, appeared to frolic with a clutch of small-mouthed parrotfish. The colors were vivid, beautiful, and dizzying, like a wedding bouquet gone wild.

Surgeonfish, with their sparkling slender bodies, exuded their potential for speed and seemed unimpressed by the visitors; they were much more distracted by a lurking barracuda that, much like the shark in the preceding scene, dominated not only the setting but also the senses. The brilliant-layered corals, stretching the length of the diorama, brought the setting to ecstatic life, offering an ebullient theater for the more friendly denizens to pose. Everything seemed so very real.

The barracuda's lean, angular body and rows of needle-like teeth provided the guests with a reminder of their chilling experience of only moments before. Mrs. Tiffany took a cursory glance over her shoulder back into the darkness, but the great white lay hidden beyond her gaze. Its disappearance seemed no less troubling than if she had seen it smiling back at her. Willie deftly sensed the chill in the room.

Their excursion into the seascapes had now fully induced a most surreal mood. Willie's ethereal, wandering cigar and his ability to create light — or throw them into utter darkness — drew them into a world that was at once both stultifying and limitless. By allowing them to focus only on one depiction at a time, the room, and their senses, swam in and out of focus at their host's whim. The effect was no less than that of being in a darkened theater, but the guests were no longer an audience. They as well had become players on Willie's stage. The outside world had ceased to exist, and inside only where a light glowed was there reality. When the light was gone, that world was gone, too. In one fleeting moment, sharks circled and viciously threatened; in another, vibrant, magical colors brought delight and teased a smile from their lips. The danger and beauty of nature swirled into one, and the thick, pristine glass that once served to separate fact from fiction, had also seemingly melted away.

Such was the beauty and accuracy of Willie's fantastical world — each scene handcrafted, full of attention to detail and loving precision — so that guest and host alike were slowly transfixed. Tour became travel through time and space. While the Vanderbilt mansion above was replete with antique furniture and all its splendid accoutrement, here, ten feet below, in the sensual glow of blue light and champagne, lived a nether world of murk and magic, a realm of the incredible and unique, where Willie ruled the light, and his cigar led the way.

Knowing they were now sufficiently absorbed, Willie asked his guests to slide a few steps to their left. As they busied themselves with careful feet, their host surreptitiously turned off the light, and the Caribbean collage all but disappeared. Again, the blue floor offered its mysterious passage to their next visual intrigue.

For a long while they witnessed little more than a blue reflection in the angled glass. They had to wait while their host fumbled to find the foot pedal that would draw the curtain on the next scene. Such unfortunate lack of choreography could certainly be forgiven for the would-be showman. After all, Willie was juggling a cigar in one hand and a fresh martini in the other. Behind him, a servant materialized with a glistening tray and everyone promptly reached for a fresh drink. Charles murmured in satisfaction as a solid Cuban appeared in his hand. Willie responded with a turn of his wrist, bringing forth a long uncanny flame, leaping out of the darkness. Its wavering glow softly illuminated the surroundings in an unintentional but nonetheless dramatic way. Rose watched, silently bemused. She could almost see the wheels in Willie's head turning; no doubt this fiery display would become a staple of his act in performances to come. In that same instant, the waiting diorama sprang to life, while scalloped moldings phosphoresced in their shimmering whiteness.

Having withstood the excess, Willie's guests were offered repose in the friendly and familiar scene of a Long Island marsh. All basked in the warm light. It was peaceful, and yet there was a magic and mystique to this quaint and comely place. It was as if Willie had brought the same sense of majesty and the exotic of the previous vista to this simple local scene. He had grown up surrounded by marshes such as these at his parents' south shore estate, Idle Hour. The memories were sweet ones. This land, then teeming with life, was his first real experience with nature. But even he would have to admit that his tightly packed collection of indigenous birds in so small a space would have made an ornithologist wither and hunters explode. It was an odd sight in such close quarters, but such was Willie's creative immoderation. Nothing was complete until it amply dripped with gilded flair, even a lowly marsh. Willie was far more interested in artistry than accuracy. Their creator was never one to suffer image for mundane fact.

In the foreground, Eider, Mallard, Wood, Black and Harlequin ducks were paired in Noah-like fashion. Pristine couples alike in kind, and set neatly side by side, ambled toward one another in a way never provided for — nor indeed intended — by nature. Closer scrutiny offered up to the observant a collection of small and large shore birds, a hog-nosed snake, and a meandering red-spotted turtle. With so much fauna only a few feet away, one felt the need to remain stock still for fear it might all take flight. Mrs. Tiffany let out a sentimental sigh, observing that she had never been underwater, but had taken much pleasure in the birds of her home. Willie then explained that his intrepid Rose had actually donned a diving helmet and could attest that the remarkable colors of the previous diorama were exact to those seen in nature. Rosamund remembered curious sergeant majors coming within inches of her face while submerged, some even eating from her hand.

But much as he relived for his guests the singular moment in these gorgeous dioramas, Willie was, in fact, painting the panorama of his life. Indeed, this pursuit, like so many of Willie's, was essentially a personal one. It was an autobiography, the story of a scientist, an adventurer, and a seeker. Willie's money had afforded him scientific excursions his limited credentials could not. He was truly fascinated by life — in all its guises, and he forever sought his place in it.

The guests each reached for another glass and followed Willie's twinkling firefly. The happy Pied Piper led his clique onward. At first, the company of friends hesitated to cross the luminescent blue glass; so beautiful and ephemeral, they assumed it must be equally delicate. Willie strode on confidently, declaring that art could be both form and function, wonderment and walkway. They floated across the blue misted glass together.

As unexpected as it was breathtaking, the next scene was dark and tropical, a tangle of rich luxuriant foliage that offered limited vision and no clear sight of the horizon. Rose explained that they had spent time in Cuba on the return from their 1926 voyage, and had found the rain forest utterly impenetrable. Indeed, the scene before them was so encroaching it had an almost oppressive grip. The effect on the guests was all too sobering. Rose prompted a servant to refresh their glasses to buoy the tourists for the rest of the journey.

The Cuban forest vanished into the eerie, blue-lit void. The quartet retreated as well, leaving the darkly uninviting tropics behind, and crossing the luminous mist once again. The guests proceeded indecorously, as eager to refresh themselves on libations as they were to take in Willie's eye for detail and indefatigable flair for the dramatic. The mercurial host strolled merrily on, the cigar light bobbing and martini glass tinkling with the play of ice. Then he stopped suddenly, arresting his followers mid-stride. Intent on the Cuban, Willie took a long draw, his concentration punctuated by a torchlight of orange.

Click — and his guests froze again, now before a vast expanse of northern forest. Across a lake, quiet hunting cabins perched in view, just as they did in Willie's memory. The pain stabbed him as he remembered a photo taken by his son at the hunting lodge. He had bagged a broadly endowed elk whose antlers would seem to have made movement through the woods impossible for the animal. With bended knee and rifle on his arm he seemed small next to the towering rack, yet it was the epitome of manhood, always to be remembered and embraced. Yet Willie was the man in the photograph and it was the memory of a little boy, *his* boy, taking the picture that poignantly pierced his conscience. Where the others enjoyed the beautiful scenery, Willie was filled with melancholy memories of a child gone. When at last someone cleared his throat, interrupting Willie's reverie, he abruptly sidestepped the menagerie — as if by removing himself from its presence he could leave the memories behind.

In contrast to the beauty of the previous scene, the next was a sense of incongruity — unmistakable tragedy, in fact. A pair of bear cubs was making their way through the snow. Something seemed immediately remiss. Cubs belonged under the protection of their mother, but she was nowhere to be found. Willie could remember Hobart Nichols' frustrated comments about "gimmickry versus accuracy." Despite the snub, Willie was quite pleased at the effect. Someone muttered, as if on cue, "Poor dears." Willie turned to Rose, knowing the same emotion was sweeping over her, as it always did. He collected Rose on his arm, and the pair walked quietly away.

Willie finally came to a stop, but did not speak; there was no overture necessary here. By this time Willie's travels abroad were legendary. The very air of expectancy that suffused the broad, infinite room required no further comment.

The light flickered on, and a rookery from the Galapagos crowded into view. The guests were quite familiar with the Vanderbilts' trip to the Galapagos— everyone in society was. However, no stories or gossip could prepare them for the exotic scene now illuminated. The seaside panorama was rugged and covered with innumerable species of strange and extraordinary birds unlike anything they'd ever seen before. While his friends talked of density, diversity, and difference, Rose and Willie gazed in solitary silence. The host and hostess were as awed as their guests, though for much different reasons.

The embarrassing silence required mitigation. It came in the next scene. Willie and Rose were suddenly flowing with words while a wild island world came into view. Miraculously, Albemarle Island, part of the chain of Galapagos Islands, suddenly appeared and, with it, the world's largest ship in a bottle, the majestic *Ara*. The yacht was a known commodity, but the guests needed some guidance to interpret the dazzling art and biology. Willie and Rose launched into a cacophony of stories and descriptions, duly recounting their exploits, simultaneously confirming the legend that surrounded their trip and correcting inaccuracies of rumor in the process. They pointed here and there. Sea lions, land and marine iguanas, boobies and the like all had personal significance to Willie and Rose—like dear old friends from a very exclusive social circle. This was more than mere champagne and martinis talking. Though the pair spoke only in the language of natural history, it was clear that each explanation was a metaphor for something much deeper and far more romantic. The guests could sense the love between Rose and Willie and patiently listened as each story quietly raised more questions than were answered.

It was getting late and the climactic scene of Albemarle Island finally and reluctantly receded into its quixotic darkness. As a single body, the group simultaneously moved on, turning toward the doors. But Willie's story was not complete. There was one final curtain. The embers swirled again as he pressed the ninth button. This last was the most surreal of them all: a night scene where a dilapidated shore met the sea's edge and a long trail of the moon was reflected in the water. Off to the side, goats raised their heads in silent bray beneath the pale yellow circle. Bones lay ominously in the foreground. And in the center, a woeful burro, clearly in an advanced state of starvation, stood muzzling the bare volcanic earth. Dead branches protruded all around, leafless.

Willie quickly explained that this, too, was the Galapagos, though a far cry from the prior vistas so teeming with life and energy. These were the introduced species that swarmed over the islands like passengers through Grand Central Terminal. By virtue of sheer numbers, they extinguished all in their path. Nothing, regardless of its rarity or beauty, was spared, until finally the invaders, too, began to starve off. Willie was obviously forlorn in the retelling, his voice slow and shallow. For Willie, the scene rekindled those feelings of restlessness that had chased him throughout his life. The habitat and his collection,

though vast, would never be complete. A world on the brink of extinction —
just as he understood his own to be.

The tour ended thus, infused with the dry taste of mortality. The lights
flickered away and the grotto sank into darkness. The journey was a great success. Willie smiled in glee as glasses were filled until champagne danced on the
floor. The Tiffanys and the Vanderbilts toasted to life and all its richness. They
toasted to their host — and his grand accomplishments. They said their good-
byes, and Willie and Rose were left to face the evening alone, as they preferred.

Chapter Notes

Chapter 1

1. Arthur T. Vanderbilt II, *Fortune's Children: The Fall of the House of Vanderbilt* (New York: William Morrow, 1989), pg. 202.
2. Cornelius V. Vanderbilt, Jr. *Queen of the Golden Age: The Fabulous Story of Grace Wilson Vanderbilt* (New York: McGraw-Hill, 1956), pg. 54.
3. "New York Central in Mammoth Deal," *New York Times*, June 26, 1899, pg. 1.
4. "New York Central in Another Deal," *New York Times*, July 7, 1899.
5. Ibid.
6. "William Kissam Vanderbilt," *New York Times*, July 9, 1899, pg. SM2.
7. Ibid.
8. Ibid.
9. Vanderbilt, Jr., pg. 65.
10. "Mr. Cornelius Vanderbilt Dead," *New York Times*, September 13, 1899, pg. 1.
11. "Mr. Vanderbilt's Funeral," *New York Times*, September 16, 1899, pg. 1.
12. "Sudden Death of Vanderbilt," *Chicago Daily*, September 13, 1899, pg. 1.
13. "Rushes from Ocean to Ocean," *Atlanta Constitution*, October 10, 1899, pg. 1.
14. Edwin P. Hoyt, *The Vanderbilts and Their Fortunes* (Garden City, NY: Doubleday, 1962), pg. 333.
15. "Vanderbilt Will Read," *Chicago Daily*, September 16, 1899, pg. 7.
16. Vanderbilt, Jr., pg. 137.
17. Vanderbilt II, pg. 223.
18. Ibid., pg. 221.
19. Ibid.

Chapter 2

1. "A Vanderbilt-Fair Union," *New York Times*, December 29, 1898, pg. 1.
2. Ibid.
3. Consuelo Vanderbilt Balsan, *The Glitter & the Gold* (English County of Kent: George Mann, 1973), pg. 7.
4. "A Vanderbilt-Fair Union," pg. 1.
5. Ibid., pg. 88.
6. "Vanderbilt's Yacht," *New York Times*, October 1, 1886, pg. 3.
7. Ibid.
8. "Willie K. Too Gay," *Chicago Daily*, August 30, 1894, pg. 7.
9. "Great Ball in Newport," *New York Times*, August 29, 1895.
10. "She Is Now a Duchess," *New York Times*, November 7, 1895, pg. 1.
11. "Know Him? Peckham of the Harvard Advocate; Had the Journalistic 'Bug' and Wouldn't Be Suppressed, So He Founded That Literary Magazine," *New York Times*, August 20, 1911, pg. SM14.
12. "Willie K., Jr. Barred Twice at Monte Carlo," Unsourced article in WKII's clipping album, ca. 1903.
13. Undated article in WKVII archives, *Boston Herald*, SCVM.
14. Ibid.
15. "A Vanderbilt-Fair Union," pg. 1.
16. *New York Times*, June 4, 1905.
17. Ibid.
18. Edwin P. Hoyt, *The Vanderbilts and Their Fortunes* (New York: Doubleday, 1962).
19. Ibid.
20. Ibid.
21. Ibid.
22. "In Honor of Miss Virginia Fair," *New York Times*, August 24, 1894, pg. 4.
23. "A Vanderbilt-Fair Union," pg. 1.
24. Oscar Lewis, *Silver Kings: The Lives and Times of MacKay, Fair, Flood, and O'Brien, Lords of the Nevada Comstock Lode* (New York: Alfred A. Knopf, 1947), pg. 164.
25. Ibid., pg. 124.
26. Ibid., pg. 141.
27. Ibid., pg. 170.
28. Ibid., pg. 171.
29. Ibid., pg. 179.
30. Ibid., pg. 182.
31. Ibid., pg. 183.

32. Ibid., pg. 186.
33. Ibid., pg. 116.
34. Ibid., pg. 117.
35. Ibid.
36. Ibid.
37. Ibid., pg. 180.
38. "Hermann Oelrich Dies on a Liner at Sea," *New York Times*, September 5, 1904.
39. Ibid.
40. "William K. Vanderbilt II," *Town Topics*, January 12, 1899.
41. Ibid.
42. "Vanderbilt Not to Be a Catholic," *Boston*, May 8, 1899.
43. "William K. Vanderbilt II."
44. "Vanderbilt Not to Be a Catholic."
45. "Vanderbilt-Fair Wedding," *New York Times*, April 12, 1899.
46. Ibid.
47. "Vanderbilt-Fair Union," *New York Times*, April 5, 1899, pg. 1.
48. Ibid.
49. Lewis, *Silver Kings: The Lives and Times of MacKay, Fair, Flood, and O'Brien, Lords of the Nevada Comstock Lode*, pg. 206.
50. Ibid.
51. "Vanderbilt-Fair Union," pg. 1.

Chapter 3

1. "Vanderbilt Villa Burned," *New York Times*, April 12, 1899, pg. 1.
2. Ibid.
3. Robert B. MacKay, Anthony Baker, and Carol Traynor, *The Long Island Country Houses and Their Architects, 1860–1940* (New York: W.B. Norton, 1997), pg. 218.
4. "Vanderbilt Villa Burned," pg. 1.
5. Ibid.
6. Ibid.
7. Ibid.
8. Ibid.
9. Ibid.
10. "Burned Vanderbilt Villa," *New York Times*, April 13, 1899, pg. 4.
11. "Vanderbilts at Oakdale," *New York Times*, April 6, 1899, pg. 7.
12. "Vanderbilt Villa Burned," pg. 1.
13. Ibid.
14. Ibid.
15. Ibid.
16. "Idle Hour in Flames," *New York Times*, April 12, 1899.
17. "Millionaires Risk Lives as Firemen to Save Village," *World*, April 9, 1906.
18. Unlabeled article in WKVII archives. SCVM.

Chapter 4

1. National Oceanic Atmospheric Administration. National Weather Review. July 1898.
2. Adonica Y. Lui, "The Machine and Social Policies: Tammany Hall and the Politics of Public Outdoor Relief, New York City, 1874–1898," *Studies in American Political Development*, 1995. Vol. 9 [2]), pp. 386–403.
3. Joseph W. Campbell, *Yellow Journalism: Puncturing the Myths, Defining the Legacies* (Westport, CT: Greenwood, 2001), pg. 122.
4. Robert Sobel, *The Entrepreneurs: Explorations within the American Business Tradition* (New York: Weybright & Talley, 1974), Chapter 4.
5. Michael P. Malone, *James J. Hill: Empire Builder of the Northwest* (Norman: University of Oklahoma Press, 1996), pp. 142–50.
6. Ron Chernow, *The House of Morgan: An American Banking Dynasty and the Rise of Modern Finance* (New York: Grove Press, 2001), pp. 100–101.
7. Jean Strouse, *MORGAN: American Financier* (New York: Harper Perennial, 1999), pp. 265–66.
8. Chernow, *The House of Morgan: An American Banking Dynasty and the Rise of Modern Finance*, pp. 100–101.
9. "$217,000,000," *Boston Daily*, February 10, 1886, pg. 5.
10. Ibid.
11. "Mr. Vanderbilt Retires," *New York Times*, May 5, 1883, pg. 8.
12. "Vanderbilt's Yacht," *New York Times*, October 1, 1886, pg. 3.
13. "Light on Two Important Questions," *Chicago Daily Tribune*, May 5, 1895, pg. 47.
14. Ibid.
15. Ibid.

Chapter 5

1. "Carmita at Lawley's Yard," *Boston Daily Globe*, April 18, 1899, pg. 7.
2. "Young Vanderbilt's Modest Honeymoon," *Newport Herald*, April 20, 1899.
3. Ibid.
4. Ibid.
5. Sidney Kirkpatrick, *The Revenge of Thomas Eakins* (New Haven, CT: Yale University Press, 2006), pg. 157.
6. Ibid.
7. William K. Vanderbilt, Jr., *The Log of My Motor 1899–1908: Being A Record of Many Delightful Days Spent in Touring the Continent* (New York: Privately published, 1908).
8. Ibid., pg. x.
9. Ibid.
10. Ibid., pg. xii.
11. Ibid., pg. xiii.
12. Ibid.
13. Ibid., pg. xv.

14. Ibid.

15. Ibid., pg. xvi.

16. Ibid., pg. 17.

17. Ibid., pg. xix.

18. Ibid., pg. 18.

19. Ibid., pp. 74–5.

20. Ibid., pg. 72.

21. Ibid., pg. 70.

22. Ibid., pg. 26.

23. Ibid., pg. 118.

24. Ibid., pg. 76.

25. Ibid., pg. 82.

26. Beverly Rae Kimes, "Willie K.: The Saga of a Racing Vanderbilt," *Automotive Quarterly* 40, no. 3 (1904).

27. Ibid.

28. Ibid.

29. Ibid.

30. Ibid.

31. Ibid.

32. Ibid.

33. Frederick Lewis Allen and William L. O'Neill, *The Big Change: America Transforms Itself 1900–1950* (New Brunswick, NJ: Transaction, 1992), pg. 7.

34. Vanderbilt, Jr., *The Log of My Motor 1899–1908: Being A Record of Many Delightful Days Spent in Touring the Continent*, pg. 56.

35. Kimes, "Willie K.: The Saga of a Racing Vanderbilt."

36. Ibid.

37. "Vanderbilt Fined for Scorching," *New York Journal*, June 1900.

38. Kimes, "Willie K.: The Saga of a Racing Vanderbilt."

39. "Newport's Automobile Races; William K. Vanderbilt, Jr.'s, French Vehicle Carried Off Two Prizes," *New York Times*, September 7, 1900, pg. 7.

40. "Almost a Tragedy at Newport," *Newport Herald*, September 7, 1900.

41. Kimes, "Willie K.: The Saga of a Racing Vanderbilt."

42. "Willie Vanderbilt Near Death on an Automobile," *New York Journal*, July 5, 1899.

43. Untitled article, *New York World*, 1903. WKVII collection, SCVM.

44. Ibid.

45. Howard Kroplick, *Vanderbilt Cup Races of Long Island* (Chicago: Arcadia, 2008), pg. 14.

46. Lloyd R. Morris, *Not So Long Ago* (New York: Random House, 1949), pg. 271.

47. Michael L. Berger, *The Devil Wagon in God's Country — The Automobile and Social Change in Rural America, 1893–1929* (Hamden, CT: Archon Books, 1979), pg. 25.

48. "Young Vanderbilt Warned at Police Station," *New York Journal*, June 12, 1899.

49. "'Arrest Me Every Day, if You Want To,' Says Mr. Vanderbilt," Copyright 1900 by W.R. Hearst.

50. *New York Times*, June 8, 1900.

51. Ibid.

52. "Vanderbilt Tells Why He Quits Newport," *Newport Journal*, September 16, 1901.

53. Michael L. Bromley, *William Howard Taft and the First Motoring Presidency, 1909–1913* (Jefferson, NC: McFarland, 2003), pg. 89.

54. "A Dog from the Machine," Unlabeled article, WKVII collection SCVM, May 5, 1905.

55. Unlabeled article, *St. Louis Star*, WKVII collection, SCVM.

56. Ibid.

57. Berger, *The Devil Wagon in God's Country — The Automobile and Social Change in Rural America, 1893–1929*, pg. 19.

58. Murine Eye Drops advertisement. WKVII collection, SCVM.

59. "One Woman Who Did Not Jump" (Cartoon) WKVII collection, SCVM.

60. Ibid.

61. "William K. Vanderbilt, Jr.'s French Vehicle Carried Off Two Prizes," *New York Times*, September 7, 1900, pg. 7.

Chapter 6

1. *The World*, September 15, 1901.

2. "Vanderbilt's Yacht Launched," May 27, 1900, pg. 8.

3. "First Race for Four Seventy-Footers," *Town Topics*, July 15, 1900.

4. "Vanderbilts in Match Race," *The World*, July 12, 1900.

5. *New York Herald*, August 6, 1901.

6. *The World*, July 13, 1900.

7. *New York Journal*, July 15, 1900.

8. *New York Journal*, August 8, 1900.

9. "New Vanderbilt Heiress," *New York Times*, November 25, 1900, pg. 12.

10. "W.K. Vanderbilt, Jr. Seriously Burned by Exploding Lamp," *Post Telegram*, July 7, 1900, pg. 15.

11. *New York Telegraph*, July 23, 1903.

12. "The Red Devil," *The Hartford Courant*, July 27, 1901, pg. 14.

13. William Randolph Hearst, "'Arrest Me Every Day if You Want To' Says Mr. Vanderbilt," copyright 1900 by W.R. Hearst.

14. "The American Locomotive versus Fournier," *Life*, December 5, 1901, pg. 499.

15. Beverly Raes Kimes, "Willie K.: The Saga of a Racing Vanderbilt," *Automotive Quarterly* 40, no. 3 (1904).

16. "The Red Devil," *The Hartford Courant*, July 27, 1901, pg. 14.

17. "W.K. Vanderbilt, Jr. a Bold Life Saver," *New York Times*, Sept 14, 1901, pg. 7.

18. *New York Times*, September 14, 1901, pg. 7.

19. Kimes, "Willie K.: The Saga of a Racing Vanderbilt."

20. *New York World*, March 23, 1903.
21. Ibid.
22. Ibid.
23. Ibid.
24. *New York Herald*, August 12, 1903.
25. *New York Evening Post*, 1903, Box 1346, WKII, pg. 131.
26. *Automobile Topics*, March 5, 1904.
27. Ibid.
28. *New York American*, September 27, 1904.
29. Ibid.
30. Ibid.
31. *Town Topics*, December 29, 1904.
32. *The World*, December 10, 1905.

Chapter 7

1. *New York Times*, November 25, 1900.
2. *The Hartford Courant*, June 12, 1902, pg. 10.
3. "W.K. Vanderbilt, Jr., Seeking to Buy Mysterious Lake," New York Times, June 15, 1902, pg. 28.
4. Ibid.
5. "One of those Bottomless Lakes," *The Hartford Courant*, June 12, 1902, pg. 10.
6. Ibid.
7. Ibid.
8. Ibid.
9. *Sun*, August 5, 1902.
10. *Brooklyn Eagle*, July 20, 1902.
11. "Birdseye View of Mr. Vanderbilt's New Estate at Success Lake," *New York Herald*, February 15, 1903.
12. "William Vanderbilt, Jr. to Beautify Lake Success," *Brooklyn Eagle*, July 20, 1902.
13. Ibid.
14. *New York Herald*, August 7, 1902.
15. "William Vanderbilt, Jr. to Beautify Lake Success."
16. Ibid.
17. *Town Topics*, November 13, 1902.
18. *New York Telegram*, June 5, 1902.
19. *Town Topics*, November 13, 1902.
20. "Vanderbilt Fails to Get Lake He Covets," *Journal*, September 17, 1902.
21. Ibid.
22. Ibid.
23. "As to Lake Success," *Brooklyn Standard Union*, September 17, 1902.
24. "Vanderbilt, Jr. Seizes Lake Success," *Journal*, September 18, 1902.
25. Ibid.
26. Ambrose Bierce, *Town Topics*, 1902.
27. Ibid.
28. Ibid.
29. "A Very Knotty Question Raised in the Lake Success Matter," *Brooklyn Eagle*, October 23, 1903.
30. "Vanderbilt's Land Purchase," *New York Times*, March 14, 1903, pg. 2.
31. "Vanderbilt as Speech Maker," *New York Journal*, October 31, 1903.
32. "A Very Knotty Question Raised in the Lake Success Matter."
33. "Vanderbilt Gets Right of Way to the Lake," *New York Press*, October 31, 1903.
34. "W.K. Vanderbilt Gets Lease," *New York Times*, October 31, 1903, pg. 6.
35. "Vanderbilt Wins Fight for Road," *New York Herald*, October 31, 1903.
36. Ibid.
37. "Vanderbilt to Close Road," *New York Times*, July 7, 1904, pg. 9.
38. "Millionaires' Estates That Cut Off the Growth of New York," *The World*, March 15, 1903.
39. Ibid.
40. Ibid.
41. Ibid.

Chapter 8

1. Unlabelled article in WKVII collection, *Louisville Herald*, SCVM.
2. Ibid.
3. Ibid.
4. "American Gold May Help Russian Loan," *New York Times*, June 12, 1904, pg. FS1.
5. Ibid.
6. "Personal and Otherwise," *New York Times*, March 11, 1906, pg. X6.
7. "Vanderbilts Well Pleased," *New York Journal*, April 28, 1903.
8. W.K. Vanderbilt, Jr. Training," *New York Sun*, December 4, 1903.
9. Article 23 — No Title, *New York Times*, February 2, 1913, pg. T3.
10. Kurt C. Schlichting, *Grand Central Terminal* (Baltimore and London: Johns Hopkins University Press, 2001).
11. "Topics of the Times," *New York Times*, September 20, 1899, pg. 6.
12. Ibid.
13. Ibid.
14. Ibid.
15. "New York Central," *Wall Street Journal*, December 4, 1903.
16. Unidentified clipping in William K. Vanderbilt II's scrapbook, SCVM.
17. Schlichting, *Grand Central Terminal*, pg. 60.
18. Ibid., pg. 66.
19. "Façade of the Terminal the Keynote to the Structure," *New York Times*, February 2, 1913, pg. T2.
20. Schlichting, *Grand Central Terminal*, pg. 124.
21. "W.K. Vanderbilt, Jr.: 'Every Man Should Work — Any One Tires Soon of Frivolity — I Haven't Been Devoted to Pleasure,'" *The World*, December 6, 1903.

22. Ibid.
23. Ibid.
24. Ibid.
25. Ibid.
26. *New York Herald*, February 8, 1905.
27. Milton J. Platt, "New York Central," *New York Times*, October 11, 1903, pg. F1.
28. Schlichting, *Grand Central Terminal*, pg. 66.
29. Ibid.
30. Ibid.
31. Ibid.
32. *New York World*, April 23, 1903.
33. Ibid.
34. Unattributed article in WKVII archive, SCVM.
35. *New York Evening Journal*, pg. 49. (Album 1643, WKV, dated in heading as 9/4/01— probable misprint, with other articles in 1903.)
36. Ibid.
37. Ibid., pp. 82–84.
38. Ibid., pg. 87.
39. "Town Topics," October 27, 1904.
40. *Post of Grand Rapids*, July 8, 1905.
41. *The Herald* (unattributed article in WKVII archive, SCVM).
42. *Syracuse Journal*, June 1, 1905.
43. *Post-Standard*, August 4, 1905.
44. Ibid.
45. Ibid.
46. *Plain Dealer*, June 17, 1905.
47. *New York American*, July 1, 1906.
48. Ibid.
49. "My, Oh My, There'll Be Doings When Willie K., Jr., Comes to Syracuse," *Syracuse Telegram* (unattributed article in WKVII archive, SCVM.)
50. "Vanderbilt Smashes Record on Trolley," *New York American*, July 8, 1905.
51. *The Washington Post*, July 10, 1905.
52. *Rochester Post Express*, December 1905.
53. *Buffalo Times*, December 18, 1905.
54. Schlichting, *Grand Central Terminal*, pp. 82–84.
55. Ibid., pg. 100.
56. "Twenty-five Killed and Seventy-Five Injured," *New York Herald*, February 17, 1907, pg. 1.
57. Schlichting, *Grand Central Terminal*, pg. 101.
58. Ibid., pp. 102–3.

Chapter 9

1. William Kissam Vanderbilt, *Log of My Motor 1899–1908* (New York: Privately published, 1908), pg. xvii.
2. "W.K. Vanderbilt Jr., Proud of Last Race," New York World, August 2, 1902.
3. "Six Persons Killed in Automobile Race," *New York Times*, May 25, 1903, pg. 1.

4. Ibid., pp. 96–8.
5. Ibid., pg. 97.
6. Ibid., pg. 98.
7. Ibid., pg. 102.
8. Ibid.
9. John Tennell and Jackie Stewart, *Motor Racing: The Golden Age: Extraordinary Images from 1900 to 1970* (London: Cassell Illustrated, 2006).
10. "Vanderbilt Did a Mile in .39 Flat," *Boston Herald*, January 27, 1904.
11. "World's Auto Record Beaten by Vanderbilt," *New York World*, January 27, 1904.
12. Ibid.
13. Edwin P. Hoyt, *The Vanderbilts and Their Fortunes* (New York: Doubleday, 1962).
14. "New Auto Records Expected at Ormond," *New York Times*, January 22, 1904, pg. 8.
15. "World's Fastest Mile by Stanley Automobile," *New York Times*, January 27, 1906, pg. 1.
16. "Vanderbilt Cup Rules," *New York Times*, July 7, 1904, pg. 7.

Chapter 10

1. Robert Casey, "The Vanderbilt Cup, 1908." *Technology and Culture* 40, no. 2 (April 1999): 359–362.
2. William Kissam Vanderbilt, Jr., *Log of My Motor: 1899–1908* (New York: Privately published, 1908), pg. 139.
3. Ibid.
4. Ibid.
5. Vanderbilt, Jr., *Log of My Motor: 1899–1901*, pp. 140–141.
6. W.K. Vanderbilt, Jr. Back," *New York Times*, April 4, 1906, pg. 18.
7. Ibid.
8. "Vanderbilt Not a Catholic," *Town Topics*, July 13, 1899.
9. Ibid.
10. "Fair Case Settled, Lump Sum to Nelsons," *New York Times*, May 1904.
11. "Further Details of the Automobile Accident," *New York Herald* (European Edition: Paris). August 16, 1902.
12. Ibid.
13. Ibid.
14. Ibid.
15. Ibid.
16. Oscar Lewis, *Silver Kings: The Lives and Times of Mackay, Fair, Flood, and O'Brien, Lords of the Nevada Comstock Lode* (New York: Alfred A. Knopf, 1947), pp. 206–8.
17. "Costs $2,000,000 to End the Fair Will Contest," *New York World*, May 11, 1904.
18. "Contest for Vanderbilt Cup Will Be America's Greatest Automobile Event," *New York Times*, October 2, 1904, pg. SMA4.

19. Ibid.

20. "American Car Gains Friends," *Motoring and Boating*, November 17, 1904, pg. 265.

21. "Contest for Vanderbilt Cup Will Be America's Greatest Automobile Event."

22. "Heath Auto Wins; One Man Killed," *New York Times*, October 9, 1904, pg. 1.

23. Ibid.

24. Ibid.

25. E.P. Ingersoll, "Observations on the Vanderbilt Cup," *The Horseless Age* 14, no. 15 (October 12, 1904).

26. "Heath Auto Wins; One Man Killed," *New York Times*, October 9, 1904, pg. 1.

27. "The 'Great' Race," *New York Times*, October 9, 1904.

28. Ibid.

29. Ibid.

30. "Vanderbilt's Racer Altered," *Automobile Topics* IX, no. 12 (December 31, 1904).

31. Howard Kroplick, *Vanderbilt Cup Races of Long Island* (Chicago: Arcadia Publishing), 2008, pg. 38.

32. Ibid.

33. "French Racers Arrive for Vanderbilt Cup," *New York Times*, October 1, 1905, pg. 12.

34. "Vanderbilt Race Won by Hemery," *New York Times*, October 15, 1905, pg. 1.

35. Ibid.

36. "The Racing Effect in 'The Vanderbilt Cup,'" *New York Times*, March 12, 1904.

37. Ibid.

38. Henry Austin Clark, Jr., "Vanderbilt Cup Races 1904–1937."

39. "Autoists Are Anxious About Vanderbilt Cup," *New York Times*, April 9, 1906, pg. 6.

40. "Vanderbilt Buys Car and Will Race for Cup," *New York Times*, September 19, 1906, pg. 7.

41. "Vanderbilt Out of Race," *New York Times*, September 20, 1906, pg. 1.

42. "Auto Cup Race Won by Wagner," *New York Times*, October 7, 1908, pg. 1.

43. "Shepard Sells Auto," *New York Times*, October 26, 1906, pg. 1.

44. Erwin Lessner, *Famous Auto Races and Rallies* (New York: Hanover House, 1956).

45. *Chicago Daily Tribune*, October 26, 1906.

46. *New York Times*, October 7, 1906.

47. "Auto Race Next Year Over Private Course," *New York Times*, October 9, 1906.

Chapter 11

1. Richard D. Stone, *The Interstate Commerce Commission and the Railroad Industry: A History of Regulatory Policy* (New York: Praeger, 1991), pg. 31.

2. Robert B. Carson, *Main Line to Oblivion: The Disintegration of the New York Railroads in the Twentieth Century* (Port Washington, NY: Kennikat Press, 1971), pg. 47.

3. Albro Martin, *Enterprise Denied: Origins of the Decline of American Railroads, 1897–1917* (New York: Columbia University Press, 1978).

4. Carson, *Main Line to Oblivion: The Disintegration of the New York Railroads in the Twentieth Century*, pg. 40.

5. C.M. Keys.

6. Ibid.

7. Carson, *Main Line to Oblivion: The Disintegration of the New York Railroads in the Twentieth Century*, pg. 37.

8. Kurt C. Schlichting, *Grand Central Terminal: Railroads, Engineering, and Architecture in New York City* (Baltimore: John Hopkins University Press, 2001), pg. 196.

9. Carson, *Main Line to Oblivion: The Disintegration of the New York Railroads in the Twentieth Century*, pg. 47.

10. Ibid., pg. 48.

11. Ibid., pg. 44.

Chapter 12

1. Al Velocci, *The Toll Lodges of the Long Island Motor Parkway* (Mount Pleasant, SC: Arcadia Press, 2004).

2. "Varied Auto Advice at Annual Dinner," *New York Times*, December 9, 1906, pg. 10.

3. Ibid.

4. "60-Mile Auto Road to Cost $2,000,000," *New York Times*, October 21, 1906.

5. Ibid.

6. *New York Times*, October 9, 1906.

7. "60-Mile Auto Road to Cost $2,000,000," *New York Times*, October 21, 1906.

8. Ibid.

9. "60-Mile Auto Road to Cost $2,000,000."

10. Ibid.

11. "Long Island Speedway Assumes More Definite Shape," *New York Times*, November 1906.

12. *The Journal of Long Island History*.

13. "Millions for a Race Road," *Motor-Print*, Vol. I, No. 9, November 1906.

14. Ibid.

15. Ibid.

16. "Long Island Speedway Assumes More Definite Shape."

17. Ibid.

18. "No 1907 Cup," *Automobile Topics*, November 3, 1906.

19. "'The Apostle of High Speed' Is Young Vanderbilt's Just Title," *Washington Post*, November 18, 1906, pg. R12.

20. Ibid.

21. Ibid.

22. Ibid.

23. Ibid.

24. Ibid.

25. Velocci, *The Toll Lodges of the Long Island Motor Parkway.*

26. Ibid.

27. *New York Times*, May 19, 1908.

28. Ibid.

29. David Kahn, "The Granddaddy of Superhighways," *Lincoln-Mercury Times*, September-October 1955.

30. Typed notes of speech, Smithtown Public Library, Pardington Collection.

31. "The Modern Appian Way for the Motorist," *Harpers Weekly*, March 16, 1907.

32. "Thirty-three Cars Start in Five Sweepstake Races," *New York Times*, October 11, 1908, pg. S1.

33. *The National Monthly Magazine of Motoring*, 1907.

34. "Vanderbilt Back Without Entries," *New York Times*, September 9, 1908, pg. 6.

35. "Will Not Abandon Vanderbilt Race," *New York Times*, September 10, 1908, pg. 7.

36. "Motor Parkway Is Progressing Fast," *New York Times*, September 6, 1908, pg. S4.

37. Ibid.

38. Ibid.

39. *The Motor World*, September 10, 1908.

40. *The New York Times*, October 20, 1908.

41. Ibid.

42. Ibid.

43. "Vanderbilt Cup's Bad Management," *New York* Times, October 26, 1908, pg. 7.

44. *Evening Post*, October 24, 1908.

45. "May Be Last Vanderbilt Race," *Globe*, November 2, 1909.

46. *New York Times*, November 1, 1909.

47. "Changes Suggested in Auto Cup Race," *New York Times*, November 1, 1909, pg. 9.

48. "History of the Vanderbilt Race," New York Times, September 11, 1910.

49. "No Beds, Few Chairs, and the Crowds Out in the Rain," *Evening Post*, October 24, 1910.

50. Ibid.

51. Ibid.

52. "4 Dead, 20 Hurt, in Vanderbilt Race," *New York Times*, October 2, 1910, pg. 1.

53. "Met Death at Hicksville," *New York Times*, October 2, 1910, pg. C6.

54. "Little slip between the Cup," *Club Journal*, October 15, 1910.

55. *New York Times*, October 7, 1934.

56. Robert Casey, "The Vanderbilt Cup, 1908," *Technology and Culture* 40, no. 2 (April 1999), pp. 359–362.

Chapter 13

1. Edmund Morris, *Theodore Rex* (New York: Random House, 2001), pp. 496–503.

2. Jean Strouse, *Morgan American Financier* (New York: Random House, 1999), pp. 572–596.

3. Ron Chernow, *The House of Morgan* (New York: Grove Press, 1990), pp. 121–126.

4. Morris, *Theodore Rex*, pp. 496–503.

5. Strouse, *Morgan American Financier*, pp. 572–96.

6. Morris, *Theodore Rex*, pp. 496–503.

7. Strouse, *Morgan American Financier*, pp. 572–96.

8. Chernow, *The House of Morgan*, pp. 121–126.

9. William K. Vanderbilt, Jr., *Log of My Motor, 1899–1908* (New York: Privately published, 1908), pg. 171.

10. "Vacuum Cleaner Co. Fails," *New York Times*, May 16, 1908, pg. 16.

11. *New York Times*, March 8, 1908.

12. Arthur H. Lewis, *The Day They Shook the Plum Tree* (Cutchogue, New York: Buccaneer Books, 1963), pg. 2.

13. Ibid., pg. 1.

14. *Evening Journal*, September 29, 1909.

15. *New York American*, March 8, 1908.

16. Ibid.

17. Unattributed article, circa 1908, WKVII clipping collection, SCVM.

18. Unattributed article, New York Press, 1905, WKVII clipping collection, SCVM.

19. "Hard Times Bust Vacuum Cleaner Company," *New York Times*, 1908, pg. 165.

20. "Newport Preparing for Summer Season," *New York Times*, April 19, 1908, pg. C5.

Chapter 14

1. Edwin P. Hoyt, *The Vanderbilts and Their Fortunes* (Garden City, New York: Doubleday, 1963), pg. 351.

2. Ibid., pg. 353.

3. Cornelius V. Vanderbilt, Jr., *Queen of the Golden Age: The Fabulous Story of Grace Wilson Vanderbilt* (New York: McGraw-Hill, 1956), pg. 224.

4. "Son Born to the House of Young W.K. Vanderbilt," *New York Times*, October 31, 1907.

5. Unlabeled articles, October 31, 1907, WKVII clipping album, SCVM.

6. *New York Times*, August 2, 1908.

7. *New York Times*, December 12, 1908.

8. *New York Times*, March 17, 1909.

9. *New York Times*, December 19, 1908.

10. *New York Times*, February 1, 1909.

11. "Formal Separation Agreement Making Provision as to the Disposition of Their Two Children Drawn Up — Understanding Regarding Financial Affairs," *Evening Journal*, September 21, 1909.

12. "Mrs. Oelrich Pens Tribute to 'Frisco," *The World*, April 23, 1906.

13. *New York Times*, April 14, 1909.
14. *New York Times*, April 22, 1909.
15. "Vanderbilt Caught Speeding," *New York Times*, April 22, 1909, pg. 3.
16. "Fear Islands Are Gone: Acapulco Thinks 'Quake Sunk Clipperton Group in the Sea," *New York Times*, August 24, 1909, pg.1.
17. *New York Times*, August 25, 1909.
18. Ibid.
19. "W.K. Vanderbilt, Jr. and Wife Parted?" *New York Times*, September 22, 1909, pg. 9.
20. *Evening Journal*, September 21, 1909.
21. Ibid.
22. *New York Herald*, February 28, 1910.
23. *Evening Journal*, September 19, 1910.
24. *New York Herald*, February 28, 1910.
25. "Mrs. Vanderbilt in Peril on Trip in Air," *New York Times*, September 1909.
26. "Vanderbilt Jr. and His Wife Are Separated," *Evening Journal*, September 21, 1909.
27. *New York American*, April 4, 1910.
28. *New York Times*, April 10, 1910.
29. *New York American*, April 4, 1910.
30. *New York Times*, April 10, 1910.
31. Ibid.
32. Ibid.
33. Ibid.
34. "Pretty Young Wife to Be Nearest Neighbor of Her Husband's First Cousin," *Evening Journal* (no date).
35. *Washington Post*, September 25, 1909.
36. *Washington Post*, October 9, 1909.
37. *New York Times*, February 5, 1910.
38. *The World*, March 15, 1910.
39. Ibid.
40. Ibid.
41. *The World*, March 19, 1910.
42. *Washington Post*, March 31, 1910.
43. Ibid.
44. Ibid.
45. Ibid.
46. *The World*, April 19, 1910.
47. *Washington Post*, May 5, 1910.
48. *New York Times*, May 22, 1910.
49. *New York Times*, June 30, 1910.

Chapter 15

1. "Eagle's Nest: The William K. Vanderbilt, Jr. Estate: An Historic Structure Report," Society for the Preservation of Long Island Antiquities, 1982.
2. *New York Times*, October 16, 1910.
3. *Washington Post*, January 1, 1911.
4. *New York Times*, March 19, 1911.
5. "Eagle's Nest: The William K. Vanderbilt Jr. Estate: An Historic Structure Report."

Chapter 16

1. Financial section, *The Independent*, October 21, 1909, pg. 946.

2. "Harriman, Stillman, and the New York Central," *Washington Post*, February 3, 1909, pg. 4.
3. "Harriman to Rule Central," *Washington Post*, January 15, 1909, pg. 6.
4. "Vanderbilt Regime Endures in New York Central Lines," *Wall Street Journal*, October 9, 1909, pg. 2.
5. Ibid.
6. "Holland's Letter," *Wall Street Times*, October 16, 1909, pg. 1.
7. "'Tis 'Vanderbilt Road' Again; Family Name Back in Central," *The Herald*, 1910.
8. Ibid.
9. Ibid.
10. Ibid.
11. Ibid.
12. Ibid.
13. Ibid.
14. Ibid.
15. Ibid.
16. E.J. Edwards, "W.K. Vanderbilt, Jr. Wins His Spurs in Rail World," *New York Times*, July 17, 1910, pg. SM7.
17. *New York Times*, July 17, 1910, pg. 57.
18. *New York Times*, March 22, 1911.
19. "Central Retrenches After Rate Decision," *New York Times*, March 22, 1911, pg. 12.
20. "W.K. Vanderbilt, Jr. Wins a Promotion," *The World*, March 7, 1912.
21. "W.K. Vanderbilt, Jr. Goes Up," *New York Press*, March 7, 1912.
22. Edwin P. Hoyt, *The Vanderbilts and Their Fortunes* (New York: Doubleday & Company, Inc., 1962).
23. Robert B. Carson, *Main Line to Oblivion: The Disintegration of the New York Railroads in the Twentieth Century* (Port Washington, NY: Kennikat Press, 1971), pg 63.
24. Ibid.
25. Ibid.
26. Gabriel Kolko, *Railroads and Regulation* (Princeton, NJ: Princeton University Press, 1965), pg. 211.
27. Ibid.
28. Carson, *Main Line to Oblivion: The Disintegration of the New York Railroads in the Twentieth Century*, pg. 63.
29. "The People Don't Intend That the Railroads Shall Rob Them," *New York Evening Journal*, March 28, 1913.
30. "Wm. Kissam Vanderbilt, Jr. Escapes," *New York Times*, 1913.
31. "S. Osgood Pell Killed in Train and Motor Crash," *New York Times*, August 4, 1913.
32. "Mrs. Laimbeer's Hurt May Not Mar Beauty," *New York Times*, August 4, 1913.
33. "S. O. Pell Killed as Train Hits Auto," *New York Times*, August 4, 1913, pg. 1.
34. *New York Herald*, August 6, 1913.

35. Charles Edward Russell, "Railroad Revolution," *Pearson's*, 1913, pg. 565.

36. "New Steel Yacht After Launching," *Christian Science Monitor*, January 29, 1913, pg. 10.

37. "William K. Vanderbilt, Jr.," *New York Times*, 1913.

38. "The Tarantula, Thought Destined for Use in War, Halted by U.S. at Boston," *New York Times*, August 21, 1913.

39. Kurt C. Schlichting, *Grand Central Terminal-Railroads, Engineering and Architecture in New York City* (Baltimore and London: Johns Hopkins University Press, 2001), pp. 196–7.

40. Ibid.

41. Ibid.

42. Carson, *Main Line to Oblivion The Disintegration of the New York Railroads in the Twentieth Century*, pg. 58.

43. Ibid., pg. 62.

44. Ibid., pg. 59.

45. *The Herald*, July 19, 1917.

46. *Wall Street Journal*, October 11, 1918.

47. Ibid.

48. Hoyt, *The Vanderbilts and Their Fortunes*, pg. 353.

49. Ibid., pg. 358.

Chapter 17

1. Robert B. Carson, *Main Line to Oblivion: The Disintegration of the New York Railroads in the Twentieth Century* (Port Washington, NY: Kennikat Press, 1971).

2. Ibid.

3. Kurt C. Schlichting, *Grand Central Terminal-Railroads, Engineering and Architecture in New York City* (Baltimore: Johns Hopkins University Press, 2001), pg 197.

4. Ibid.

5. Carson, *Main Line to Oblivion: The Disintegration of the New York Railroads in the Twentieth Century*.

6. "The End of a Railway Dynasty," *New York Times*, June 2, 1918, pg. 24.

Chapter 18

1. "W.K. Vanderbilt Dead at Paris," *Boston Daily Globe*, July 23, 1920, pg. 1.

2. "W.K. Vanderbilt Left $54,530,966 Estate in 1920," *Chicago Daily Tribune*, March 7, 1923, pg. 7.

3. "Vanderbilt Bequeaths Estate to His Family," *Wall Street Journal*, August 28, 1920, pg. 1.

4. W.K. Vanderbilt, Jr., *A Trip Through Italy, Sicily, Tunisia, Algeria, and Southern France* (New York: Privately published, 1918), pg. 40.

5. Ibid., pg. 47.

6. Ibid., pg. 45.

7. Ibid., pg. 64.

8. Ibid., pg. 74.

9. Ibid., pg. 115.

10. "How Vanderbilt Captured That Sea Devil," *The World Magazine*, April 19, 1925.

11. "Independents Open Annual Exhibition," *New York Times*, March 1, 1925, pg. 15.

12. "The Great Society Machine," *Atlanta Constitution*, March 19, 1922, pg. E8.

13. *Worcester Telegram*, May 31, 1925.

14. Ibid.

15. "How Vanderbilt Captured That Sea Devil."

16. Ibid.

17. Ibid.

18. Ibid.

19. Ibid.

20. "Sea-Devil Romance of the Dare-Devil Debutante," *Worcester Telegram*, May 31, 1925.

21. "Engagement Announced of Miss Muriel Vanderbilt," *Chicago Daily Tribune*, April 18, 1925, pg. 13.

Chapter 19

1. "W.K. Vanderbilt Unique Museum of Sea," *New York Evening Post*, March 15, 1924.

2. "Mr. Vanderbilt to Fathom Deep Sea: How the Millionaire Is Going to Continue the Interesting and Valuable Scientific Research Which the Late Prince of Monaco Made His Lifelong Hobby," *Philadelphia Inquirer* (Magazine Section), October 19, 1923.

3. Ibid.

4. "Hancock Plans Great Cruise to Galapagos," *New York Times*, January 8, 1923, pg. III.

5. "In Pursuit of an Elusive Sea," *New York Times*, April 19, 1925, pg. SM1.

6. Ibid.

7. Ibid.

8. "Off to the Fabled Sargasso," *New York Times*, February 15, 1925, pg. SM1.

9. "In Pursuit of an Elusive Sea."

10. Zane Grey, *Tales of Fishing Virgin Seas* (London: Derrydale Press, 1925).

11. Ibid.

12. Ibid.

13. Ibid.

14. Amanda Mackenzie Stuart, *Consuelo & Alva: Love and Power in the Gilded Age* (London: Harper Collins, 2005), pg. 306.

15. "Vanderbilt Sails for Strange Seas," *New York Times*, August 19, 1923, pg. 17.

16. "Mr. Vanderbilt to Fathom Deep Sea: How the Millionaire Is Going to Continue the Interesting and Valuable Scientific Research Which the Late Prince of Monaco Made His Lifelong Hobby."

17. Ibid.
18. Ibid.
19. "Vanderbilt Sails for Strange Seas."
20. "W.K. Vanderbilt, Jr. in Far North Quest of Marine Life," *Chicago Daily Tribune*, August 19, 1923, pg. 6.
21. "Quest for Rare Fish by W.K. Vanderbilt, Jr.," *Washington Post*, March 31, 1926, pg. 4.
22. "W.K. Vanderbilt Off to Seek Sea Wonders," *Washington Post*, August 19, 1923, pg. 1.
23. "Photo Standalone," *Chicago Daily Tribune*, March 1, 1925, pg. 15.
24. "History Museum Needs $10,000,000," *New York Times*, January 5, 1926, pg. 29.
25. Charles H. Townsend, "Giant Tortoise Finds That Man Is Friendly," The New York Zoological Society, 1928.
26. "Quest for Rare Fish by W.K. Vanderbilt, Jr.," pg. 4.
27. "Florida Bringing Its Fish Industry to the Front," *Wall Street Journal*, February 19, 1923, pg. 13.
28. "These Fascinating Ladies," *New York Journal*, 1926.
29. Ibid.
30. William Kissam Vanderbilt, *To the Galapagos on the Ara* (New York: Privately published, 1927).
31. Ibid.
32. Ibid.
33. Ibid.
34. Ibid.
35. Ibid.
36. Ibid., pg. 54.
37. Ibid., pg. 59.
38. Ibid.
39. Ibid., pg. 54.
40. "Vanderbilt Back with Sea Marvels: Commodore at Miami After a Two-Month Scientific Cruise, Which Found Many Rarities," *New York Times*, April 1, 1926, pg. 1.
41. Vanderbilt, Jr., *To the Galapagos on the Ara*, pg. 64.
42. Ibid., pg. 65.
43. "Vanderbilt Back with Sea Marvels: Commodore at Miami After a Two-Month Scientific Cruise, Which Found Many Rarities," pg. 1.
44. Vanderbilt, Jr., *To the Galapagos on the Ara*, pg. 62.
45. Ibid., pg. 59.
46. Ibid., pg. 63.
47. Ibid.
48. Ibid., pp. 51–60.
49. Ibid., pg. 63.
50. Ibid., pg. 81.
51. Ibid.
52. Ibid.
53. Ibid.
54. Ibid., pg. 70.

55. Ibid., pg. 82.
56. Ibid., pg. 85.
57. Ibid.
58. Ibid.
59. "Saw Volcanic Eruption," *New York Times*, March 18, 1926, pg 9.
60. Vanderbilt, Jr., *To the Galapagos on the Ara*, pg. 85.
61. Ibid., pg. 99.
62. Ibid.
63. "Vanderbilt Back with Sea Marvels: Commodore at Miami After a Two-Month Scientific Cruise, Which Found Many Rarities," pg. 1.
64. "Vanderbilt's Cruises Net South Sea Specimens," *New York Journal*, March 22, 1928.
65. "Vanderbilts Due Home," *New York Times*, March 27, 1928, pg. 13.
66. "Vanderbilt Back with Sea Trophies," *New York Times*, March 17, 1929, pg. 9.
67. "Rare Fishes Arrive on Vanderbilt Yacht," *Washington Post*, April 1, 1926, pg. 3.
68. "Vanderbilt Back with Sea Marvels: Commodore at Miami After a Two-Month Scientific Cruise, Which Found Many Rarities," pg. 1.
69. Ibid.

Chapter 20

1. *New York Evening Journal*, July 25, 1925.
2. Cholly Knickerbocker, *New York Times*, July 25, 1925.
3. *New York American*, July 28, 1925.
4. Knickerbocker.
5. "Will Change Her Name of Miss Consuelo Vanderbilt to Mrs. Smith," *Dallas Journal*, August 17, 1926.
6. *New York Herald Tribune*, November 22, 1926.
7. Amanda Mackenzie Stuart, *Consuelo and Alva: Love and Power in the Gilded Age* (London: Harper Collins, 2005).
8. "W.K. Vanderbilt to Wed Mrs. Warburton; Secret Arrangements in Paris Revealed," *New York Times*, August 26, 1927, pg. 6.
9. William Kissam Vanderbilt, *15,000 Miles Cruise with Ara* (New York: Privately published, 1928), pg. 5.
10. "Denial by W.K. Vanderbilt," *New York Times*, January 6, 1927, pg. E8.
11. Vanderbilt, Jr., *15,000 Miles Cruise with Ara*, pg. 13.
12. "Mrs. W.K. Vanderbilt to Have Racing Stable," *Washington Post*, July 28, 1923, pg. 12.
13. "Zev and Sarazen Won't Race Until Next Year," *Washington Post*, November 9, 1923, pg. 19.
14. "Sarazen Is Race Winner," *Atlanta Constitution*, October 27, 1923, pg. 8.

15. Ibid., pg 16.
16. Ibid., pp. 22–3.
17. "Vanderbilt Divorce Unlikely," *New York Times*, April 12, 1927.
18. Ibid.
19. "Divorce Is Granted to Mrs. Vanderbilt," *New York Times*, June 3, 1927.
20. Ibid.
21. Ibid.
22. Ibid.
23. "W.K. Vanderbilt to Wed Mrs. Warburton; Secret Arrangements in Paris Revealed," *New York Times*, August 26, 1927, pg. 6.
24. *New York American*, September 5, 1927.
25. The graffiti at Tower Island is now (2004) approximately two feet from the beach level. Apparently the 1982 El Niño drove sand up on the beach. In addition, the carving has been worn severely by tidal motion and will soon disappear. The house-flag is now almost gone. The rock chosen for carving, having been shortened by rising sands, no longer appears significant among the others surrounding it.
26. "Eagle's Nest: The William K. Vanderbilt Jr. Estate: An Historic Structure Report." Society for the Preservation of Long Island Antiquities, 1982.
27. Ibid.
28. Ibid.
29. "Paris Experts Pick 20 'Best Dressed,'" *New York Times*, November 26, 1935, pg. 27.
30. Ibid.
31. *Los Angeles Times*, November 26, 1935, pg. 9.

Chapter 21

1. "Vanderbilt Writes Book About Cruise," *Christian Science Monitor*, December 26, 1930, pg. 3.
2. Ibid.
3. Lord Byron, *The Sea*.
4. William Kissam Vanderbilt, Jr., *Taking One's Own Ship Around the World* (New York: Privately published, 1929), pg. 1.
5. Ibid., pg. 5.
6. Ibid., pg. 6.
7. Ibid., pg. 9.
8. Ibid., pg. 8
9. Ibid., pg. 19.
10. Ibid., pg. 9.
11. Ibid., pg. 13.
12. Ibid., pg. 21.
13. Ibid., pg. 32.
14. "Impressions and Observations of the Journal Man," *Oregon Daily Journal*," February 23, 1929.
15. Ibid.
16. Vanderbilt, Jr., *Taking One's Own Ship Around the World*, pg. 39.
17. Ibid., pg. 54.

18. Ibid., pg. 55.
19. Ibid., pg. 57.
20. Ibid., pg. 59.
21. Ibid., pg. 70.
22. Ibid., pp. 83–5.
23. Ibid., pg. 84.
24. Ibid.
25. Ibid., pg. 94.
26. Ibid., pg. 85.
27. Ibid., pg. 101.
28. Ibid., pg. 103.
29. Ibid., pg. 128.
30. Ibid., pp. 128–9.
31. Ibid., pg. 111.
32. "Former Muriel Vanderbilt Seeks Divorce from Frederic C. Church, Jr. for Non-Support," *New York Times*, February 3, 1929, pg. 1.
33. Ibid., pg. 137.
34. Ibid., pp. 137–41.
35. Ibid., pg. 146.
36. Ibid., pg. 152.
37. Ibid., pg. 158.
38. Ibid., pg. 162.
39. Ibid., pg. 168.
40. Ibid., pg. 155.
41. Ibid., pg. 195.
42. Ibid., pg. 200.
43. Ibid., pg. 203.
44. "Vanderbilt Shuns 'Germs,'" *New York Times*, April 24, 1929, pg. 3.
45. Ibid., pg. 215.
46. Ibid., pg. 223.
47. Ibid., pg. 222.
48. Ibid., pg. 223.
49. Ibid.
50. Ibid., pg. 173.
51. Ibid., pg. 227.
52. Ibid., pg. 180.
53. Ibid., pg. 156.
54. Ibid., pg. 228.
55. Ibid., pg. 229.
56. Vanderbilt, Jr., *Taking One's Own Ship Around the World*, pg. viii.
57. "Vanderbilt Writes on Sea Travel," *Los Angeles Times*, December 28, 1930, pg. A5.
58. Vanderbilt, Jr., *Taking One's Own Ship Around the World*, pg. xii.
59. "W.K. Vanderbilt Tells Own Story of World Cruise," *Chicago Daily Tribune*, December 20, 1930, pg. 15.
60. "Vanderbilt Writes Book About Cruise," *Christian Science Monitor*, December 26, 1930, pg. 3.
61. "Vanderbilt Writes on Sea Travel," *Los Angeles Times*, December 28, 1930, pg. A5.
62. Ibid.
63. Ibid., pg. 173.

Chapter 22

1. William Kissam Vanderbilt, Jr., *West Made East with the Loss of a Day* (New York: Privately published, 1933), pp. 3–5.
2. "Yacht Alva Launched," *Christian Science Monitor*, November 18, 1930, pg. 4.
3. "Yacht Trips on Nile Lure Americans," *New York Times*, March 2, 1930, pg 62.
4. "Vanderbilt's Yacht at Newport," *New York Times*, July 21, 1899, pg. 3.
5. "W.K. Vanderbilts Sail," *New York Times*, January 20, 1931, pg. 6.
6. "Vanderbilt Accepts Yacht," *New York Times*, March 3, 1931, pg. 15.
7. Ibid., pg. 11.
8. Ibid., pp. 14–15.
9. "Wm. Vanderbilt Builds 3,500 Ton Luxury Yacht," *Chicago Daily Tribune*, February 22, 1931, pg. 22.
10. "Vanderbilt Plans Cruise," *New York Times*, April 13, 1931, pg. 5.
11. Ibid., pg. 42.
12. Ibid., pg. 41.
13. "Vanderbilt Cup Reposted," *New York Times*, January 15, 1930, pg. 21.
14. "Tagore, Here Hails Advance in Russia," *New York Times*, October 10, 1930, pg. 12.
15. "To Put Whale in Museum," *New York Times*, August 26, 1930, pg. 12.
16. "Wanamakers Land Whale at Montauk," *New York Times*, August 17, 1930, pg. 16.
17. Ibid., pg. 5.
18. Ibid., pg. 47.
19. "Mrs. Muriel Church to Wed H.D. Phelps," *New York Times*, July 4, 1931, pg. 20.
20. "Vanderbilts Set Out on Scientific Cruise," *New York Times*, July 8, 1931, pg. 24.
21. Ibid., pg. 45.
22. Ibid., pg. 49.
23. Ibid.
24. "W.K. Vanderbilt in Cristobal," *New York Times*, July 22, 1931, pg. 12.
25. Ibid., pg. 43.
26. Ibid., pg. 38.
27. Vanderbilt, Jr., *West Made East with the Loss of a Day*, pg. 59.
28. "Black and White Still Favorites," *Chicago Daily Tribune*, June 3, 1931, pg. 23.
29. "Women of the World Styles Are in Vogue," *Chicago Daily Tribune*, November 7, 1937, pg. D6.
30. Vanderbilt, Jr., *West Made East with the Loss of a Day*, pg. 50.
31. Ibid., pg. 317.
32. Ibid., pg. 347.
33. Ibid., pg. 351.
34. Ibid., pg. vii.
35. Ibid., pg. 40.
36. Robert Bronner, "Letters to Father" (Courtesy of Suffolk County Vanderbilt Museum), July 2, 1931.
37. Ibid., pg. 62.
38. Ibid.
39. Ibid., pg. 63.
40. Ibid., pg. 67.
41. Ibid., pp. 68–69.
42. Ibid., pg. 73.
43. Ibid., pg. 71.
44. Ibid., pg. 73.
45. Ibid., pg. 116.
46. Ibid., pg. 109.
47. Ibid., pg. 112.
48. Ibid., pg. 113.
49. Ibid., pg. 138.
50. Ibid., pg. 151.
51. Ibid.
52. Ibid., pg. 145.
53. "Yacht Crew Suit Fails," *New York Times*, September 6, 1931, pg. 15.
54. Vanderbilt, Jr., *West Made East with the Loss of a Day*, pg. 174.
55. Ibid.
56. Ibid., pg. 226.
57. Ibid., pp. 218–219.
58. Joseph Gollomb, *Crimes of the Year* (New York: Horace Liveright, 1931).
59. Vanderbilt, Jr., *West Made East with the Loss of a Day*, pg. 221.
60. Ibid.
61. Ibid., pg. 222.
62. Ibid., pg. 30.
63. Ibid., pg. 339.
64. Ibid., pp. 361–2.
65. Ibid., pg. 177.

Chapter 23

1. Elsa Maxwell, *R.S.V.P* (Boston, MA: Little, Brown, 1954).
2. Edwin P. Hoyt, *The Vanderbilts and Their Fortunes* (New York: Doubleday, 1962).
3. *New York Times*, January 25, 1933, pg. 14.
4. *New York Times*, January 26, 1933, pg. 17.
5. Ibid.
6. Amanda Mackenzie Stuart, *Consuelo & Alva: Love and Power in the Gilded Age* (London: Harper Collins, 2005), pg. 444.
7. "Belmont Funeral a National Tribute," *New York Times*, February 13, 1933, pg. 17.
8. *New York Times*, March 1, 1933, pg. 15.
9. Stuart, *Consuelo & Alva: Love and Power in the Gilded Age*.
10. "Mrs. Belmont Left Most to Daughter," *New York Times*, March 1, 1933, pg. 15.
11. Louis Auchincloss, *The Vanderbilt Era: Profiles of a Gilded Age* (New York: Charles Scribner's Sons, 1989).
12. *New York Times*, June 5, 1933, pg. 12.
13. *New York Times*, November 9, 1933, pg. 25.

14. *Chicago Daily Tribune*, November 16, 1933, pg. 5.

15. "Vanderbilt III Killed in Auto Crash: Two Hurt," *New York Times*, November 16, 1933, pg. 1.

16. "Had Been in Accident Tuesday," *New York Times*, November 16, 1933, pg. 12.

17. *Washington Post*, November 19, 1933, pg. 12.

18. Ibid.

19. "Eagle's Nest, The William K. Vanderbilt Jr. Estate: An Historic Structure Report," Society for the Preservation of Long Island Antiquities, 1982, pp. 81–84.

20. *Washington Post*, July 8, 1935.

21. "Mrs. Vanderbilt Dies in Home Here," *New York Times*, July 8, 1935, pg. 15.

22. "Ex-Wife of Vanderbilt," *Los Angeles Times*, July 8, 1935, pg. 1.

23. "Mrs. Vanderbilt Dies in Home Here," pg. 15.

24. *New York Times*, July 18, 1935, pg. 17.

25. *Washington Post*, July 8, 1935.

26. Ibid.

27. *New York Times*, April 26, 1933.

28. *New York Times*, May 24, 1933.

29. Mordaunt Hall, "Motion Picture Record of William K. Vanderbilt's World Cruise Shown at the Plaza," *New York Times*, May 24, 1933, pg. 24.

30. *New York Times*, September 24, 1933, pg. 14.

31. *New York Times*, August 6, 1935, pg. 25.

32. *New York Times*, August 7, 1935, pg. 1.

33. Cornelius Vanderbilt III, *Farewell to Fifth Avenue* (New York: Simon and Schuster, 1935), pg. 237.

Chapter 24

1. "Vanderbilt Cup Now in Museum," *New York Times*, December 16, 1934, pg. XX12.

2. *New York Times*, June 20, 1936.

3. *New York Times*, June 14, 1936.

4. "Marine Museum Open," *New York Times*, July 11, 1940, pg. 41.

5. William Kissam Vanderbilt, Jr., *West Made East with the Loss of a Day* (New York: Privately published, 1933), pg. 78.

6. Ibid.

7. Ibid.

8. Ibid.

9. Ibid., pg. 122.

10. Ibid., pg. 125.

11. Ibid., pg. 122.

12. Ibid., pp. 193–6.

13. Ibid.

Chapter 25

1. "Miami Charity Day Has Many Patrons," *New York Times*, March 8, 1936, pg. N4.

2. "Mrs. Muriel Phelps Gets Divorce in Reno," *New York Times*, June 18, 1936, pg. 9.

3. William K. Vanderbilt, *Flying Lanes* (New York: Privately published, 1937).

4. "Vanderbilts Buying Two Family Planes," *New York Times*, August 19, 1936, pg. 43.

5. Ibid.

6. Ibid., pg. 4.

7. Vanderbilt, Jr., *Flying Lanes*, pg. 9.

8. Ibid., pg. 26.

9. Ibid.

10. Ibid., pp. 46–7.

11. Ibid., pg. 28.

12. Ibid., pg. 56.

13. Ibid., pg. 15.

14. Ibid., pg. 24.

15. Ibid., pg. 39.

16. Ibid., pg. 29.

17. Ibid., pg. 59.

18. Ibid., pg. 85.

19. Ibid., pg. 90.

20. Ibid., pg. 106.

21. "Yacht Sold to Ecuador," *Los Angeles Times*, August 22, 1935, pg. 21.

22. Ibid., pg. 34.

23. Ibid., pg. 41.

24. Ibid., pg. 114.

25. Ibid., pp. 37–8.

26. Ibid., pg. 90.

27. Ibid., pp. 118–19.

28. Ibid., pg. 120.

29. Ibid., pg. 81.

30. Ibid., pg. 126.

31. Ibid.

32. Ibid.

33. Ibid.

34. Ibid., pg. 129.

35. Ibid., pg. 135.

Chapter 26

1. Marcia Winn, "N.Y. Café Society Finds Peace in Gin and Rummy—Dancing, Too, Helps Ease Worries Over War," *Chicago Daily Tribune*, July 17, 1942, pg. 3.

2. Ibid.

3. "The New Yorker," *Washington Post*, January 3, 1941, pg. 18.

4. "W.K. Vanderbilt Gives Yacht Alva to Navy; $3,000,000 Craft Has Thrice Circled the Globe," *New York Times*, October 27, 1941, pg. 13.

5. *New York Times*, October 28, 1941.

6. *New York Times*, November 20, 1944.

7. "468 Flivver Planes Set for Southward Hop to St. Petersburg," *Chicago Daily Tribune*, January 3, 1940, pg. 4.

8. "Dinner to Assist French," *New York Times*, February 4, 1940, pg. 47.

9. "Mrs. H.G. Davis at Reno," *New York Times*, February 14, 1940, pg. 10.

10. "W.K. Vanderbilt Heir Wins Divorce at Reno," *Los Angeles Times*, April 5, 1940, pg. 1.

11. "Wedding at Home for Mrs. C.V. Fair," *New York Times*, January 16, 1941, pg. 26.

12. "Mrs. W.K. Vanderbilt, Sr. Dies in New York Hospital," *Los Angeles Times*, April 21, 1940, pg. 3.

13. "Vanderbilt Rites Held in St. Thomas," *New York Times*, April 24, 1940.

14. "Chatterbox," *Los Angeles Times*, April 26, 1940, pg. A8.

15. "Arthur E. Harding," *New York Times*, January 8, 1941, pg. 19.

16. "The New Yorker," Washington Post, January 20, 1941, pg. 18.

17. "Chatterbox," *Los Angeles Times*, September 2, 1941, pg. A5.

18. "Ball at Newport Assists Red Cross," *New York Times*, July 19, 1941, pg. 17.

19. "Miami Beach Seeks to Aid U.S. Morale," *Christian Science Monitor*, January 6, 1942, pg. 14.

20. Reginald Cleveland, "At the Wheel," *New York Times*, August 4, 1940, pg. 118.

21. "Nation's Auto Show Opens Here Today," *New York Times*, October 2, 1940, pg. 10.

22. "Honoring a Pioneer at Automotive Old Timers' Association," *New York Times*, October 16, 1941, pg. 18.

23. "Rain Fails to Halt Frolic of Colonial Dames," *Chicago Daily Tribune*, May 24, 1942, pg. G2.

24. "Navy Bares Loss of Six Ships, Including Sub and Destroyer," *Washington Post*, August 16, 1943, pg. 1.

25. *New York Times*, January 8, 1944.

26. "Vanderbilt Rites Draw Thousands,"
New York Times, January 12, 1944, pg. 23.

27. "Taxes Reduce W.K. Vanderbilt Estate $30,000,000," *Los Angeles Times*, July 19, 1945, pg. 1.

28. "Mrs. Vanderbilt Has 'Only 5 Million' Left after Taxes," Washington Post, July 19, 1945, pg. 1.

29. "Transition," *Washington Post*, July 23, 1945, pg. 8.

30. *New York Times*, August 18, 1941, pg. A7.

31. "Vanderbilt Estate to Be a Public Park," *New York Times*, January 21, 1944, pg. 19.

32. "State Not to Take Vanderbilt Tract," *New York Times*, February 10, 1944, pg. 17.

33. *New York Times*, August 31, 1948, pg. 25.

34. *New York Times*, July 9, 1950.

35. *New York Times*, August 29, 1947, pg. 17.

36. *New York Times*, September 20, 1947.

37. "'Consuela's [sic] marriage'" (Belmont Memoirs).

38. Ibid.

39. Consuelo Vanderbilt Balsan, *The Glitter and the Gold* (United Kingdom: William Heinemann, 1953), pg. 158.

40. "W.K. Vanderbilt Dies in N.Y. of Heart Disease," *Chicago Daily Tribune*, January 8, 1944, pg. 19.

41. "The Vanishing Vanderbilts," *Chicago Daily Tribune*, July 7, 1938, pg. 10.

42. "Transition," pg. 8.

43. William Kissam Vanderbilt, *West Made East with the Loss of a Day* (New York: Privately published, 1933), pg. 39.

44. Ibid., pg. vii.

45. Ibid., pg. 5.

Bibliography

Articles

"Almost Tragedy at Newport." *The Newport Herald*, September 7, 1900.

"American Car Gains Friends." *Motoring and Boating*, November 17, 1904.

"American Gold May Help Russian Loan; New York May Send Gold to Berlin." *New York Times*, June 12, 1904.

"The Apostle of High Speed Is Young Vanderbilt's Just Title." *The Washington Post*, November 18, 1906.

"Auto Cup Won by Wagner; Vanderbilt Trophy Goes to a Frenchman Again. The Course Given Up After E.F. Shepard Kills a Man — Others Hurt. 250,000 at the Contest First Five Racers to Finish All Foreigners — Tracy Makes the Fastest Lap." *New York Times*, October 7, 1908.

"Auto Race Next Year Over Private Course." *New York Times*, October 9, 1906.

"Autoists Are Anxious About Vanderbilt Cup." *New York Times*, April 9, 1906.

"Ball at Newport Assists Red Cross." *New York Times*, July 19, 1941.

"Belmont Funeral a National Tribute; Hundreds of Associates of Woman's Party President in Procession at Service. In Robes, Carry Banners Jubilant Funeral Hymn Written by Mrs. Belmont Sung — Taps Sounded at the Tomb." *New York Times*, February 13, 1933.

"Birdseye View of Mr. Vanderbilt's New Estate at Success Lake." *New York Herald*, February 15, 1903.

"Black and White Still Favorites." *The Chicago Daily Tribune*, June 3, 1931.

"Carmita's at Lawley's Yard." *Boston Daily Globe*, April 18, 1899.

Casey, Robert. "The Vanderbilt Cup 1908." *Technology and Culture* 40, no. 2 (April 1999).

"Central Retrenches After Rate Decision; Divided Rate Reduced to 5% Because of Denial of Right to Increase Freight Charges." *New York Times*, March 22, 1911.

"Changes Suggested in Auto Cup Race; Disappointing Attendance Makes It Necessary to Adopt New Methods to Revive Interest. Small Cars Show Up Well Second Section of Motor Parkway Covering 9 Miles, Thrown Open to Public." *New York Times*, November 1, 1909.

"Chatterbox." *Los Angeles Times*, September 2, 1941.

Cleveland, Reginald. "At the Wheel." *New York Times*. August, 1940, pg. 118.

"Contest for Vanderbilt Cup Will Be America's Greatest Automobile Event." *New York Times*, October 2, 1904.

"Costs $2,000,000 to End the Fair Will Contest." *New York Times*, May 11, 1904.

"Details of Central's Electric Road Plans." *New York Times*, November 22, 1903.

"Dinner to Assist French." *New York Times*, February 4, 1940.

Edwards, E.J. "W.K. Vanderbilt, Jr. Wins His Spurs in Rail World." *New York Times*, July 1910, pg. 7.

"The End of the Railway Dynasty." *New York Times*, June 2, 1918, pg. 24.

"Engagement Announced of Miss Muriel Vanderbilt." *The Chicago Daily Tribune*, April 18, 1925.

"Ex-Wife of Vanderbilt." *Los Angeles Times,* July 8 1935.

"Façade of the Terminal the Keynote to the Structure." *New York Times,* February 2, 1913.

"Fair Case Settled, Lump Sum to Nelsons." *New York Times,* May 1904.

"Fifteen Killed in Rear End Collision." *New York Times,* January 9, 1902.

"First Race for Four Seventy-Footers." *Town Topics,* July 15, 1900.

"Florida Bringing Its Fish Industry to the Front." *The Wall Street Journal,* February 19, 1923.

"Formal Separation Agreement Making Provision as to the Disposition of Their Two Children Drawn Up — Understanding Regarding Financial Affairs." *Evening Journal,* September 21, 1909.

"Former Muriel Vanderbilt Seeks Divorce from Frederic C. Church, Jr. for Non-Support." *New York Times.* February 2, 1929.

"4 Dead, 20 Hurt, in Vanderbilt Race; Greatest Contest in the History of the Event Marred by Many Accidents." *New York Times,* October 2, 1910.

"468 Flivver Planes Set for Southward Hop to St. Petersburg." *The Chicago Daily Tribune,* January 3, 1940.

"French Racers Arrive for Vanderbilt Cup; Henry, Wagner, Duray, and Szisz. Here with Their Cars. Excessive Speed Predicted Foreign Autoist Expect 65 Miles an Hour Over Long Island Course — Heath Due This Week." *New York Times,* October 1, 1905.

"Further Details of the Automobile Accident." *New York Herald.* (European Edition: Paris), August 16, 1902.

"Great Ball in Newport." *New York Times,* August 29, 1895.

"The 'Great' Race." *New York Times,* October 9, 1904.

"The Great Society Machine." *The Atlanta Constitution,* March 19, 1922, pg. E8.

"Had Been in Accident Tuesday." *New York Times,* November 16, 1933.

Hall, Mordaunt. "Motion Picture Record of William K. Vanderbilt's World Cruise Shown at the Plaza." *New York Times,* May 24, 1933.

"Hancock Plans Great Cruise to Galapagos." *New York Times,* January 8, 1923.

"Hard Times Bust Vacuum Cleaner Company." *New York Times,* 1908.

"Harriman, Stillman and the New York Central." *The Washington Post,* February 3, 1909.

"Harriman to Rule Central." *The Washington Post,* January 15, 1909.

Hearst, W. R. "'Arrest me everyday if you want to,' Says Mr. Vanderbilt." *New York Times,* June 8, 1900.

"Heath Auto Wins; One Man Killed; George Arents, Jr., Unconscious, Mechanician Dead Clement Second in Race Mrs. W.K. Vanderbilt, Jr. Leads Grand Stand Cheering. A Great Day for Nassau. The Course of 284.4 Miles Covered by the Winner in 5 Hours, 26 Minutes and 45 Seconds." *New York Times,* October 9, 1904.

"Hermann Oelrich Dies on a Liner at Sea." *New York Times,* September 5, 1904.

"History Museum Needs $10, 000,000." *New York Times.* January 5, 1926.

"History of the Vanderbilt Cup Races." *New York Times,* September 11, 1910.

"Holland's Letter." *The Wall Street Journal.* October 16, 1909, pg. 1.

"Honoring a Pioneer at Automotive Old Timers' Association." *New York Times,* October 16, 1941.

"How Vanderbilt Captured That Sea Devil." *The World Magazine,* April 19, 1925.

"Idle Hour in Flames," *New York Times,* April, 12 1899.

"Impressions and Observations of the Journal Man." *Oregon Daily Journal,* February 23, 1929.

"In Honor of Miss Virginia Fair." *New York Times,* August 24, 1894.

"In Pursuit of an Elusive Sea." *New York Times,* April 19, 1925.

"Independents Open Annual Exhibition." *New York Times,* March 1, 1925, pg. 15.

Ingersoll, E.P. "Observations on the Vanderbilt Cup." *The Horseless Age* 14, no. 15 (October 12, 1904).

Kimes, Beverly Rae. "Willie K.: The Saga of a Racing Vanderbilt." *Automotive Quarterly* 40, no. 3 (1904).

"Know Him? Peckham of the Harvard Advocate; Had the Journalistic 'Bug' and Wouldn't Be Suppressed, So He Founded That Literary Magazine." *New York Times,* August 20, 1911.

"Light on Two Important Questions." *The Chicago Daily Tribune,* May 5, 1895.

"Long Island Speedway Assumes More Definite Shape." *New York Times,* November 3, 1906.

"Marine Museum Open." *New York Times*, July 11, 1940.
"May Be Last Vanderbilt Race." *Globe*, November 2, 1909.
"Met Death at Hicksville; Miller Killed and Spectators Hurt on Dangerous Curve." *New York Times*, October 2, 1910, pg. 6.
"Miami Beach Seeks to Aid U.S. Morale." *The Christian Science Monitor*, January 6, 1942.
"Miami Charity Day Has Many Patrons." *New York Times*, March 8, 1936.
"Millionaires Risk Lives as Firemen to Save Village," *World*, April 9, 1906.
"Millions for a Race Road." *Motor-Print*, November 1906, Vol. 1, No. 9.
"Mr. Cornelius Vanderbilt Dead." *New York Times*, September 13, 1899.
"Mr. Vanderbilt Retires." *New York Times*, May 5, 1883.
"Mr. Vanderbilt to Fathom Deep Sea: How the Millionaire Is Going to Continue the Interesting and Valuable Scientific Research Which the Late Prince of Monaco Made His Lifelong Hobby." *The Philadelphia Inquirer*, October 19, 1923.
"The Modern Appian Way for the Modest." *Harpers Weekly*, March 16, 1907.
"Motor Parkway Is Progressing Fast." *New York Times*, September 6, 1908.
"Mrs. Belmont Left Most to Daughter; Mme. Jacques Balsan Is Chief Beneficiary — Woman's Party Gets Only Public Bequest. Sons Are Executors Harold Vanderbilt Receives Only the 'Marble House,' Sold After Will Was Drawn." *New York Times*, March 1, 1933.
"Mrs. H.G. Davis at Reno." *New York Times*, February 14, 1940.
"Mrs. Laimbeer's Hurt May Not Mar Beauty." *New York Times*, August 4, 1913.
"Mrs. Muriel Church to Wed H.D. Phelps." *New York Times*, July 4, 1931.
"Mrs. Muriel Phelps Gets Divorce in Reno." *New York Times*, June 18, 1936.
"Mrs. Oelrich Pens Tribute to 'Frisco.'" *The World*, April 23, 1906.
"Mrs. Vanderbilt Dies in Home Here; Former Wife of W.K. 2d, Long Social Leader in New York, Had Been Ill Nine Weeks." *New York Times*, July 8, 1935.
"Mrs. Vanderbilt Has 'Only 5 Million' Left After Taxes." *The Washington Post*, July 19, 1945.
"Mrs. Vanderbilt in Peril on Trip in Air." *New York Times*, September 1909.
"Mrs. W.K. Vanderbilt, Sr. Dies in New York Hospital." *Los Angeles Times*, April 21, 1940.
"Nation's Auto Show Opens Here Today." *New York Times*, October 12, 1940.
"Navy Bares Loss of Six Ships, Including Sub and Destroyer." *The Washington Post*, August 16, 1943.
"New Auto Records Expected at Ormond." *New York Times*, January 22, 1904.
"New Steel Yacht After Launching." *Christian Science Monitor*, January 29, 1913, pg. 10.
"New Vanderbilt Heiress." *New York Times*, November 25, 1900.
"New York Central in Another Deal." *New York Times*, July 7, 1899.
"New York Central in Mammoth Deal." *New York Times*, June 26, 1899.
"Newport Preparing for Summer Season." *New York Times*, April 19. 1908.
"Newport's Automobile Races; William K. Vanderbilt, Jr.'s French Vehicle Carried Off Two Prizes." *New York Times*, September 7, 1900.
"No Beds, Few Chairs, and the Crowds Out in the Rain." *Evening Post*, October 24, 1910.
"Off to the Fabled Sargasso." *New York Times*, February 15, 1925.
"One of Those Bottomless Lakes." *The Hartford Courant*, June 12, 1902.
"Paris Experts Pick 20 'Best Dressed'; Ten American Women Among Those Considered Leaders in Smart Attire." *New York Times*, November 26, 1935.
"The People Don't Intend That the Railroads Shall Rob Them." *The Evening Journal*, March 28, 1913.
Platt, Milton J. "New York Central." *New York Times*. October 11, 1903.
"Quest for Rare Fish by W.K. Vanderbilt, Jr." *The Washington Post*, March 31, 1926.
"The Racing Effect in 'The Vanderbilt Cup.'" *New York Times*, March 12, 1904.
"Rain Fails to Halt Frolic of Colonial Dames." *The Chicago Daily Tribune*, May 24, 1942.
"Rare Fishes Arrive on Vanderbilt Yacht." *The Washington Post*, April 1, 1926.
"The Red Devil." *The Hartford Courant*, July 27, 1901.
"Rushes from Ocean to Ocean." *The Atlanta Constitution*, October 10, 1899.
"S.O. Pell Killed as Train Hits Auto; Mr. and Mrs. William Laimbeer, His Guests, Seriously Hurt, and Chauffeur Also Killed." *New York Times*, August 4, 1913.
"Saw Volcanic Eruption." *New York Times*, March 18, 1926.

"Sea-Devil Romance of the Dare-Devil Debutante." *Worcester Telegram*, May 31, 1925.

"She Is Now a Duchess." *New York Times*, November 7, 1895.

"Shepard Sells Auto; E.R. Thomas Buys Vanderbilt Cup Racer and May Compete at Ormond." *New York Times*, October 26, 1906.

"Six Persons Killed in Automobile Race; Shocking Accidents in Record-Breaking Paris-Madrid Contest. Automobilist Marcel Renault and Barrows Probably Dying—Continuance of Race on French Territory Forbidden." *New York Times*, May 25, 1903.

"60-Mile Auto Road to Cost $2,000,000." *New York Times*, October 21, 1906.

"Son Born to the House of Young W.K. Vanderbilt." *New York Times*, October 31, 1907.

"State Not to Take Vanderbilt Tract." *New York Times*, February 10, 1944.

"Sudden Death of Vanderbilt." *The Chicago Daily*, September 13.1899.

"Tagore, Here, Hails Advance in Russia." *New York Times*, October 10, 1930.

"The Tarantula, Thought Destined for Use in War, Halted by U.S. at Boston." *New York Times*, August 21, 1913.

"Taxes Reduce W.K. Vanderbilt Estate $30,000,000." *Los Angeles Times*, July 19, 1945.

"Thirty-Three Cars Start in Five Sweepstake Races; Herbert Lytle, Driving the Winning Car in Stellar Event, Averages Better Than 64 Miles an Hour for the Vanderbilt Cup Distance." *New York Times*, October 11, 1908.

"'Tis 'Vanderbilt Road' Again; Family Name Back in Central." *The Herald*, 1910.

"To Put Whale in Museum." *New York Times*, August 26, 1930.

"Topics of the Times." *New York Times*, September 20, 1899.

"Transition." *The Washington Post*, July 23, 1945.

"Twenty-five Killed and Seventy-five Injured." *The New York Herald*, February 17, 1907.

"$217,000,000." *The Boston Daily*, February 10, 1886.

"Vacuum Cleaner Co. Fails—Hasn't Been Making Expenses Lately—W.K. Vanderbilt, Jr. a Director." *New York Times*, May 16, 1908.

"Vanderbilt Accepts Yacht." *New York Times*, March 3, 1931.

"Vanderbilt as Speech Maker." *New York Journal*, October 31, 1903.

"Vanderbilt Back with Sea Marvels: Commodore at Miami After a Two-Month Scientific Cruise, Which Found Many Rarities." *New York Times*, April 1, 1926.

"Vanderbilt Back with Sea Trophies." *New York Times*, March 17, 1929.

"Vanderbilt Back Without Entries; Has Brought No Additional European Competitors for the Cup Race. Confers with Pardington This Afternoon; He Will Need the Cup Commission to Decide What Course Shall Be Pursued." *New York Times*, September 9, 1908.

"Vanderbilt Bequeaths Estate to His Family." *The Wall Street Journal*, August 28, 1920, pg. 1.

"Vanderbilt Buys Car and Will Race for Cup." *New York Times*, September 19, 1906.

"Vanderbilt Caught Speeding." *New York Times*, April 22, 1909.

"Vanderbilt Cup Now in Museum." *New York Times*, December 16, 1934.

"Vanderbilt Cup Race Won by Hemery; Frenchman in Darracq Car Captures the Trophy Lancia Lost by Ill-Luck When 30 Miles Ahead His Machine Is Wrecked. Beat a Mile a Minute Italian Driver Made Better Than 80 and Hour in Straight Sections—Two Protests—100,000 See the Race." *New York Times*, October 15, 1905.

"Vanderbilt Cup Reposted." *New York Times*, January 15, 1930.

"Vanderbilt Cup Rules." *New York Times*, July 7, 1904.

"Vanderbilt Cups Bad Management; Great Automobile Contest of Long Island Fails to Meet Expectations. Fine Opportunity Missed Organization and Foresight Would Have Kept Road Clear and Provided Accommodations for Spectators." *New York Times*, October 26, 1908.

"Vanderbilt Did a Mile in .39 Flat." *New York World*, January 27, 1904.

"Vanderbilt Estate to Be a Public Park." *New York Times*, January 21, 1944.

"Vanderbilt Fined for Scorching." *The New York Journal*, June 1900.

"Vanderbilt Gets Right of Way to the Lake." *New York Press*, October 31, 1903.

"Vanderbilt III Killed in Auto Crash: Two Hurt." *New York Times*, November 16, 1933.

"Vanderbilt, Jr. and His Wife Are Separated." *The Evening Journal*, September 21, 1909.

"Vanderbilt Out of Race." *New York Times*, September 20, 1906.

"Vanderbilt Plans Cruise." *New York Times*, April 13, 1931.

"Vanderbilt Regime Endures in New York Central Lines." *The Wall Street Journal*, Oct 9. 1909, pg. 2.

"Vanderbilt Rites Draw Thousands." *New York Times*, January 12, 1944.

"Vanderbilt Rites Held in St. Thomas." *New York Times*, April 24, 1940.

"Vanderbilt Sails for Strange Seas." *New York Times*, August 19, 1923.

"Vanderbilt Shuns 'Germs.'" *New York Times*, April 24, 1929.

"Vanderbilt Smashes Record on Trolley." *The New York American*, July 8, 1905.

"Vanderbilt to Close Road." *New York Times*, July 7, 1904.

"Vanderbilt Villa Burned." *New York Times*, April 12, 1899.

"Vanderbilt Wins Fight for Road." *New York Times*, October 31, 1903.

"Vanderbilt Writes Book About Cruise." *The Christian Science Monitor*, December 26, 1930, pg. 3.

"Vanderbilt Writes on Sea Travel." *Los Angeles Times*, December 28, 1930.

"Vanderbilt-Fair Union." *New York Times*, April 5, 1899.

"A Vanderbilt-Fair Union; Rumored Engagement Is Confirmed by Hermann Oelrichs." *New York Times*, December 29, 1898.

"Vanderbilt-Fair Wedding." *New York Times*, April 12, 1899.

"Vanderbilts at Oakdale." *New York Times*, April 6, 1899.

"Vanderbilts Buying Two Family Planes." *New York Times*, August 19, 1936.

"Vanderbilt's Cruises Net South Sea Specimens." *The New York Journal*, March 22, 1928.

"Vanderbilts Due Home." *New York Times*, March 27, 1928.

"Vanderbilts Set Out on Scientific Cruise." *New York Times*, July 8, 1931.

"Vanderbilts Well Pleased." *New York Journal*, April 28, 1903.

"Vanderbilt's Yacht." *New York Times*, October 1, 1886.

"Vanderbilt's Yacht at Newport." *New York Times*, July 21, 1899.

"Vanderbilt's Yacht Launched." *New York Times*, May 27, 1900.

"The Vanishing Vanderbilts." *The Chicago Daily Tribune*, July 7, 1938.

"Varied Auto Advice at Annual Dinner; Gen. Porter Condemns the Reckless, Conscience-less Driver. W.K. Vanderbilt, Jr.'s Debut Donor of the World's Greatest Racing Trophy Cities Advantages of Proposed Long Island Speedway." *New York Times*, December 9, 1906.

"A Very Knotty Question Raised in the Lake Success Matter." *Brooklyn Eagle*, October 23, 1903.

"W.K. Vanderbilt Dead at Paris." *The Boston Daily Globe*, July 23, 1920.

"W.K. Vanderbilt Dies in N.Y. of Heart Disease." *The Chicago Daily Tribune*, January 8, 1944.

"W.K. Vanderbilt Gets Lease." *New York Times*, October 31, 1903.

"W.K. Vanderbilt Gives Yacht Alva to Navy; $3,000,000 Craft Has Thrice Circled the Globe." *New York Times*, October 27, 1941.

"W.K. Vanderbilt Heir Wins Divorce at Reno." *Los Angeles Times*, April 5, 1940.

"W.K. Vanderbilt in Cristobal." *New York Times*, July 22, 1931.

"W.K. Vanderbilt, Jr. a Bold Life Saver." *New York Times*, September 14, 1901.

"W.K. Vanderbilt, Jr. and Wife Parted?" *New York Times*, September 22, 1909.

"W.K. Vanderbilt, Jr. Back." *New York Times*, April 4, 1906.

"W.K. Vanderbilt, Jr. Goes Up." *New York Press*, March 7, 1912.

"W.K. Vanderbilt, Jr. in Far North Quest of Marine Life." *The Chicago Daily Tribune*, August 19, 1923.

"W.K. Vanderbilt, Jr., Seeking to Buy Mysterious Lake." *New York Times*, June 15. 1902.

"W.K. Vanderbilt, Jr. Training." *New York Sun*, December 4, 1903.

"W.K. Vanderbilt, Jr. Wins Promotion." *The World*, March 7, 1912.

"W.K. Vanderbilt Left $54,430,966 Estate in 1920." *The Chicago Daily Tribune*, March 7, 1923, pg. 7.

"W.K. Vanderbilt Off to Seek Sea Wonders." *The Washington Post*, August 19, 1923.

"W.K. Vanderbilt Proud of Last Race." *New York World*, August 2, 1902.

"W.K. Vanderbilt Seriously Burned by Exploding Lamp." *Post Telegram*, July 7, 1900.

"W.K. Vanderbilt Tells Own Story of World Cruise." *The Chicago Daily Tribune*, December 20, 1930.

"W.K. Vanderbilt to Wed Mrs. Warburton; Secret Arrangements in Paris Revealed." *New York Times*, August 26, 1927.
"W.K. Vanderbilt Unique Museum of the Sea." *New York Evening Post*, March 15, 1924.
"W.K. Vanderbilts Sail" *New York Times*, January 20, 1931.
"Wanamakers Land Whale at Montauk." *New York Times*, August 17, 1930.
"Wedding at Home for Mrs. C.V. Fair." *New York Times*, January 16, 1941.
"Will Change Her Name of Miss Consuelo Vanderbilt to Mrs. Smith." *The Dallas Journal*, August 17, 1926.
"Will Not Abandon Vanderbilt Race: Cup Commission Meets Donor and Unanimously Decides to Hold Contest. Parkway Ready on Time A.R. Pardington Makes Official Announcements—Says Four Additional American Entries Are Assured." *New York Times*, September 10, 1908.
"William K. Vanderbilt II." *Town Topics*, January 12, 1899.
"William Kissam Vanderbilt." *New York Times*, July 9, 1899.
"William Vanderbilt, Jr. to Beautify Lake Success." *Brooklyn Eagle*, July 20, 1902.
"Willie K. Too Gay." *Chicago Daily*, August 30, 1894.
"Willie Vanderbilt Near Death on an Automobile." *The New York Journal*, July 5, 1899.
"Wm. Kissam Vanderbilt, Jr. Escapes." *New York Times*, 1913.
"Wm. Vanderbilt Builds 3,500 Ton Luxury Yacht." *The Chicago Daily Tribune*, February 22, 1931.
Winn, Marcia. "N.Y. Café Society Finds Peace in Gin and Rummy—Dancing, Too, Helps Ease Worries Over War." *The Chicago Daily Tribune*, July 17, 1942.
"Women of the World Styles Are in Vogue." *The Chicago Daily Tribune*, November 7, 1937.
"World's Auto Record Beaten by Vanderbilt." *New York World*, January 27, 1904.
"World's Fastest Mile by Stanley Automobile; Mariott Drives Steam Car on Ormond Beach in 0:28 1–5. Makes Kilometer Record Dewar Cup Winner Travels at Rate of Over 127 Miles an Hour—Chevrolet's Good Time." *New York Times*, January 27, 1906.
"Yacht Alva Launched." *The Christian Science Monitor*, November 18, 1930.
"Yacht Crew Suit Fails" *New York Times*, September 6, 1931.
"Yacht Sold to Ecuador." *Los Angeles Times*, August 22, 1935.
"Young Vanderbilt Warned at Police Station." *The New York Journal*, June 12, 1899.
"Young Vanderbilt's Modest Honeymoon." *The Newport Herald*, April 20, 1899.

Books and Manuscripts

Allen, Frederick Lewis, and William L. O'Neill. *The Big Change: America Transforms Itself 1900–1950*. New Brunswick: Transaction, 1992.
Amory, Cleveland. *The Vanderbilt Legend: The Story of the Vanderbilt Family, 1794–1940*. New York: Harcourt, Brace, 1941.
_____. *Who Killed Society?* New York: Harper and Brothers, 1960.
Andrews, Wayne. *The Vanderbilt Legend*. New York: Harcourt Brace, 1941.
Auchincloss, Louis. *The Book Class*. Boston: Houghton Mifflin, 1984.
_____. *The Vanderbilt Era*. New York: Charles Scribner's Sons, 1989.
Balsan, Consuelo Vanderbilt. *The Glitter & the Gold*. New York: Harper and Brothers, 1952.
Beebe, Lucius. *The Big Spenders*. Garden City, NY: Doubleday, 1966.
_____. *Mansions on Rails*. Berkeley, CA: Howell-North, 1959.
Beebe, William. *Galapagos: World's End*. New York: Dover, 1988.
Benson, Lee. *Merchants, Farmers and Railroads: Railroad Regulation and New York Politics, 1850–1887*. Cambridge, MA: Russell & Russell, 1955.
Berger, Michael, L. *The Devil Wagon in God's Country—The Automobile and Social Change in Rural America, 1893–1929*. Hamden, CT: Archon Books, 1979.
Bromley, Michael L. *William Howard Taft and the First Motoring Presidency, 1909–1913*. Jefferson, NC: McFarland, 2003.
Brough, James. *Counsuelo: Portrait of an American Heiress*. New York: Coward, McCann, and Geoghegan, 1979.
Campbell, W. Joseph. *Yellow Journalism: Puncturing the Myths, Defining the Legacies*. Westport, CT: Greenwood, 2001.

Carson, Robert B. *Main Line to Oblivion; The Disintegration of the New York Railroads in the Twentieth Century*. Port Washington, NY: Kennikat Press, 1971.

Chernow, Ron. *The House of Morgan: An American Banking Dynasty and the Rise of Modern Finance*. New York: Grove Press, 2001.

Clews, Henry. *Fifty Years in Wall Street*. Hoboken, NJ: John Wiley, 2006.

Croffert, William A. *The Leisure Class in America*. New York: Arno Press, 1975.

Croffut, William. *The Vanderbilts and the Story of Their Fortune*. London: Griffith, Farran, Okeden, & Welsh, 1886.

Depew, Chauncey M. *My Memories of Eighty Years*. New York: Scribner's, 1922.

Dixon, Frank Haigh. *Railroads and Government*. New York: Scribner's, 1922.

"Eagle's Nest; The William K. Vanderbilt Jr. Estate: An Historic Structure Report." Society for the Preservation of Long Island Antiquities, 1982.

Faulkner, Harold U. *The Decline of Laissez Faire*. New York: Holt, Rinehart and Winston, 1962.

Foreman, John, and Robbe Pierce Stimson. *The Vanderbilts and the Gilded Age: Architectural Aspirations, 1879–1901*. New York: St. Martin Press, 1991.

Gavan, Terrence. *The Barrons of Newport. A Guide to the Gilded Age*. Newport, RI: Pineapple, 1988.

Goldsmith, Barbara. *Little Gloria ... Happy at Last*. New York: Alfred A. Knopf, 1980.

Gollomb, Joseph. *Crimes of the Year*. New York: Horace Liveright, 1931.

Grey, Zane. *Tales of Fishing Virgin Seas*. London: Derrydale Press, 1925.

Harlow, Alvin F. *The Road of the Century: The Story of the New York Central*. New York: Creative Age Press, 1947.

Hines, Walker D. *War History of American Railroads*. New Haven: Yale University Press, 1928.

Hoyt, Edwin P. *The Vanderbilts and Their Fortunes*. New York: Doubleday, 1962.

Hungerford, Edward. "The Greatest Railway Terminal in the World." *Outlook 102* (December 28, 1912).

_____. *Men and Iron: The Story of the New York Central*. New York: Thomas C. Crowell, 1938.

_____. *The Story of the Baltimore and Ohio Railroad, 1827–1927*. New York: G.P. Putnam, 1928.

Jackson, Michael H. *Galapagos: A Natural History*. Calgary, Alberta: University of Calgary Press, 1993.

Josephson, Matthew. *The Robber Barons*. New York: Harcourt Press, 1934.

Kahn, David. "The Granddaddy of the Superhighways." *Lincoln-Mercury Times*. September-October 1955.

King, Robert B. *The Vanderbilt Homes*. New York: Rizzoli International Publications, 1989.

Kirkpatrick, Sidney. *The Revenge of Thomas Eakins*. New Haven: Yale University Press, 2006.

Kolko, Gabriel. *Railroads and Regulation*. Princeton, NJ: Princeton University Press, 1965.

_____. *The Triumph of Conservatism*. New York: The Free Press: A Division of Macmillan, 1963.

Kroplick, Howard. *Vanderbilt Cup Races of Long Island*. Chicago, IL: Arcadia, 2008.

_____, and Al Velocci. *Images of America: The Long Island Motor Parkway*. Mount Pleasant, SC: Arcadia, 2008.

Lane, Wheaton. *Commodore Vanderbilt: An Epic of the Steam Age*. New York: Knopf, 1942.

Latorre, Octavio. *The Curse of the Giant Tortoise*. Quito, Ecuador: National Culture Fund, 2003.

Lehr, Elizabeth Drexel. *King Lehr and the Gilded Age*. London: J.P. Lippincott, 1935.

Leonard, William Norris. *Railroad Consolidation Under the Transportation Act of 1920*. New York: Columbia University Press, 1946.

Lessner, Erwin. *Famous Auto Races and Rallies*. New York: Hanover House, 1956.

Lewis, Arthur H. *The Day They Shook the Plum Tree*. Cutchogue, NY: Buccaneer Books, 1963.

Lewis, Oscar. *Silver Kings: The Lives and Times of Mackay, Fair Flood and O'Brian, Lords of the Nevada Comstock Lode*. New York: Alfred A. Knopf, 1947.

Lewis, R.W.B. *Edith Wharton*. New York: Harper & Row, 1975.

Logan, Andy. *The Man Who Robbed the Robber Barons*. New York: Akadine Press, 2001.

Lui, Adonica Y. "The Machine and Social Policies: Tammany Hall and the Politics of Public Outdoor Relief, New York City, 1874–1889." *Studies in American Political Development* (Vol. 9), 1995.

MacDowell, Dorothy K. *Commodore Vanderbilt and His Family*. Hendersonville, NC: D.K. MacDowell, 1989.

MacKay, Robert B., Anthony Baker, and Carol Traynor. *The Long Island Country Houses and Their Architects, 1860–1940*. New York: B.W. Norton, 1997.

Malone, Michael P., and James J. Hill. *Empire Builder of the Northwest*. Norman: University of Oklahoma Press, 1996.

Martin, Albro. *Enterprise Denied: Origins of the Decline of American Railroads, 1897–1917*. New York: Columbia University Press, 1978.

Martin, Frederick Townsend. *The Passing of the Idle Rich*. Garden City, NY: Doubleday, Page, 1911.

Maurice, Arthur Bartlett. *Fifth Avenue*. New York: Dodd, Mead, 1918.

Maxwell, Elsa. *The Celebrity Circus*. New York: Appleton-Century, 1963.

_____. *R.S.V.P.* Boston: Little, Brown, 1954.

McAllister, Ward. *Society as I Have Found It*. New York: Cassell, 1890.

Morris, Edmund. *Theodore Rex*. New York: Random House, 2001.

Morris, Loyd R. *Not So Long Ago*. New York: Random House, 1949.

Moulton, H.G. *The American Transportation Problem*. Washington: Brookings Institution, 1933.

Myers, Gustavus. *The Ending of Hereditary American Fortunes*. New York: Julian Messner, 1939.

National Oceanic Atmospheric Administration. *National Weather Review*, July 1898.

Nelson, James C. *Railroad Transportation and Public Policy*. Washington, D.C.: Brookings Institution, 1959.

Patterson, Jerry E. *The Vanderbilts*. New York: Harry N. Abrams, 1989.

Rector, Margaret Hayden. *Alva, That Vanderbilt-Belmont Woman*. Wickford, RI: Dutch Island Press, 1992.

Renehan, Edward, Jr. *Commodore: The Life of Cornelius Vanderbilt*. New York: Basic Books, 2007.

Ripley, William Z. *Railroads: Finance and Organization*. New York: Longmans, Green, 1915.

_____. *Railroads: Rates and Regulation*. New York: Longmans, Green, 1912.

Rousmaniese, John. *The Luxury Yachts*. Alexandria, VA: Time-Life Books, 1981.

Schlichting, Kurt C. *Grand Central Terminal*. Baltimore and London: Johns Hopkins University Press, 2001.

Simon, Kate. *Fifth Avenue: A Very Social History*. New York: Harcourt Brace Jovanovich, 1978.

Smith, Arthur D. Howden. *Commodore Vanderbilt: An Epic of American Achievement*. New York: Robert M. McBride, 1927.

Sobel, Robert. *The Entrepreneurs: Explorations Within the American Business Tradition*. New York: Weybright & Talley, 1974.

Spearman, Frank H. *The Strategy of Great Railroads*. New York: Scribner's, 1912.

Splawn, W.M.W. *Consolidation of Railroads*. New York: Macmillan, 1924.

Stasz, Clarice. *The Vanderbilt Women, Dynasty of Wealth, Glamour and Tragedy*. New York: St. Martin's Press, 1991.

Stone, Richard D. *The Interstate Commerce Commission and the Railroad Industry: A History of Regulatory Policy*. New York: Praeger, 1991.

Strouse, Jean. *Morgan American Financier*. New York: Random House, 1999.

Stuart, Amanda Mackenzie. *Consuelo & Alva; Love and Power in the Gilded Age*. London: HarperCollins, 2005.

Tarbell, Ida M. *The History of the Standard Oil Company* (Vol. 2). New York: McClure, Phillips, 1904.

_____. *The Nationalization of Business, 1878–1898*. New York: Macmillan, 1936.

Tennell, John, and Jackie Stewart. *Motor Racing: The Golden Age: Extraordinary Images from 1900 to 1970*. London: Cassell Illustrated, 2006.

Thompson, Slason. *A Short History of American Railroads*. New York: Appleton, 1925.

Townsend, Charles H. *Giant Tortoise Finds That Man Is Friendly*. New York: The New York Zoological Society, 1928.

Vanderbilt, Arthur T., II. *Fortune's Children: The Fall of the House of Vanderbilt*. New York: William Morrow, 1989

Vanderbilt, Cornelius, Jr. *Farewell to Fifth Avenue*. New York: Simon and Schuster, 1935.
_____. *The Living Past of America*. New York: Crown, 1960.
_____. *Man of the World: My Life on Five Continents*. New York: Crown, 1959.
_____. *Queen of the Golden Age: The Fabulous Story of Grace Wilson Vanderbilt*. New York: McGraw-Hill, 1956.
_____. *The Vanderbilt Feud*. London: Hutchenson, 1957.
Vanderbilt, Gloria. *Black Knight, White Knight*. New York: Alfred A. Knopf, 1987.
_____. *Once Upon a Time*. New York: Alfred A. Knopf, 1985.
Vanderbilt, Gloria Morgan. *Without Prejudice*. New York: E.P. Dutton, 1936.
_____, and Lady Thelma Furness. *Double Exposure*. New York: David McKay, 1958.
Vanderbilt, William K., Jr. *Across the Atlantic with Ara*. New York: Privately published, 1925.
_____. *Across the Atlantic with Ara*. New York: Privately published, 1924.
_____. *Flying Lanes*. New York: Privately printed, 1937.
_____. *The Log of My Motor* (1899–1908). New York: Privately published, 1908.
_____. *Taking One's Own Ship Around the World*. New York: Privately published, 1929.
_____. *To the Galapagos on the Ara*. New York: Privately published, 1927.
_____. *A Trip Through Italy, Sicily, Tunisia, Algeria, and Southern France*. New York: Privately printed, 1918.
_____. *West Made East with the Loss of a Day*. New York: Privately published, 1933.
Van Pelt, John, and Eugene Clute. *A Monograph of the W.K. Vanderbilt House*. New York: John Van Pelt, 1925.
Velocci, Al. *The Toll Lodges of the Long Island Motor Parkway*. Mount Pleasant, SC: Arcadia, 2004.
Wharton, Edith. *The Age of Innocence*. New York: The Library of America, 1985.
_____. *A Backward Glance*. New York: Appleton-Century, 1934.
Wilgus, William J. "The Grand Central Terminal in Perspective." Transactions of the American Society of Civil Engineers 106, October, 1940.

Index